THIS LOG BOOK BELONGS TO:

Name:
....

Company:
....

Establishment:
....

Address:
....

....

....

Phone:
....

Fax:
....

Email:
....

LOG BOOK START & END DATE:

Log Book Number:
....

Log Book Start Date:
....

Log Book End Date:
....

Log Book Notes:
....

....

....

D1560684

www.FyldeMerchandise.com

ESSENTIAL OFFICE CLEANING *Checklist*

Location/Building	Department	Office Number	Week Number

Start Date & Time	Finnish Date & Time	Name	Signature

	Daily/Weekly Office Cleaning Tasks	M	T	W	T	F	S	S	Cleaned By	Date/Time
1	Clean And Sanitize All The Desks And Tables									
2	Clean And Sanitize All The Counter Tops And Surface Areas									
3	Disinfect All Point-Of-Sale Terminals And Touch Screens									
4	Disinfect Touch Points, Light Switches And Other Switches									
5	Clean And Sanitize All Keyboards And Computer Mice									
6	Wipe Down The Walls Wherever There Are Spills And Splashes									
7	Clean And Disinfect All Doors, Door Handles And Doorknobs									
8	Re-Stock Protective Clothing, Face Masks/Shields, Gloves									
9	Clean And Sanitize All The Chairs, Seats And Benches									
10	Clean All The Mirrors, Glass Cabinets/Displays									
11	Replace And Change Burned Out Light Bulbs/Broken Lights									
12	Sweep The Floors To Ensure They're Free From Debris									
13	Mop Tiled And Laminate Floors With Disinfectant Cleaner									
14	Vacuum And Hoover The Carpets, Mats And Rugs									
15	Place Wet Floor Signs If Floors Are Wet After Mopping									
16	Wash & Clean Dirty Cups, Drinking Bottles And Glasses									
17	Clean & Re-Stock Paper Dispensers & Paper Towel Rolls									
18	Wipe Down Equipment & Sanitize Tea And Coffee Makers									
19	Refill Soap Dispensers, Sanitizers And Hand Gels									
20	Clean And Dust Furniture And Office Equipment									
21	Take Out The Rubbish/Trash, Remove Waste And Recycling									
22	Clean & Disinfectant Bins/Waste Disposal Area & Trash Cans									
23	Clean And Wipe Down Windowsills									
24	Vacuum Furnishings, Cushions, Chairs, Sofas And Couches									
25	Spray Air Freshener									
26	Clean And Disinfect Any Cabinets, Shelves And Units									
27	Clean Surfaces And Desk/Work Dividers									
28	Clean And Disinfect Telephones And Headsets									
29	Polish Any Wooden Furniture And Hardwood Surfaces									

	Monthly Office Cleaning Tasks	M	T	W	T	F	S	S	Cleaned By	Date/Time
1	Clean Skirting Boards/Baseboards And Corners									
2	Clean And Disinfect All The Walls From Top To Bottom									
3	Clean Blinds (Take Down And Wash If Possible)									
4	Wash And Clean Windows (Inside And Outside)									
5	Clean And Disinfect Shared Surfaces									
6	Steam Clean Carpets And Rugs									
7	Dust And Clean Ceilings, Ceiling Corners And Ceiling Tiles									
8	Check For Broken Chairs And Tables									
9	Dust And Wash Radiator Covers									
10	Clean And Disinfect Ceiling Wall Vents									
11	Clean And Vacuum Central Heating Units									
12	Wash And Clean Light Covers									
13	Clean Drapes And Curtains (Take Down And Wash if Possible)									
14	Check Cleaning Supplies And Re-Stock As Necessary									
15	Check Ceiling Fans, Fire Sprinklers And Smoke Alarms									
16	Check Hardware, Door Stops And Lock Mechanisms									
17	Fire Exit Lights And Emergency Lights Checked & Functioning									
18	Organize And De-Clutter Office Drawers									
19	Organize And De-Clutter Storeroom									
	Daily/Weekly Toilets/Restroom Cleaning Tasks	M	T	W	T	F	S	S	Cleaned By	Date/Time
1	Clean And Disinfect All Doors, Door Handles And Doorknobs									
2	Disinfect Touch Points, Light Switches And Other Switches									
3	Toilet Roll Holders Cleaned And Disinfected And Re-Stocked									
4	Wipe Down The Walls Wherever There Are Spills And Splashes									
5	Electric Hand Dryers Cleaned, Disinfected & Operating Correctly									
6	Sweep The Floors To Ensure They're Free From Debris									
7	Mop Tiled And Laminate Floors With Disinfectant Cleaner									
8	Paper Dispensers & Paper Towel Rolls Cleaned & Re-Stocked									
9	Take Out The Rubbish/Trash, Remove Waste And Recycling									
10	Clean & Disinfectant Bins/Waste Disposal Area & Trash Cans									
11	Feminine Hygiene Bins/Containers Cleaned And Disinfected									
12	Toilets Cleaned & Disinfected, Outside, Inside And Handles									
13	Urinals & Urinal Screens Cleaned, Disinfected & Blocks Replaced									
14	Wall Mirrors Cleaned With Glass Cleaner									
15	Clean And Re-Stock Paper Dispensers & Paper Towel Rolls									
16	Refill Soap Dispensers, Sanitizers And Hand Gels									
17	Sinks, Taps, Fixtures, Surface Areas Cleaned And Disinfected									

	Daily/Weekly Toilets/Restroom Cleaning Tasks Con	M	T	W	T	F	S	S	Cleaned By	Date/Time
18	Windowsills Clean And Wiped Down									
19	Check Plumbing And Schedule Work If Required									
20	Air Fresheners Checked And Replaced									
21	Fire Exit Lights And Emergency Lights Checked & Functioning									
22	Place Wet Floor Signs If Floors Are Wet After Mopping									
23	Cabinets Cleaned And Disinfected									
	Monthly Toilets/Restroom Cleaning Tasks	M	T	W	T	F	S	S	Cleaned By	Date/Time
1	Toilet/Restroom Service Storeroom/Cupboard Clean And Tidy									
2	Walls Free Of Graffiti, Stickers, Gum And Residue									
3	Wash And Clean Windows (Inside And Outside)									
4	Check Hardware, Door Stops And Lock Mechanisms									
5	All Fittings Securely Fixed (Schedule Maintenance If Not)									
6	Dust And Clean Ceilings, Ceiling Corners And Ceiling Tiles									
7	Clean Skirting Boards/Baseboards And Corners									
8	Thoroughly Clean Grout And Tiles									
9	Ceiling Wall Vents Cleaned And Disinfected									
10	Clean And Vacuum Central Heating Units									
11	Wash And Clean Light Covers									
12	Wash All Toilet And Restroom Mats									
	Daily/Weekly Kitchen Cleaning Tasks	M	T	W	T	F	S	S	Cleaned By	Date/Time
1	Wash And Sanitize All Counter Tops And Prep Area Surfaces									
2	Empty Dishwasher, Run The Dishwasher/Dish Drainer									
3	Disinfect Touch Points, Light Switches And Other Switches									
4	Take Out The Rubbish/Trash, Remove Waste And Recycling									
5	Clean & Disinfectant Bins/Waste Disposal Area & Trash Cans									
6	Wipe Down The Walls Wherever There Are Spills And Splashes									
7	Sweep The Floors To Ensure They're Free From Debris									
8	Mop Tiled And Laminate Floors With Disinfectant Cleaner									
9	Wet Floor Signs In Place If Floors Are Wet After Mopping									
10	Thoroughly Clean And Disinfect The Sinks And Taps									
11	Clean Exterior Of Appliances, Check For Spilled Food									
12	Replace Empty Paper Towel Rolls And Cloth Roller Towels									
13	Refill Soap Dispensers And Hand Sanitizers/Hand Gels									
14	Wipe Down Equipment, Tea And Coffee Makers, Toasters Etc									
15	Fire Exit Lights And Emergency Lights Checked & Functioning									
16	Pour Drain Cleaner Down Floor And Sink Drains									
17	Clean Inside Microwave, Check For Spilled Food									

	Daily/Weekly Kitchen Cleaning Tasks Continued	M	T	W	T	F	S	S	CLEANED BY	DATE/TIME
18	Replace Wash Rags, Cloths And Tea Towels With Clean Ones									
19	Wash Rags, Cloths, Tea Towels And Towels In Washing Machine									
20	Replace And Change Burned Out Light Bulbs/Broken Lights									
21	Clean Inside Of Dishwasher									
22	Sanitise Sponges Or Replace Damaged Sponges With New									
23	Dishes, Pots, Pans, And Utensils To Be Stored Away Properly									
24	Clean Out Refrigerator And Wipe Down Shelves And Drawers									
	Monthly Kitchen Cleaning Tasks	M	T	W	T	F	S	S	Cleaned By	Date/Time
1	Wash And Clean Air Vents									
2	Sort Through And Organize Cooking Utensils, Pans And Pots									
3	Wash And Clean Air Vents									
4	Check Plates, Cups And Glasses And Bin Anything Chipped									
5	Clean And Vacuum Central Heating Units									
6	Wash And Clean Light Covers									
7	Clean And De-Lime Dishwasher									
8	Dust And Clean Ceilings, Ceiling Corners And Ceiling Tiles									
9	Thoroughly Clean Grout And Tiles									
10	Clean Refrigerator Coils To Remove Dust, Unplug First									
11	Run Cleaning & Sanitizing Chemicals Through Coffee Machine									
12	Disinfect And Clean All The Walls From Top To Bottom									
13	Check For Out Of Date Food In Cabinets/Cupboards									
14	Clean Skirting Boards/Baseboards And Corners									
15	Clean Under Refrigerator									
16	Wash And Clean Doors, Door Frames And Glass									
17	Sort Through Leftover Items In The Fridge/Refrigerators									
18	Wash And Clean Windows (Inside And Outside)									
19	Replace Pest Traps									

ESSENTIAL CLEANING NOTES

....

....

....

....

....

....

....

....

ESSENTIAL OFFICE CLEANING *Checklist*

Location/Building	Department	Office Number	Week Number

Start Date & Time	Finnish Date & Time	Name	Signature

	Daily/Weekly Office Cleaning Tasks	M	T	W	T	F	S	S	Cleaned By	Date/Time
1	Clean And Sanitize All The Desks And Tables									
2	Clean And Sanitize All The Counter Tops And Surface Areas									
3	Disinfect All Point-Of-Sale Terminals And Touch Screens									
4	Disinfect Touch Points, Light Switches And Other Switches									
5	Clean And Sanitize All Keyboards And Computer Mice									
6	Wipe Down The Walls Wherever There Are Spills And Splashes									
7	Clean And Disinfect All Doors, Door Handles And Doorknobs									
8	Re-Stock Protective Clothing, Face Masks/Shields, Gloves									
9	Clean And Sanitize All The Chairs, Seats And Benches									
10	Clean All The Mirrors, Glass Cabinets/Displays									
11	Replace And Change Burned Out Light Bulbs/Broken Lights									
12	Sweep The Floors To Ensure They're Free From Debris									
13	Mop Tiled And Laminate Floors With Disinfectant Cleaner									
14	Vacuum And Hoover The Carpets, Mats And Rugs									
15	Place Wet Floor Signs If Floors Are Wet After Mopping									
16	Wash & Clean Dirty Cups, Drinking Bottles And Glasses									
17	Clean & Re-Stock Paper Dispensers & Paper Towel Rolls									
18	Wipe Down Equipment & Sanitize Tea And Coffee Makers									
19	Refill Soap Dispensers, Sanitizers And Hand Gels									
20	Clean And Dust Furniture And Office Equipment									
21	Take Out The Rubbish/Trash, Remove Waste And Recycling									
22	Clean & Disinfectant Bins/Waste Disposal Area & Trash Cans									
23	Clean And Wipe Down Windowsills									
24	Vacuum Furnishings, Cushions, Chairs, Sofas And Couches									
25	Spray Air Freshener									
26	Clean And Disinfect Any Cabinets, Shelves And Units									
27	Clean Surfaces And Desk/Work Dividers									
28	Clean And Disinfect Telephones And Headsets									
29	Polish Any Wooden Furniture And Hardwood Surfaces									

	Monthly Office Cleaning Tasks	M	T	W	T	F	S	S	Cleaned By	Date/Time
1	Clean Skirting Boards/Baseboards And Corners									
2	Clean And Disinfect All The Walls From Top To Bottom									
3	Clean Blinds (Take Down And Wash If Possible)									
4	Wash And Clean Windows (Inside And Outside)									
5	Clean And Disinfect Shared Surfaces									
6	Steam Clean Carpets And Rugs									
7	Dust And Clean Ceilings, Ceiling Corners And Ceiling Tiles									
8	Check For Broken Chairs And Tables									
9	Dust And Wash Radiator Covers									
10	Clean And Disinfect Ceiling Wall Vents									
11	Clean And Vacuum Central Heating Units									
12	Wash And Clean Light Covers									
13	Clean Drapes And Curtains (Take Down And Wash if Possible)									
14	Check Cleaning Supplies And Re-Stock As Necessary									
15	Check Ceiling Fans, Fire Sprinklers And Smoke Alarms									
16	Check Hardware, Door Stops And Lock Mechanisms									
17	Fire Exit Lights And Emergency Lights Checked & Functioning									
18	Organize And De-Clutter Office Drawers									
19	Organize And De-Clutter Storeroom									
	Daily/Weekly Toilets/Restroom Cleaning Tasks	M	T	W	T	F	S	S	Cleaned By	Date/Time
1	Clean And Disinfect All Doors, Door Handles And Doorknobs									
2	Disinfect Touch Points, Light Switches And Other Switches									
3	Toilet Roll Holders Cleaned And Disinfected And Re-Stocked									
4	Wipe Down The Walls Wherever There Are Spills And Splashes									
5	Electric Hand Dryers Cleaned, Disinfected & Operating Correctly									
6	Sweep The Floors To Ensure They're Free From Debris									
7	Mop Tiled And Laminate Floors With Disinfectant Cleaner									
8	Paper Dispensers & Paper Towel Rolls Cleaned & Re-Stocked									
9	Take Out The Rubbish/Trash, Remove Waste And Recycling									
10	Clean & Disinfectant Bins/Waste Disposal Area & Trash Cans									
11	Feminine Hygiene Bins/Containers Cleaned And Disinfected									
12	Toilets Cleaned & Disinfected, Outside, Inside And Handles									
13	Urinals & Urinal Screens Cleaned, Disinfected & Blocks Replaced									
14	Wall Mirrors Cleaned With Glass Cleaner									
15	Clean And Re-Stock Paper Dispensers & Paper Towel Rolls									
16	Refill Soap Dispensers, Sanitizers And Hand Gels									
17	Sinks, Taps, Fixtures, Surface Areas Cleaned And Disinfected									

	Daily/Weekly Toilets/Restroom Cleaning Tasks Con	M	T	W	T	F	S	S	Cleaned By	Date/Time
18	Windowsills Clean And Wiped Down									
19	Check Plumbing And Schedule Work If Required									
20	Air Fresheners Checked And Replaced									
21	Fire Exit Lights And Emergency Lights Checked & Functioning									
22	Place Wet Floor Signs If Floors Are Wet After Mopping									
23	Cabinets Cleaned And Disinfected									
	Monthly Toilets/Restroom Cleaning Tasks	M	T	W	T	F	S	S	Cleaned By	Date/Time
1	Toilet/Restroom Service Storeroom/Cupboard Clean And Tidy									
2	Walls Free Of Graffiti, Stickers, Gum And Residue									
3	Wash And Clean Windows (Inside And Outside)									
4	Check Hardware, Door Stops And Lock Mechanisms									
5	All Fittings Securely Fixed (Schedule Maintenance If Not)									
6	Dust And Clean Ceilings, Ceiling Corners And Ceiling Tiles									
7	Clean Skirting Boards/Baseboards And Corners									
8	Thoroughly Clean Grout And Tiles									
9	Ceiling Wall Vents Cleaned And Disinfected									
10	Clean And Vacuum Central Heating Units									
11	Wash And Clean Light Covers									
12	Wash All Toilet And Restroom Mats									
	Daily/Weekly Kitchen Cleaning Tasks	M	T	W	T	F	S	S	Cleaned By	Date/Time
1	Wash And Sanitize All Counter Tops And Prep Area Surfaces									
2	Empty Dishwasher, Run The Dishwasher/Dish Drainer									
3	Disinfect Touch Points, Light Switches And Other Switches									
4	Take Out The Rubbish/Trash, Remove Waste And Recycling									
5	Clean & Disinfectant Bins/Waste Disposal Area & Trash Cans									
6	Wipe Down The Walls Wherever There Are Spills And Splashes									
7	Sweep The Floors To Ensure They're Free From Debris									
8	Mop Tiled And Laminate Floors With Disinfectant Cleaner									
9	Wet Floor Signs In Place If Floors Are Wet After Mopping									
10	Thoroughly Clean And Disinfect The Sinks And Taps									
11	Clean Exterior Of Appliances, Check For Spilled Food									
12	Replace Empty Paper Towel Rolls And Cloth Roller Towels									
13	Refill Soap Dispensers And Hand Sanitizers/Hand Gels									
14	Wipe Down Equipment, Tea And Coffee Makers, Toasters Etc									
15	Fire Exit Lights And Emergency Lights Checked & Functioning									
16	Pour Drain Cleaner Down Floor And Sink Drains									
17	Clean Inside Microwave, Check For Spilled Food									

	Daily/Weekly Kitchen Cleaning Tasks Continued	M	T	W	T	F	S	S	CLEANED BY	DATE/TIME
18	Replace Wash Rags, Cloths And Tea Towels With Clean Ones									
19	Wash Rags, Cloths, Tea Towels And Towels In Washing Machine									
20	Replace And Change Burned Out Light Bulbs/Broken Lights									
21	Clean Inside Of Dishwasher									
22	Sanitise Sponges Or Replace Damaged Sponges With New									
23	Dishes, Pots, Pans, And Utensils To Be Stored Away Properly									
24	Clean Out Refrigerator And Wipe Down Shelves And Drawers									
	Monthly Kitchen Cleaning Tasks	M	T	W	T	F	S	S	Cleaned By	Date/Time
1	Wash And Clean Air Vents									
2	Sort Through And Organize Cooking Utensils, Pans And Pots									
3	Wash And Clean Air Vents									
4	Check Plates, Cups And Glasses And Bin Anything Chipped									
5	Clean And Vacuum Central Heating Units									
6	Wash And Clean Light Covers									
7	Clean And De-Lime Dishwasher									
8	Dust And Clean Ceilings, Ceiling Corners And Ceiling Tiles									
9	Thoroughly Clean Grout And Tiles									
10	Clean Refrigerator Coils To Remove Dust, Unplug First									
11	Run Cleaning & Sanitizing Chemicals Through Coffee Machine									
12	Disinfect And Clean All The Walls From Top To Bottom									
13	Check For Out Of Date Food In Cabinets/Cupboards									
14	Clean Skirting Boards/Baseboards And Corners									
15	Clean Under Refrigerator									
16	Wash And Clean Doors, Door Frames And Glass									
17	Sort Through Leftover Items In The Fridge/Refrigerators									
18	Wash And Clean Windows (Inside And Outside)									
19	Replace Pest Traps									

ESSENTIAL CLEANING NOTES

....

....

....

....

....

....

....

....

ESSENTIAL OFFICE CLEANING *Checklist*

Location/Building	Department	Office Number	Week Number

Start Date & Time	Finnish Date & Time	Name	Signature

	Daily/Weekly Office Cleaning Tasks	M	T	W	T	F	S	S	Cleaned By	Date/Time
1	Clean And Sanitize All The Desks And Tables									
2	Clean And Sanitize All The Counter Tops And Surface Areas									
3	Disinfect All Point-Of-Sale Terminals And Touch Screens									
4	Disinfect Touch Points, Light Switches And Other Switches									
5	Clean And Sanitize All Keyboards And Computer Mice									
6	Wipe Down The Walls Wherever There Are Spills And Splashes									
7	Clean And Disinfect All Doors, Door Handles And Doorknobs									
8	Re-Stock Protective Clothing, Face Masks/Shields, Gloves									
9	Clean And Sanitize All The Chairs, Seats And Benches									
10	Clean All The Mirrors, Glass Cabinets/Displays									
11	Replace And Change Burned Out Light Bulbs/Broken Lights									
12	Sweep The Floors To Ensure They're Free From Debris									
13	Mop Tiled And Laminate Floors With Disinfectant Cleaner									
14	Vacuum And Hoover The Carpets, Mats And Rugs									
15	Place Wet Floor Signs If Floors Are Wet After Mopping									
16	Wash & Clean Dirty Cups, Drinking Bottles And Glasses									
17	Clean & Re-Stock Paper Dispensers & Paper Towel Rolls									
18	Wipe Down Equipment & Sanitize Tea And Coffee Makers									
19	Refill Soap Dispensers, Sanitizers And Hand Gels									
20	Clean And Dust Furniture And Office Equipment									
21	Take Out The Rubbish/Trash, Remove Waste And Recycling									
22	Clean & Disinfectant Bins/Waste Disposal Area & Trash Cans									
23	Clean And Wipe Down Windowsills									
24	Vacuum Furnishings, Cushions, Chairs, Sofas And Couches									
25	Spray Air Freshener									
26	Clean And Disinfect Any Cabinets, Shelves And Units									
27	Clean Surfaces And Desk/Work Dividers									
28	Clean And Disinfect Telephones And Headsets									
29	Polish Any Wooden Furniture And Hardwood Surfaces									

	Monthly Office Cleaning Tasks	M	T	W	T	F	S	S	Cleaned By	Date/Time
1	Clean Skirting Boards/Baseboards And Corners									
2	Clean And Disinfect All The Walls From Top To Bottom									
3	Clean Blinds (Take Down And Wash If Possible)									
4	Wash And Clean Windows (Inside And Outside)									
5	Clean And Disinfect Shared Surfaces									
6	Steam Clean Carpets And Rugs									
7	Dust And Clean Ceilings, Ceiling Corners And Ceiling Tiles									
8	Check For Broken Chairs And Tables									
9	Dust And Wash Radiator Covers									
10	Clean And Disinfect Ceiling Wall Vents									
11	Clean And Vacuum Central Heating Units									
12	Wash And Clean Light Covers									
13	Clean Drapes And Curtains (Take Down And Wash if Possible)									
14	Check Cleaning Supplies And Re-Stock As Necessary									
15	Check Ceiling Fans, Fire Sprinklers And Smoke Alarms									
16	Check Hardware, Door Stops And Lock Mechanisms									
17	Fire Exit Lights And Emergency Lights Checked & Functioning									
18	Organize And De-Clutter Office Drawers									
19	Organize And De-Clutter Storeroom									
	Daily/Weekly Toilets/Restroom Cleaning Tasks	M	T	W	T	F	S	S	Cleaned By	Date/Time
1	Clean And Disinfect All Doors, Door Handles And Doorknobs									
2	Disinfect Touch Points, Light Switches And Other Switches									
3	Toilet Roll Holders Cleaned And Disinfected And Re-Stocked									
4	Wipe Down The Walls Wherever There Are Spills And Splashes									
5	Electric Hand Dryers Cleaned, Disinfected & Operating Correctly									
6	Sweep The Floors To Ensure They're Free From Debris									
7	Mop Tiled And Laminate Floors With Disinfectant Cleaner									
8	Paper Dispensers & Paper Towel Rolls Cleaned & Re-Stocked									
9	Take Out The Rubbish/Trash, Remove Waste And Recycling									
10	Clean & Disinfectant Bins/Waste Disposal Area & Trash Cans									
11	Feminine Hygiene Bins/Containers Cleaned And Disinfected									
12	Toilets Cleaned & Disinfected, Outside, Inside And Handles									
13	Urinals & Urinal Screens Cleaned, Disinfected & Blocks Replaced									
14	Wall Mirrors Cleaned With Glass Cleaner									
15	Clean And Re-Stock Paper Dispensers & Paper Towel Rolls									
16	Refill Soap Dispensers, Sanitizers And Hand Gels									
17	Sinks, Taps, Fixtures, Surface Areas Cleaned And Disinfected									

	Daily/Weekly Toilets/Restroom Cleaning Tasks Con	M	T	W	T	F	S	S	Cleaned By	Date/Time
18	Windowsills Clean And Wiped Down									
19	Check Plumbing And Schedule Work If Required									
20	Air Fresheners Checked And Replaced									
21	Fire Exit Lights And Emergency Lights Checked & Functioning									
22	Place Wet Floor Signs If Floors Are Wet After Mopping									
23	Cabinets Cleaned And Disinfected									
	Monthly Toilets/Restroom Cleaning Tasks	M	T	W	T	F	S	S	Cleaned By	Date/Time
1	Toilet/Restroom Service Storeroom/Cupboard Clean And Tidy									
2	Walls Free Of Graffiti, Stickers, Gum And Residue									
3	Wash And Clean Windows (Inside And Outside)									
4	Check Hardware, Door Stops And Lock Mechanisms									
5	All Fittings Securely Fixed (Schedule Maintenance If Not)									
6	Dust And Clean Ceilings, Ceiling Corners And Ceiling Tiles									
7	Clean Skirting Boards/Baseboards And Corners									
8	Thoroughly Clean Grout And Tiles									
9	Ceiling Wall Vents Cleaned And Disinfected									
10	Clean And Vacuum Central Heating Units									
11	Wash And Clean Light Covers									
12	Wash All Toilet And Restroom Mats									
	Daily/Weekly Kitchen Cleaning Tasks	M	T	W	T	F	S	S	Cleaned By	Date/Time
1	Wash And Sanitize All Counter Tops And Prep Area Surfaces									
2	Empty Dishwasher, Run The Dishwasher/Dish Drainer									
3	Disinfect Touch Points, Light Switches And Other Switches									
4	Take Out The Rubbish/Trash, Remove Waste And Recycling									
5	Clean & Disinfectant Bins/Waste Disposal Area & Trash Cans									
6	Wipe Down The Walls Wherever There Are Spills And Splashes									
7	Sweep The Floors To Ensure They're Free From Debris									
8	Mop Tiled And Laminate Floors With Disinfectant Cleaner									
9	Wet Floor Signs In Place If Floors Are Wet After Mopping									
10	Thoroughly Clean And Disinfect The Sinks And Taps									
11	Clean Exterior Of Appliances, Check For Spilled Food									
12	Replace Empty Paper Towel Rolls And Cloth Roller Towels									
13	Refill Soap Dispensers And Hand Sanitizers/Hand Gels									
14	Wipe Down Equipment, Tea And Coffee Makers, Toasters Etc									
15	Fire Exit Lights And Emergency Lights Checked & Functioning									
16	Pour Drain Cleaner Down Floor And Sink Drains									
17	Clean Inside Microwave, Check For Spilled Food									

	Daily/Weekly Kitchen Cleaning Tasks Continued	M	T	W	T	F	S	S	CLEANED BY	DATE/TIME
18	Replace Wash Rags, Cloths And Tea Towels With Clean Ones									
19	Wash Rags, Cloths, Tea Towels And Towels In Washing Machine									
20	Replace And Change Burned Out Light Bulbs/Broken Lights									
21	Clean Inside Of Dishwasher									
22	Sanitise Sponges Or Replace Damaged Sponges With New									
23	Dishes, Pots, Pans, And Utensils To Be Stored Away Properly									
24	Clean Out Refrigerator And Wipe Down Shelves And Drawers									
	Monthly Kitchen Cleaning Tasks	M	T	W	T	F	S	S	Cleaned By	Date/Time
1	Wash And Clean Air Vents									
2	Sort Through And Organize Cooking Utensils, Pans And Pots									
3	Wash And Clean Air Vents									
4	Check Plates, Cups And Glasses And Bin Anything Chipped									
5	Clean And Vacuum Central Heating Units									
6	Wash And Clean Light Covers									
7	Clean And De-Lime Dishwasher									
8	Dust And Clean Ceilings, Ceiling Corners And Ceiling Tiles									
9	Thoroughly Clean Grout And Tiles									
10	Clean Refrigerator Coils To Remove Dust, Unplug First									
11	Run Cleaning & Sanitizing Chemicals Through Coffee Machine									
12	Disinfect And Clean All The Walls From Top To Bottom									
13	Check For Out Of Date Food In Cabinets/Cupboards									
14	Clean Skirting Boards/Baseboards And Corners									
15	Clean Under Refrigerator									
16	Wash And Clean Doors, Door Frames And Glass									
17	Sort Through Leftover Items In The Fridge/Refrigerators									
18	Wash And Clean Windows (Inside And Outside)									
19	Replace Pest Traps									

ESSENTIAL CLEANING NOTES

....

....

....

....

....

....

....

....

ESSENTIAL OFFICE CLEANING *Checklist*

Location/Building	Department	Office Number	Week Number

Start Date & Time	Finnish Date & Time	Name	Signature

	Daily/Weekly Office Cleaning Tasks	M	T	W	T	F	S	S	Cleaned By	Date/Time
1	Clean And Sanitize All The Desks And Tables									
2	Clean And Sanitize All The Counter Tops And Surface Areas									
3	Disinfect All Point-Of-Sale Terminals And Touch Screens									
4	Disinfect Touch Points, Light Switches And Other Switches									
5	Clean And Sanitize All Keyboards And Computer Mice									
6	Wipe Down The Walls Wherever There Are Spills And Splashes									
7	Clean And Disinfect All Doors, Door Handles And Doorknobs									
8	Re-Stock Protective Clothing, Face Masks/Shields, Gloves									
9	Clean And Sanitize All The Chairs, Seats And Benches									
10	Clean All The Mirrors, Glass Cabinets/Displays									
11	Replace And Change Burned Out Light Bulbs/Broken Lights									
12	Sweep The Floors To Ensure They're Free From Debris									
13	Mop Tiled And Laminate Floors With Disinfectant Cleaner									
14	Vacuum And Hoover The Carpets, Mats And Rugs									
15	Place Wet Floor Signs If Floors Are Wet After Mopping									
16	Wash & Clean Dirty Cups, Drinking Bottles And Glasses									
17	Clean & Re-Stock Paper Dispensers & Paper Towel Rolls									
18	Wipe Down Equipment & Sanitize Tea And Coffee Makers									
19	Refill Soap Dispensers, Sanitizers And Hand Gels									
20	Clean And Dust Furniture And Office Equipment									
21	Take Out The Rubbish/Trash, Remove Waste And Recycling									
22	Clean & Disinfectant Bins/Waste Disposal Area & Trash Cans									
23	Clean And Wipe Down Windowsills									
24	Vacuum Furnishings, Cushions, Chairs, Sofas And Couches									
25	Spray Air Freshener									
26	Clean And Disinfect Any Cabinets, Shelves And Units									
27	Clean Surfaces And Desk/Work Dividers									
28	Clean And Disinfect Telephones And Headsets									
29	Polish Any Wooden Furniture And Hardwood Surfaces									

	Monthly Office Cleaning Tasks	M	T	W	T	F	S	S	Cleaned By	Date/Time
1	Clean Skirting Boards/Baseboards And Corners									
2	Clean And Disinfect All The Walls From Top To Bottom									
3	Clean Blinds (Take Down And Wash If Possible)									
4	Wash And Clean Windows (Inside And Outside)									
5	Clean And Disinfect Shared Surfaces									
6	Steam Clean Carpets And Rugs									
7	Dust And Clean Ceilings, Ceiling Corners And Ceiling Tiles									
8	Check For Broken Chairs And Tables									
9	Dust And Wash Radiator Covers									
10	Clean And Disinfect Ceiling Wall Vents									
11	Clean And Vacuum Central Heating Units									
12	Wash And Clean Light Covers									
13	Clean Drapes And Curtains (Take Down And Wash if Possible)									
14	Check Cleaning Supplies And Re-Stock As Necessary									
15	Check Ceiling Fans, Fire Sprinklers And Smoke Alarms									
16	Check Hardware, Door Stops And Lock Mechanisms									
17	Fire Exit Lights And Emergency Lights Checked & Functioning									
18	Organize And De-Clutter Office Drawers									
19	Organize And De-Clutter Storeroom									
	Daily/Weekly Toilets/Restroom Cleaning Tasks	M	T	W	T	F	S	S	Cleaned By	Date/Time
1	Clean And Disinfect All Doors, Door Handles And Doorknobs									
2	Disinfect Touch Points, Light Switches And Other Switches									
3	Toilet Roll Holders Cleaned And Disinfected And Re-Stocked									
4	Wipe Down The Walls Wherever There Are Spills And Splashes									
5	Electric Hand Dryers Cleaned, Disinfected & Operating Correctly									
6	Sweep The Floors To Ensure They're Free From Debris									
7	Mop Tiled And Laminate Floors With Disinfectant Cleaner									
8	Paper Dispensers & Paper Towel Rolls Cleaned & Re-Stocked									
9	Take Out The Rubbish/Trash, Remove Waste And Recycling									
10	Clean & Disinfectant Bins/Waste Disposal Area & Trash Cans									
11	Feminine Hygiene Bins/Containers Cleaned And Disinfected									
12	Toilets Cleaned & Disinfected, Outside, Inside And Handles									
13	Urinals & Urinal Screens Cleaned, Disinfected & Blocks Replaced									
14	Wall Mirrors Cleaned With Glass Cleaner									
15	Clean And Re-Stock Paper Dispensers & Paper Towel Rolls									
16	Refill Soap Dispensers, Sanitizers And Hand Gels									
17	Sinks, Taps, Fixtures, Surface Areas Cleaned And Disinfected									

	Daily/Weekly Toilets/Restroom Cleaning Tasks Con	M	T	W	T	F	S	S	Cleaned By	Date/Time
18	Windowsills Clean And Wiped Down									
19	Check Plumbing And Schedule Work If Required									
20	Air Fresheners Checked And Replaced									
21	Fire Exit Lights And Emergency Lights Checked & Functioning									
22	Place Wet Floor Signs If Floors Are Wet After Mopping									
23	Cabinets Cleaned And Disinfected									
	Monthly Toilets/Restroom Cleaning Tasks	M	T	W	T	F	S	S	Cleaned By	Date/Time
1	Toilet/Restroom Service Storeroom/Cupboard Clean And Tidy									
2	Walls Free Of Graffiti, Stickers, Gum And Residue									
3	Wash And Clean Windows (Inside And Outside)									
4	Check Hardware, Door Stops And Lock Mechanisms									
5	All Fittings Securely Fixed (Schedule Maintenance If Not)									
6	Dust And Clean Ceilings, Ceiling Corners And Ceiling Tiles									
7	Clean Skirting Boards/Baseboards And Corners									
8	Thoroughly Clean Grout And Tiles									
9	Ceiling Wall Vents Cleaned And Disinfected									
10	Clean And Vacuum Central Heating Units									
11	Wash And Clean Light Covers									
12	Wash All Toilet And Restroom Mats									
	Daily/Weekly Kitchen Cleaning Tasks	M	T	W	T	F	S	S	Cleaned By	Date/Time
1	Wash And Sanitize All Counter Tops And Prep Area Surfaces									
2	Empty Dishwasher, Run The Dishwasher/Dish Drainer									
3	Disinfect Touch Points, Light Switches And Other Switches									
4	Take Out The Rubbish/Trash, Remove Waste And Recycling									
5	Clean & Disinfectant Bins/Waste Disposal Area & Trash Cans									
6	Wipe Down The Walls Wherever There Are Spills And Splashes									
7	Sweep The Floors To Ensure They're Free From Debris									
8	Mop Tiled And Laminate Floors With Disinfectant Cleaner									
9	Wet Floor Signs In Place If Floors Are Wet After Mopping									
10	Thoroughly Clean And Disinfect The Sinks And Taps									
11	Clean Exterior Of Appliances, Check For Spilled Food									
12	Replace Empty Paper Towel Rolls And Cloth Roller Towels									
13	Refill Soap Dispensers And Hand Sanitizers/Hand Gels									
14	Wipe Down Equipment, Tea And Coffee Makers, Toasters Etc									
15	Fire Exit Lights And Emergency Lights Checked & Functioning									
16	Pour Drain Cleaner Down Floor And Sink Drains									
17	Clean Inside Microwave, Check For Spilled Food									

	Daily/Weekly Kitchen Cleaning Tasks Continued	M	T	W	T	F	S	S	CLEANED BY	DATE/TIME
18	Replace Wash Rags, Cloths And Tea Towels With Clean Ones									
19	Wash Rags, Cloths, Tea Towels And Towels In Washing Machine									
20	Replace And Change Burned Out Light Bulbs/Broken Lights									
21	Clean Inside Of Dishwasher									
22	Sanitise Sponges Or Replace Damaged Sponges With New									
23	Dishes, Pots, Pans, And Utensils To Be Stored Away Properly									
24	Clean Out Refrigerator And Wipe Down Shelves And Drawers									
	Monthly Kitchen Cleaning Tasks	M	T	W	T	F	S	S	Cleaned By	Date/Time
1	Wash And Clean Air Vents									
2	Sort Through And Organize Cooking Utensils, Pans And Pots									
3	Wash And Clean Air Vents									
4	Check Plates, Cups And Glasses And Bin Anything Chipped									
5	Clean And Vacuum Central Heating Units									
6	Wash And Clean Light Covers									
7	Clean And De-Lime Dishwasher									
8	Dust And Clean Ceilings, Ceiling Corners And Ceiling Tiles									
9	Thoroughly Clean Grout And Tiles									
10	Clean Refrigerator Coils To Remove Dust, Unplug First									
11	Run Cleaning & Sanitizing Chemicals Through Coffee Machine									
12	Disinfect And Clean All The Walls From Top To Bottom									
13	Check For Out Of Date Food In Cabinets/Cupboards									
14	Clean Skirting Boards/Baseboards And Corners									
15	Clean Under Refrigerator									
16	Wash And Clean Doors, Door Frames And Glass									
17	Sort Through Leftover Items In The Fridge/Refrigerators									
18	Wash And Clean Windows (Inside And Outside)									
19	Replace Pest Traps									

ESSENTIAL CLEANING NOTES

....

....

....

....

....

....

....

....

ESSENTIAL OFFICE CLEANING *Checklist*

Location/Building	Department	Office Number	Week Number

Start Date & Time	Finnish Date & Time	Name	Signature

	Daily/Weekly Office Cleaning Tasks	M	T	W	T	F	S	S	Cleaned By	Date/Time
1	Clean And Sanitize All The Desks And Tables									
2	Clean And Sanitize All The Counter Tops And Surface Areas									
3	Disinfect All Point-Of-Sale Terminals And Touch Screens									
4	Disinfect Touch Points, Light Switches And Other Switches									
5	Clean And Sanitize All Keyboards And Computer Mice									
6	Wipe Down The Walls Wherever There Are Spills And Splashes									
7	Clean And Disinfect All Doors, Door Handles And Doorknobs									
8	Re-Stock Protective Clothing, Face Masks/Shields, Gloves									
9	Clean And Sanitize All The Chairs, Seats And Benches									
10	Clean All The Mirrors, Glass Cabinets/Displays									
11	Replace And Change Burned Out Light Bulbs/Broken Lights									
12	Sweep The Floors To Ensure They're Free From Debris									
13	Mop Tiled And Laminate Floors With Disinfectant Cleaner									
14	Vacuum And Hoover The Carpets, Mats And Rugs									
15	Place Wet Floor Signs If Floors Are Wet After Mopping									
16	Wash & Clean Dirty Cups, Drinking Bottles And Glasses									
17	Clean & Re-Stock Paper Dispensers & Paper Towel Rolls									
18	Wipe Down Equipment & Sanitize Tea And Coffee Makers									
19	Refill Soap Dispensers, Sanitizers And Hand Gels									
20	Clean And Dust Furniture And Office Equipment									
21	Take Out The Rubbish/Trash, Remove Waste And Recycling									
22	Clean & Disinfectant Bins/Waste Disposal Area & Trash Cans									
23	Clean And Wipe Down Windowsills									
24	Vacuum Furnishings, Cushions, Chairs, Sofas And Couches									
25	Spray Air Freshener									
26	Clean And Disinfect Any Cabinets, Shelves And Units									
27	Clean Surfaces And Desk/Work Dividers									
28	Clean And Disinfect Telephones And Headsets									
29	Polish Any Wooden Furniture And Hardwood Surfaces									

	Monthly Office Cleaning Tasks	M	T	W	T	F	S	S	Cleaned By	Date/Time
1	Clean Skirting Boards/Baseboards And Corners									
2	Clean And Disinfect All The Walls From Top To Bottom									
3	Clean Blinds (Take Down And Wash If Possible)									
4	Wash And Clean Windows (Inside And Outside)									
5	Clean And Disinfect Shared Surfaces									
6	Steam Clean Carpets And Rugs									
7	Dust And Clean Ceilings, Ceiling Corners And Ceiling Tiles									
8	Check For Broken Chairs And Tables									
9	Dust And Wash Radiator Covers									
10	Clean And Disinfect Ceiling Wall Vents									
11	Clean And Vacuum Central Heating Units									
12	Wash And Clean Light Covers									
13	Clean Drapes And Curtains (Take Down And Wash if Possible)									
14	Check Cleaning Supplies And Re-Stock As Necessary									
15	Check Ceiling Fans, Fire Sprinklers And Smoke Alarms									
16	Check Hardware, Door Stops And Lock Mechanisms									
17	Fire Exit Lights And Emergency Lights Checked & Functioning									
18	Organize And De-Clutter Office Drawers									
19	Organize And De-Clutter Storeroom									

	Daily/Weekly Toilets/Restroom Cleaning Tasks	M	T	W	T	F	S	S	Cleaned By	Date/Time
1	Clean And Disinfect All Doors, Door Handles And Doorknobs									
2	Disinfect Touch Points, Light Switches And Other Switches									
3	Toilet Roll Holders Cleaned And Disinfected And Re-Stocked									
4	Wipe Down The Walls Wherever There Are Spills And Splashes									
5	Electric Hand Dryers Cleaned, Disinfected & Operating Correctly									
6	Sweep The Floors To Ensure They're Free From Debris									
7	Mop Tiled And Laminate Floors With Disinfectant Cleaner									
8	Paper Dispensers & Paper Towel Rolls Cleaned & Re-Stocked									
9	Take Out The Rubbish/Trash, Remove Waste And Recycling									
10	Clean & Disinfectant Bins/Waste Disposal Area & Trash Cans									
11	Feminine Hygiene Bins/Containers Cleaned And Disinfected									
12	Toilets Cleaned & Disinfected, Outside, Inside And Handles									
13	Urinals & Urinal Screens Cleaned, Disinfected & Blocks Replaced									
14	Wall Mirrors Cleaned With Glass Cleaner									
15	Clean And Re-Stock Paper Dispensers & Paper Towel Rolls									
16	Refill Soap Dispensers, Sanitizers And Hand Gels									
17	Sinks, Taps, Fixtures, Surface Areas Cleaned And Disinfected									

	Daily/Weekly Toilets/Restroom Cleaning Tasks Con	M	T	W	T	F	S	S	Cleaned By	Date/Time
18	Windowsills Clean And Wiped Down									
19	Check Plumbing And Schedule Work If Required									
20	Air Fresheners Checked And Replaced									
21	Fire Exit Lights And Emergency Lights Checked & Functioning									
22	Place Wet Floor Signs If Floors Are Wet After Mopping									
23	Cabinets Cleaned And Disinfected									
	Monthly Toilets/Restroom Cleaning Tasks	M	T	W	T	F	S	S	Cleaned By	Date/Time
1	Toilet/Restroom Service Storeroom/Cupboard Clean And Tidy									
2	Walls Free Of Graffiti, Stickers, Gum And Residue									
3	Wash And Clean Windows (Inside And Outside)									
4	Check Hardware, Door Stops And Lock Mechanisms									
5	All Fittings Securely Fixed (Schedule Maintenance If Not)									
6	Dust And Clean Ceilings, Ceiling Corners And Ceiling Tiles									
7	Clean Skirting Boards/Baseboards And Corners									
8	Thoroughly Clean Grout And Tiles									
9	Ceiling Wall Vents Cleaned And Disinfected									
10	Clean And Vacuum Central Heating Units									
11	Wash And Clean Light Covers									
12	Wash All Toilet And Restroom Mats									
	Daily/Weekly Kitchen Cleaning Tasks	M	T	W	T	F	S	S	Cleaned By	Date/Time
1	Wash And Sanitize All Counter Tops And Prep Area Surfaces									
2	Empty Dishwasher, Run The Dishwasher/Dish Drainer									
3	Disinfect Touch Points, Light Switches And Other Switches									
4	Take Out The Rubbish/Trash, Remove Waste And Recycling									
5	Clean & Disinfectant Bins/Waste Disposal Area & Trash Cans									
6	Wipe Down The Walls Wherever There Are Spills And Splashes									
7	Sweep The Floors To Ensure They're Free From Debris									
8	Mop Tiled And Laminate Floors With Disinfectant Cleaner									
9	Wet Floor Signs In Place If Floors Are Wet After Mopping									
10	Thoroughly Clean And Disinfect The Sinks And Taps									
11	Clean Exterior Of Appliances, Check For Spilled Food									
12	Replace Empty Paper Towel Rolls And Cloth Roller Towels									
13	Refill Soap Dispensers And Hand Sanitizers/Hand Gels									
14	Wipe Down Equipment, Tea And Coffee Makers, Toasters Etc									
15	Fire Exit Lights And Emergency Lights Checked & Functioning									
16	Pour Drain Cleaner Down Floor And Sink Drains									
17	Clean Inside Microwave, Check For Spilled Food									

	Daily/Weekly Kitchen Cleaning Tasks Continued	M	T	W	T	F	S	S	CLEANED BY	DATE/TIME
18	Replace Wash Rags, Cloths And Tea Towels With Clean Ones									
19	Wash Rags, Cloths, Tea Towels And Towels In Washing Machine									
20	Replace And Change Burned Out Light Bulbs/Broken Lights									
21	Clean Inside Of Dishwasher									
22	Sanitise Sponges Or Replace Damaged Sponges With New									
23	Dishes, Pots, Pans, And Utensils To Be Stored Away Properly									
24	Clean Out Refrigerator And Wipe Down Shelves And Drawers									
	Monthly Kitchen Cleaning Tasks	M	T	W	T	F	S	S	Cleaned By	Date/Time
1	Wash And Clean Air Vents									
2	Sort Through And Organize Cooking Utensils, Pans And Pots									
3	Wash And Clean Air Vents									
4	Check Plates, Cups And Glasses And Bin Anything Chipped									
5	Clean And Vacuum Central Heating Units									
6	Wash And Clean Light Covers									
7	Clean And De-Lime Dishwasher									
8	Dust And Clean Ceilings, Ceiling Corners And Ceiling Tiles									
9	Thoroughly Clean Grout And Tiles									
10	Clean Refrigerator Coils To Remove Dust, Unplug First									
11	Run Cleaning & Sanitizing Chemicals Through Coffee Machine									
12	Disinfect And Clean All The Walls From Top To Bottom									
13	Check For Out Of Date Food In Cabinets/Cupboards									
14	Clean Skirting Boards/Baseboards And Corners									
15	Clean Under Refrigerator									
16	Wash And Clean Doors, Door Frames And Glass									
17	Sort Through Leftover Items In The Fridge/Refrigerators									
18	Wash And Clean Windows (Inside And Outside)									
19	Replace Pest Traps									

ESSENTIAL CLEANING NOTES

....

....

....

....

....

....

....

....

ESSENTIAL OFFICE CLEANING *Checklist*

Location/Building	Department	Office Number	Week Number

Start Date & Time	Finnish Date & Time	Name	Signature

	Daily/Weekly Office Cleaning Tasks	M	T	W	T	F	S	S	Cleaned By	Date/Time
1	Clean And Sanitize All The Desks And Tables									
2	Clean And Sanitize All The Counter Tops And Surface Areas									
3	Disinfect All Point-Of-Sale Terminals And Touch Screens									
4	Disinfect Touch Points, Light Switches And Other Switches									
5	Clean And Sanitize All Keyboards And Computer Mice									
6	Wipe Down The Walls Wherever There Are Spills And Splashes									
7	Clean And Disinfect All Doors, Door Handles And Doorknobs									
8	Re-Stock Protective Clothing, Face Masks/Shields, Gloves									
9	Clean And Sanitize All The Chairs, Seats And Benches									
10	Clean All The Mirrors, Glass Cabinets/Displays									
11	Replace And Change Burned Out Light Bulbs/Broken Lights									
12	Sweep The Floors To Ensure They're Free From Debris									
13	Mop Tiled And Laminate Floors With Disinfectant Cleaner									
14	Vacuum And Hoover The Carpets, Mats And Rugs									
15	Place Wet Floor Signs If Floors Are Wet After Mopping									
16	Wash & Clean Dirty Cups, Drinking Bottles And Glasses									
17	Clean & Re-Stock Paper Dispensers & Paper Towel Rolls									
18	Wipe Down Equipment & Sanitize Tea And Coffee Makers									
19	Refill Soap Dispensers, Sanitizers And Hand Gels									
20	Clean And Dust Furniture And Office Equipment									
21	Take Out The Rubbish/Trash, Remove Waste And Recycling									
22	Clean & Disinfectant Bins/Waste Disposal Area & Trash Cans									
23	Clean And Wipe Down Windowsills									
24	Vacuum Furnishings, Cushions, Chairs, Sofas And Couches									
25	Spray Air Freshener									
26	Clean And Disinfect Any Cabinets, Shelves And Units									
27	Clean Surfaces And Desk/Work Dividers									
28	Clean And Disinfect Telephones And Headsets									
29	Polish Any Wooden Furniture And Hardwood Surfaces									

	Monthly Office Cleaning Tasks	M	T	W	T	F	S	S	Cleaned By	Date/Time
1	Clean Skirting Boards/Baseboards And Corners									
2	Clean And Disinfect All The Walls From Top To Bottom									
3	Clean Blinds (Take Down And Wash If Possible)									
4	Wash And Clean Windows (Inside And Outside)									
5	Clean And Disinfect Shared Surfaces									
6	Steam Clean Carpets And Rugs									
7	Dust And Clean Ceilings, Ceiling Corners And Ceiling Tiles									
8	Check For Broken Chairs And Tables									
9	Dust And Wash Radiator Covers									
10	Clean And Disinfect Ceiling Wall Vents									
11	Clean And Vacuum Central Heating Units									
12	Wash And Clean Light Covers									
13	Clean Drapes And Curtains (Take Down And Wash if Possible)									
14	Check Cleaning Supplies And Re-Stock As Necessary									
15	Check Ceiling Fans, Fire Sprinklers And Smoke Alarms									
16	Check Hardware, Door Stops And Lock Mechanisms									
17	Fire Exit Lights And Emergency Lights Checked & Functioning									
18	Organize And De-Clutter Office Drawers									
19	Organize And De-Clutter Storeroom									

	Daily/Weekly Toilets/Restroom Cleaning Tasks	M	T	W	T	F	S	S	Cleaned By	Date/Time
1	Clean And Disinfect All Doors, Door Handles And Doorknobs									
2	Disinfect Touch Points, Light Switches And Other Switches									
3	Toilet Roll Holders Cleaned And Disinfected And Re-Stocked									
4	Wipe Down The Walls Wherever There Are Spills And Splashes									
5	Electric Hand Dryers Cleaned, Disinfected & Operating Correctly									
6	Sweep The Floors To Ensure They're Free From Debris									
7	Mop Tiled And Laminate Floors With Disinfectant Cleaner									
8	Paper Dispensers & Paper Towel Rolls Cleaned & Re-Stocked									
9	Take Out The Rubbish/Trash, Remove Waste And Recycling									
10	Clean & Disinfectant Bins/Waste Disposal Area & Trash Cans									
11	Feminine Hygiene Bins/Containers Cleaned And Disinfected									
12	Toilets Cleaned & Disinfected, Outside, Inside And Handles									
13	Urinals & Urinal Screens Cleaned, Disinfected & Blocks Replaced									
14	Wall Mirrors Cleaned With Glass Cleaner									
15	Clean And Re-Stock Paper Dispensers & Paper Towel Rolls									
16	Refill Soap Dispensers, Sanitizers And Hand Gels									
17	Sinks, Taps, Fixtures, Surface Areas Cleaned And Disinfected									

	Daily/Weekly Toilets/Restroom Cleaning Tasks Con	M	T	W	T	F	S	S	Cleaned By	Date/Time
18	Windowsills Clean And Wiped Down									
19	Check Plumbing And Schedule Work If Required									
20	Air Fresheners Checked And Replaced									
21	Fire Exit Lights And Emergency Lights Checked & Functioning									
22	Place Wet Floor Signs If Floors Are Wet After Mopping									
23	Cabinets Cleaned And Disinfected									
	Monthly Toilets/Restroom Cleaning Tasks	M	T	W	T	F	S	S	Cleaned By	Date/Time
1	Toilet/Restroom Service Storeroom/Cupboard Clean And Tidy									
2	Walls Free Of Graffiti, Stickers, Gum And Residue									
3	Wash And Clean Windows (Inside And Outside)									
4	Check Hardware, Door Stops And Lock Mechanisms									
5	All Fittings Securely Fixed (Schedule Maintenance If Not)									
6	Dust And Clean Ceilings, Ceiling Corners And Ceiling Tiles									
7	Clean Skirting Boards/Baseboards And Corners									
8	Thoroughly Clean Grout And Tiles									
9	Ceiling Wall Vents Cleaned And Disinfected									
10	Clean And Vacuum Central Heating Units									
11	Wash And Clean Light Covers									
12	Wash All Toilet And Restroom Mats									
	Daily/Weekly Kitchen Cleaning Tasks	M	T	W	T	F	S	S	Cleaned By	Date/Time
1	Wash And Sanitize All Counter Tops And Prep Area Surfaces									
2	Empty Dishwasher, Run The Dishwasher/Dish Drainer									
3	Disinfect Touch Points, Light Switches And Other Switches									
4	Take Out The Rubbish/Trash, Remove Waste And Recycling									
5	Clean & Disinfectant Bins/Waste Disposal Area & Trash Cans									
6	Wipe Down The Walls Wherever There Are Spills And Splashes									
7	Sweep The Floors To Ensure They're Free From Debris									
8	Mop Tiled And Laminate Floors With Disinfectant Cleaner									
9	Wet Floor Signs In Place If Floors Are Wet After Mopping									
10	Thoroughly Clean And Disinfect The Sinks And Taps									
11	Clean Exterior Of Appliances, Check For Spilled Food									
12	Replace Empty Paper Towel Rolls And Cloth Roller Towels									
13	Refill Soap Dispensers And Hand Sanitizers/Hand Gels									
14	Wipe Down Equipment, Tea And Coffee Makers, Toasters Etc									
15	Fire Exit Lights And Emergency Lights Checked & Functioning									
16	Pour Drain Cleaner Down Floor And Sink Drains									
17	Clean Inside Microwave, Check For Spilled Food									

	Daily/Weekly Kitchen Cleaning Tasks Continued	M	T	W	T	F	S	S	CLEANED BY	DATE/TIME
18	Replace Wash Rags, Cloths And Tea Towels With Clean Ones									
19	Wash Rags, Cloths, Tea Towels And Towels In Washing Machine									
20	Replace And Change Burned Out Light Bulbs/Broken Lights									
21	Clean Inside Of Dishwasher									
22	Sanitise Sponges Or Replace Damaged Sponges With New									
23	Dishes, Pots, Pans, And Utensils To Be Stored Away Properly									
24	Clean Out Refrigerator And Wipe Down Shelves And Drawers									
	Monthly Kitchen Cleaning Tasks	M	T	W	T	F	S	S	Cleaned By	Date/Time
1	Wash And Clean Air Vents									
2	Sort Through And Organize Cooking Utensils, Pans And Pots									
3	Wash And Clean Air Vents									
4	Check Plates, Cups And Glasses And Bin Anything Chipped									
5	Clean And Vacuum Central Heating Units									
6	Wash And Clean Light Covers									
7	Clean And De-Lime Dishwasher									
8	Dust And Clean Ceilings, Ceiling Corners And Ceiling Tiles									
9	Thoroughly Clean Grout And Tiles									
10	Clean Refrigerator Coils To Remove Dust, Unplug First									
11	Run Cleaning & Sanitizing Chemicals Through Coffee Machine									
12	Disinfect And Clean All The Walls From Top To Bottom									
13	Check For Out Of Date Food In Cabinets/Cupboards									
14	Clean Skirting Boards/Baseboards And Corners									
15	Clean Under Refrigerator									
16	Wash And Clean Doors, Door Frames And Glass									
17	Sort Through Leftover Items In The Fridge/Refrigerators									
18	Wash And Clean Windows (Inside And Outside)									
19	Replace Pest Traps									

ESSENTIAL CLEANING NOTES

....

....

....

....

....

....

....

....

....

ESSENTIAL OFFICE CLEANING *Checklist*

Location/Building	Department	Office Number	Week Number

Start Date & Time	Finnish Date & Time	Name	Signature

	Daily/Weekly Office Cleaning Tasks	M	T	W	T	F	S	S	Cleaned By	Date/Time
1	Clean And Sanitize All The Desks And Tables									
2	Clean And Sanitize All The Counter Tops And Surface Areas									
3	Disinfect All Point-Of-Sale Terminals And Touch Screens									
4	Disinfect Touch Points, Light Switches And Other Switches									
5	Clean And Sanitize All Keyboards And Computer Mice									
6	Wipe Down The Walls Wherever There Are Spills And Splashes									
7	Clean And Disinfect All Doors, Door Handles And Doorknobs									
8	Re-Stock Protective Clothing, Face Masks/Shields, Gloves									
9	Clean And Sanitize All The Chairs, Seats And Benches									
10	Clean All The Mirrors, Glass Cabinets/Displays									
11	Replace And Change Burned Out Light Bulbs/Broken Lights									
12	Sweep The Floors To Ensure They're Free From Debris									
13	Mop Tiled And Laminate Floors With Disinfectant Cleaner									
14	Vacuum And Hoover The Carpets, Mats And Rugs									
15	Place Wet Floor Signs If Floors Are Wet After Mopping									
16	Wash & Clean Dirty Cups, Drinking Bottles And Glasses									
17	Clean & Re-Stock Paper Dispensers & Paper Towel Rolls									
18	Wipe Down Equipment & Sanitize Tea And Coffee Makers									
19	Refill Soap Dispensers, Sanitizers And Hand Gels									
20	Clean And Dust Furniture And Office Equipment									
21	Take Out The Rubbish/Trash, Remove Waste And Recycling									
22	Clean & Disinfectant Bins/Waste Disposal Area & Trash Cans									
23	Clean And Wipe Down Windowsills									
24	Vacuum Furnishings, Cushions, Chairs, Sofas And Couches									
25	Spray Air Freshener									
26	Clean And Disinfect Any Cabinets, Shelves And Units									
27	Clean Surfaces And Desk/Work Dividers									
28	Clean And Disinfect Telephones And Headsets									
29	Polish Any Wooden Furniture And Hardwood Surfaces									

	Monthly Office Cleaning Tasks	M	T	W	T	F	S	S	Cleaned By	Date/Time
1	Clean Skirting Boards/Baseboards And Corners									
2	Clean And Disinfect All The Walls From Top To Bottom									
3	Clean Blinds (Take Down And Wash If Possible)									
4	Wash And Clean Windows (Inside And Outside)									
5	Clean And Disinfect Shared Surfaces									
6	Steam Clean Carpets And Rugs									
7	Dust And Clean Ceilings, Ceiling Corners And Ceiling Tiles									
8	Check For Broken Chairs And Tables									
9	Dust And Wash Radiator Covers									
10	Clean And Disinfect Ceiling Wall Vents									
11	Clean And Vacuum Central Heating Units									
12	Wash And Clean Light Covers									
13	Clean Drapes And Curtains (Take Down And Wash if Possible)									
14	Check Cleaning Supplies And Re-Stock As Necessary									
15	Check Ceiling Fans, Fire Sprinklers And Smoke Alarms									
16	Check Hardware, Door Stops And Lock Mechanisms									
17	Fire Exit Lights And Emergency Lights Checked & Functioning									
18	Organize And De-Clutter Office Drawers									
19	Organize And De-Clutter Storeroom									
	Daily/Weekly Toilets/Restroom Cleaning Tasks	M	T	W	T	F	S	S	Cleaned By	Date/Time
1	Clean And Disinfect All Doors, Door Handles And Doorknobs									
2	Disinfect Touch Points, Light Switches And Other Switches									
3	Toilet Roll Holders Cleaned And Disinfected And Re-Stocked									
4	Wipe Down The Walls Wherever There Are Spills And Splashes									
5	Electric Hand Dryers Cleaned, Disinfected & Operating Correctly									
6	Sweep The Floors To Ensure They're Free From Debris									
7	Mop Tiled And Laminate Floors With Disinfectant Cleaner									
8	Paper Dispensers & Paper Towel Rolls Cleaned & Re-Stocked									
9	Take Out The Rubbish/Trash, Remove Waste And Recycling									
10	Clean & Disinfectant Bins/Waste Disposal Area & Trash Cans									
11	Feminine Hygiene Bins/Containers Cleaned And Disinfected									
12	Toilets Cleaned & Disinfected, Outside, Inside And Handles									
13	Urinals & Urinal Screens Cleaned, Disinfected & Blocks Replaced									
14	Wall Mirrors Cleaned With Glass Cleaner									
15	Clean And Re-Stock Paper Dispensers & Paper Towel Rolls									
16	Refill Soap Dispensers, Sanitizers And Hand Gels									
17	Sinks, Taps, Fixtures, Surface Areas Cleaned And Disinfected									

	Daily/Weekly Toilets/Restroom Cleaning Tasks Con	M	T	W	T	F	S	S	Cleaned By	Date/Time
18	Windowsills Clean And Wiped Down									
19	Check Plumbing And Schedule Work If Required									
20	Air Fresheners Checked And Replaced									
21	Fire Exit Lights And Emergency Lights Checked & Functioning									
22	Place Wet Floor Signs If Floors Are Wet After Mopping									
23	Cabinets Cleaned And Disinfected									
	Monthly Toilets/Restroom Cleaning Tasks	M	T	W	T	F	S	S	Cleaned By	Date/Time
1	Toilet/Restroom Service Storeroom/Cupboard Clean And Tidy									
2	Walls Free Of Graffiti, Stickers, Gum And Residue									
3	Wash And Clean Windows (Inside And Outside)									
4	Check Hardware, Door Stops And Lock Mechanisms									
5	All Fittings Securely Fixed (Schedule Maintenance If Not)									
6	Dust And Clean Ceilings, Ceiling Corners And Ceiling Tiles									
7	Clean Skirting Boards/Baseboards And Corners									
8	Thoroughly Clean Grout And Tiles									
9	Ceiling Wall Vents Cleaned And Disinfected									
10	Clean And Vacuum Central Heating Units									
11	Wash And Clean Light Covers									
12	Wash All Toilet And Restroom Mats									
	Daily/Weekly Kitchen Cleaning Tasks	M	T	W	T	F	S	S	Cleaned By	Date/Time
1	Wash And Sanitize All Counter Tops And Prep Area Surfaces									
2	Empty Dishwasher, Run The Dishwasher/Dish Drainer									
3	Disinfect Touch Points, Light Switches And Other Switches									
4	Take Out The Rubbish/Trash, Remove Waste And Recycling									
5	Clean & Disinfectant Bins/Waste Disposal Area & Trash Cans									
6	Wipe Down The Walls Wherever There Are Spills And Splashes									
7	Sweep The Floors To Ensure They're Free From Debris									
8	Mop Tiled And Laminate Floors With Disinfectant Cleaner									
9	Wet Floor Signs In Place If Floors Are Wet After Mopping									
10	Thoroughly Clean And Disinfect The Sinks And Taps									
11	Clean Exterior Of Appliances, Check For Spilled Food									
12	Replace Empty Paper Towel Rolls And Cloth Roller Towels									
13	Refill Soap Dispensers And Hand Sanitizers/Hand Gels									
14	Wipe Down Equipment, Tea And Coffee Makers, Toasters Etc									
15	Fire Exit Lights And Emergency Lights Checked & Functioning									
16	Pour Drain Cleaner Down Floor And Sink Drains									
17	Clean Inside Microwave, Check For Spilled Food									

	Daily/Weekly Kitchen Cleaning Tasks Continued	M	T	W	T	F	S	S	CLEANED BY	DATE/TIME
18	Replace Wash Rags, Cloths And Tea Towels With Clean Ones									
19	Wash Rags, Cloths, Tea Towels And Towels In Washing Machine									
20	Replace And Change Burned Out Light Bulbs/Broken Lights									
21	Clean Inside Of Dishwasher									
22	Sanitise Sponges Or Replace Damaged Sponges With New									
23	Dishes, Pots, Pans, And Utensils To Be Stored Away Properly									
24	Clean Out Refrigerator And Wipe Down Shelves And Drawers									
	Monthly Kitchen Cleaning Tasks	M	T	W	T	F	S	S	Cleaned By	Date/Time
1	Wash And Clean Air Vents									
2	Sort Through And Organize Cooking Utensils, Pans And Pots									
3	Wash And Clean Air Vents									
4	Check Plates, Cups And Glasses And Bin Anything Chipped									
5	Clean And Vacuum Central Heating Units									
6	Wash And Clean Light Covers									
7	Clean And De-Lime Dishwasher									
8	Dust And Clean Ceilings, Ceiling Corners And Ceiling Tiles									
9	Thoroughly Clean Grout And Tiles									
10	Clean Refrigerator Coils To Remove Dust, Unplug First									
11	Run Cleaning & Sanitizing Chemicals Through Coffee Machine									
12	Disinfect And Clean All The Walls From Top To Bottom									
13	Check For Out Of Date Food In Cabinets/Cupboards									
14	Clean Skirting Boards/Baseboards And Corners									
15	Clean Under Refrigerator									
16	Wash And Clean Doors, Door Frames And Glass									
17	Sort Through Leftover Items In The Fridge/Refrigerators									
18	Wash And Clean Windows (Inside And Outside)									
19	Replace Pest Traps									

ESSENTIAL CLEANING NOTES

....

....

....

....

....

....

....

....

ESSENTIAL OFFICE CLEANING *Checklist*

Location/Building	Department	Office Number	Week Number

Start Date & Time	Finnish Date & Time	Name	Signature

	Daily/Weekly Office Cleaning Tasks	M	T	W	T	F	S	S	Cleaned By	Date/Time
1	Clean And Sanitize All The Desks And Tables									
2	Clean And Sanitize All The Counter Tops And Surface Areas									
3	Disinfect All Point-Of-Sale Terminals And Touch Screens									
4	Disinfect Touch Points, Light Switches And Other Switches									
5	Clean And Sanitize All Keyboards And Computer Mice									
6	Wipe Down The Walls Wherever There Are Spills And Splashes									
7	Clean And Disinfect All Doors, Door Handles And Doorknobs									
8	Re-Stock Protective Clothing, Face Masks/Shields, Gloves									
9	Clean And Sanitize All The Chairs, Seats And Benches									
10	Clean All The Mirrors, Glass Cabinets/Displays									
11	Replace And Change Burned Out Light Bulbs/Broken Lights									
12	Sweep The Floors To Ensure They're Free From Debris									
13	Mop Tiled And Laminate Floors With Disinfectant Cleaner									
14	Vacuum And Hoover The Carpets, Mats And Rugs									
15	Place Wet Floor Signs If Floors Are Wet After Mopping									
16	Wash & Clean Dirty Cups, Drinking Bottles And Glasses									
17	Clean & Re-Stock Paper Dispensers & Paper Towel Rolls									
18	Wipe Down Equipment & Sanitize Tea And Coffee Makers									
19	Refill Soap Dispensers, Sanitizers And Hand Gels									
20	Clean And Dust Furniture And Office Equipment									
21	Take Out The Rubbish/Trash, Remove Waste And Recycling									
22	Clean & Disinfectant Bins/Waste Disposal Area & Trash Cans									
23	Clean And Wipe Down Windowsills									
24	Vacuum Furnishings, Cushions, Chairs, Sofas And Couches									
25	Spray Air Freshener									
26	Clean And Disinfect Any Cabinets, Shelves And Units									
27	Clean Surfaces And Desk/Work Dividers									
28	Clean And Disinfect Telephones And Headsets									
29	Polish Any Wooden Furniture And Hardwood Surfaces									

	Monthly Office Cleaning Tasks	M	T	W	T	F	S	S	Cleaned By	Date/Time
1	Clean Skirting Boards/Baseboards And Corners									
2	Clean And Disinfect All The Walls From Top To Bottom									
3	Clean Blinds (Take Down And Wash If Possible)									
4	Wash And Clean Windows (Inside And Outside)									
5	Clean And Disinfect Shared Surfaces									
6	Steam Clean Carpets And Rugs									
7	Dust And Clean Ceilings, Ceiling Corners And Ceiling Tiles									
8	Check For Broken Chairs And Tables									
9	Dust And Wash Radiator Covers									
10	Clean And Disinfect Ceiling Wall Vents									
11	Clean And Vacuum Central Heating Units									
12	Wash And Clean Light Covers									
13	Clean Drapes And Curtains (Take Down And Wash if Possible)									
14	Check Cleaning Supplies And Re-Stock As Necessary									
15	Check Ceiling Fans, Fire Sprinklers And Smoke Alarms									
16	Check Hardware, Door Stops And Lock Mechanisms									
17	Fire Exit Lights And Emergency Lights Checked & Functioning									
18	Organize And De-Clutter Office Drawers									
19	Organize And De-Clutter Storeroom									

	Daily/Weekly Toilets/Restroom Cleaning Tasks	M	T	W	T	F	S	S	Cleaned By	Date/Time
1	Clean And Disinfect All Doors, Door Handles And Doorknobs									
2	Disinfect Touch Points, Light Switches And Other Switches									
3	Toilet Roll Holders Cleaned And Disinfected And Re-Stocked									
4	Wipe Down The Walls Wherever There Are Spills And Splashes									
5	Electric Hand Dryers Cleaned, Disinfected & Operating Correctly									
6	Sweep The Floors To Ensure They're Free From Debris									
7	Mop Tiled And Laminate Floors With Disinfectant Cleaner									
8	Paper Dispensers & Paper Towel Rolls Cleaned & Re-Stocked									
9	Take Out The Rubbish/Trash, Remove Waste And Recycling									
10	Clean & Disinfectant Bins/Waste Disposal Area & Trash Cans									
11	Feminine Hygiene Bins/Containers Cleaned And Disinfected									
12	Toilets Cleaned & Disinfected, Outside, Inside And Handles									
13	Urinals & Urinal Screens Cleaned, Disinfected & Blocks Replaced									
14	Wall Mirrors Cleaned With Glass Cleaner									
15	Clean And Re-Stock Paper Dispensers & Paper Towel Rolls									
16	Refill Soap Dispensers, Sanitizers And Hand Gels									
17	Sinks, Taps, Fixtures, Surface Areas Cleaned And Disinfected									

	Daily/Weekly Toilets/Restroom Cleaning Tasks Con	M	T	W	T	F	S	S	Cleaned By	Date/Time
18	Windowsills Clean And Wiped Down									
19	Check Plumbing And Schedule Work If Required									
20	Air Fresheners Checked And Replaced									
21	Fire Exit Lights And Emergency Lights Checked & Functioning									
22	Place Wet Floor Signs If Floors Are Wet After Mopping									
23	Cabinets Cleaned And Disinfected									
	Monthly Toilets/Restroom Cleaning Tasks	M	T	W	T	F	S	S	Cleaned By	Date/Time
1	Toilet/Restroom Service Storeroom/Cupboard Clean And Tidy									
2	Walls Free Of Graffiti, Stickers, Gum And Residue									
3	Wash And Clean Windows (Inside And Outside)									
4	Check Hardware, Door Stops And Lock Mechanisms									
5	All Fittings Securely Fixed (Schedule Maintenance If Not)									
6	Dust And Clean Ceilings, Ceiling Corners And Ceiling Tiles									
7	Clean Skirting Boards/Baseboards And Corners									
8	Thoroughly Clean Grout And Tiles									
9	Ceiling Wall Vents Cleaned And Disinfected									
10	Clean And Vacuum Central Heating Units									
11	Wash And Clean Light Covers									
12	Wash All Toilet And Restroom Mats									
	Daily/Weekly Kitchen Cleaning Tasks	M	T	W	T	F	S	S	Cleaned By	Date/Time
1	Wash And Sanitize All Counter Tops And Prep Area Surfaces									
2	Empty Dishwasher, Run The Dishwasher/Dish Drainer									
3	Disinfect Touch Points, Light Switches And Other Switches									
4	Take Out The Rubbish/Trash, Remove Waste And Recycling									
5	Clean & Disinfectant Bins/Waste Disposal Area & Trash Cans									
6	Wipe Down The Walls Wherever There Are Spills And Splashes									
7	Sweep The Floors To Ensure They're Free From Debris									
8	Mop Tiled And Laminate Floors With Disinfectant Cleaner									
9	Wet Floor Signs In Place If Floors Are Wet After Mopping									
10	Thoroughly Clean And Disinfect The Sinks And Taps									
11	Clean Exterior Of Appliances, Check For Spilled Food									
12	Replace Empty Paper Towel Rolls And Cloth Roller Towels									
13	Refill Soap Dispensers And Hand Sanitizers/Hand Gels									
14	Wipe Down Equipment, Tea And Coffee Makers, Toasters Etc									
15	Fire Exit Lights And Emergency Lights Checked & Functioning									
16	Pour Drain Cleaner Down Floor And Sink Drains									
17	Clean Inside Microwave, Check For Spilled Food									

	Daily/Weekly Kitchen Cleaning Tasks Continued	M	T	W	T	F	S	S	CLEANED BY	DATE/TIME
18	Replace Wash Rags, Cloths And Tea Towels With Clean Ones									
19	Wash Rags, Cloths, Tea Towels And Towels In Washing Machine									
20	Replace And Change Burned Out Light Bulbs/Broken Lights									
21	Clean Inside Of Dishwasher									
22	Sanitise Sponges Or Replace Damaged Sponges With New									
23	Dishes, Pots, Pans, And Utensils To Be Stored Away Properly									
24	Clean Out Refrigerator And Wipe Down Shelves And Drawers									
	Monthly Kitchen Cleaning Tasks	M	T	W	T	F	S	S	Cleaned By	Date/Time
1	Wash And Clean Air Vents									
2	Sort Through And Organize Cooking Utensils, Pans And Pots									
3	Wash And Clean Air Vents									
4	Check Plates, Cups And Glasses And Bin Anything Chipped									
5	Clean And Vacuum Central Heating Units									
6	Wash And Clean Light Covers									
7	Clean And De-Lime Dishwasher									
8	Dust And Clean Ceilings, Ceiling Corners And Ceiling Tiles									
9	Thoroughly Clean Grout And Tiles									
10	Clean Refrigerator Coils To Remove Dust, Unplug First									
11	Run Cleaning & Sanitizing Chemicals Through Coffee Machine									
12	Disinfect And Clean All The Walls From Top To Bottom									
13	Check For Out Of Date Food In Cabinets/Cupboards									
14	Clean Skirting Boards/Baseboards And Corners									
15	Clean Under Refrigerator									
16	Wash And Clean Doors, Door Frames And Glass									
17	Sort Through Leftover Items In The Fridge/Refrigerators									
18	Wash And Clean Windows (Inside And Outside)									
19	Replace Pest Traps									

ESSENTIAL CLEANING NOTES

....

....

....

....

....

....

....

....

ESSENTIAL OFFICE CLEANING *Checklist*

Location/Building	Department	Office Number	Week Number

Start Date & Time	Finnish Date & Time	Name	Signature

	Daily/Weekly Office Cleaning Tasks	M	T	W	T	F	S	S	Cleaned By	Date/Time
1	Clean And Sanitize All The Desks And Tables									
2	Clean And Sanitize All The Counter Tops And Surface Areas									
3	Disinfect All Point-Of-Sale Terminals And Touch Screens									
4	Disinfect Touch Points, Light Switches And Other Switches									
5	Clean And Sanitize All Keyboards And Computer Mice									
6	Wipe Down The Walls Wherever There Are Spills And Splashes									
7	Clean And Disinfect All Doors, Door Handles And Doorknobs									
8	Re-Stock Protective Clothing, Face Masks/Shields, Gloves									
9	Clean And Sanitize All The Chairs, Seats And Benches									
10	Clean All The Mirrors, Glass Cabinets/Displays									
11	Replace And Change Burned Out Light Bulbs/Broken Lights									
12	Sweep The Floors To Ensure They're Free From Debris									
13	Mop Tiled And Laminate Floors With Disinfectant Cleaner									
14	Vacuum And Hoover The Carpets, Mats And Rugs									
15	Place Wet Floor Signs If Floors Are Wet After Mopping									
16	Wash & Clean Dirty Cups, Drinking Bottles And Glasses									
17	Clean & Re-Stock Paper Dispensers & Paper Towel Rolls									
18	Wipe Down Equipment & Sanitize Tea And Coffee Makers									
19	Refill Soap Dispensers, Sanitizers And Hand Gels									
20	Clean And Dust Furniture And Office Equipment									
21	Take Out The Rubbish/Trash, Remove Waste And Recycling									
22	Clean & Disinfectant Bins/Waste Disposal Area & Trash Cans									
23	Clean And Wipe Down Windowsills									
24	Vacuum Furnishings, Cushions, Chairs, Sofas And Couches									
25	Spray Air Freshener									
26	Clean And Disinfect Any Cabinets, Shelves And Units									
27	Clean Surfaces And Desk/Work Dividers									
28	Clean And Disinfect Telephones And Headsets									
29	Polish Any Wooden Furniture And Hardwood Surfaces									

	Monthly Office Cleaning Tasks	M	T	W	T	F	S	S	Cleaned By	Date/Time
1	Clean Skirting Boards/Baseboards And Corners									
2	Clean And Disinfect All The Walls From Top To Bottom									
3	Clean Blinds (Take Down And Wash If Possible)									
4	Wash And Clean Windows (Inside And Outside)									
5	Clean And Disinfect Shared Surfaces									
6	Steam Clean Carpets And Rugs									
7	Dust And Clean Ceilings, Ceiling Corners And Ceiling Tiles									
8	Check For Broken Chairs And Tables									
9	Dust And Wash Radiator Covers									
10	Clean And Disinfect Ceiling Wall Vents									
11	Clean And Vacuum Central Heating Units									
12	Wash And Clean Light Covers									
13	Clean Drapes And Curtains (Take Down And Wash if Possible)									
14	Check Cleaning Supplies And Re-Stock As Necessary									
15	Check Ceiling Fans, Fire Sprinklers And Smoke Alarms									
16	Check Hardware, Door Stops And Lock Mechanisms									
17	Fire Exit Lights And Emergency Lights Checked & Functioning									
18	Organize And De-Clutter Office Drawers									
19	Organize And De-Clutter Storeroom									
	Daily/Weekly Toilets/Restroom Cleaning Tasks	M	T	W	T	F	S	S	Cleaned By	Date/Time
1	Clean And Disinfect All Doors, Door Handles And Doorknobs									
2	Disinfect Touch Points, Light Switches And Other Switches									
3	Toilet Roll Holders Cleaned And Disinfected And Re-Stocked									
4	Wipe Down The Walls Wherever There Are Spills And Splashes									
5	Electric Hand Dryers Cleaned, Disinfected & Operating Correctly									
6	Sweep The Floors To Ensure They're Free From Debris									
7	Mop Tiled And Laminate Floors With Disinfectant Cleaner									
8	Paper Dispensers & Paper Towel Rolls Cleaned & Re-Stocked									
9	Take Out The Rubbish/Trash, Remove Waste And Recycling									
10	Clean & Disinfectant Bins/Waste Disposal Area & Trash Cans									
11	Feminine Hygiene Bins/Containers Cleaned And Disinfected									
12	Toilets Cleaned & Disinfected, Outside, Inside And Handles									
13	Urinals & Urinal Screens Cleaned, Disinfected & Blocks Replaced									
14	Wall Mirrors Cleaned With Glass Cleaner									
15	Clean And Re-Stock Paper Dispensers & Paper Towel Rolls									
16	Refill Soap Dispensers, Sanitizers And Hand Gels									
17	Sinks, Taps, Fixtures, Surface Areas Cleaned And Disinfected									

	Daily/Weekly Toilets/Restroom Cleaning Tasks Con	M	T	W	T	F	S	S	Cleaned By	Date/Time
18	Windowsills Clean And Wiped Down									
19	Check Plumbing And Schedule Work If Required									
20	Air Fresheners Checked And Replaced									
21	Fire Exit Lights And Emergency Lights Checked & Functioning									
22	Place Wet Floor Signs If Floors Are Wet After Mopping									
23	Cabinets Cleaned And Disinfected									
	Monthly Toilets/Restroom Cleaning Tasks	M	T	W	T	F	S	S	Cleaned By	Date/Time
1	Toilet/Restroom Service Storeroom/Cupboard Clean And Tidy									
2	Walls Free Of Graffiti, Stickers, Gum And Residue									
3	Wash And Clean Windows (Inside And Outside)									
4	Check Hardware, Door Stops And Lock Mechanisms									
5	All Fittings Securely Fixed (Schedule Maintenance If Not)									
6	Dust And Clean Ceilings, Ceiling Corners And Ceiling Tiles									
7	Clean Skirting Boards/Baseboards And Corners									
8	Thoroughly Clean Grout And Tiles									
9	Ceiling Wall Vents Cleaned And Disinfected									
10	Clean And Vacuum Central Heating Units									
11	Wash And Clean Light Covers									
12	Wash All Toilet And Restroom Mats									
	Daily/Weekly Kitchen Cleaning Tasks	M	T	W	T	F	S	S	Cleaned By	Date/Time
1	Wash And Sanitize All Counter Tops And Prep Area Surfaces									
2	Empty Dishwasher, Run The Dishwasher/Dish Drainer									
3	Disinfect Touch Points, Light Switches And Other Switches									
4	Take Out The Rubbish/Trash, Remove Waste And Recycling									
5	Clean & Disinfectant Bins/Waste Disposal Area & Trash Cans									
6	Wipe Down The Walls Wherever There Are Spills And Splashes									
7	Sweep The Floors To Ensure They're Free From Debris									
8	Mop Tiled And Laminate Floors With Disinfectant Cleaner									
9	Wet Floor Signs In Place If Floors Are Wet After Mopping									
10	Thoroughly Clean And Disinfect The Sinks And Taps									
11	Clean Exterior Of Appliances, Check For Spilled Food									
12	Replace Empty Paper Towel Rolls And Cloth Roller Towels									
13	Refill Soap Dispensers And Hand Sanitizers/Hand Gels									
14	Wipe Down Equipment, Tea And Coffee Makers, Toasters Etc									
15	Fire Exit Lights And Emergency Lights Checked & Functioning									
16	Pour Drain Cleaner Down Floor And Sink Drains									
17	Clean Inside Microwave, Check For Spilled Food									

	Daily/Weekly Kitchen Cleaning Tasks Continued	M	T	W	T	F	S	S	CLEANED BY	DATE/TIME
18	Replace Wash Rags, Cloths And Tea Towels With Clean Ones									
19	Wash Rags, Cloths, Tea Towels And Towels In Washing Machine									
20	Replace And Change Burned Out Light Bulbs/Broken Lights									
21	Clean Inside Of Dishwasher									
22	Sanitise Sponges Or Replace Damaged Sponges With New									
23	Dishes, Pots, Pans, And Utensils To Be Stored Away Properly									
24	Clean Out Refrigerator And Wipe Down Shelves And Drawers									
	Monthly Kitchen Cleaning Tasks	M	T	W	T	F	S	S	Cleaned By	Date/Time
1	Wash And Clean Air Vents									
2	Sort Through And Organize Cooking Utensils, Pans And Pots									
3	Wash And Clean Air Vents									
4	Check Plates, Cups And Glasses And Bin Anything Chipped									
5	Clean And Vacuum Central Heating Units									
6	Wash And Clean Light Covers									
7	Clean And De-Lime Dishwasher									
8	Dust And Clean Ceilings, Ceiling Corners And Ceiling Tiles									
9	Thoroughly Clean Grout And Tiles									
10	Clean Refrigerator Coils To Remove Dust, Unplug First									
11	Run Cleaning & Sanitizing Chemicals Through Coffee Machine									
12	Disinfect And Clean All The Walls From Top To Bottom									
13	Check For Out Of Date Food In Cabinets/Cupboards									
14	Clean Skirting Boards/Baseboards And Corners									
15	Clean Under Refrigerator									
16	Wash And Clean Doors, Door Frames And Glass									
17	Sort Through Leftover Items In The Fridge/Refrigerators									
18	Wash And Clean Windows (Inside And Outside)									
19	Replace Pest Traps									

ESSENTIAL CLEANING NOTES

....

....

....

....

....

....

....

....

ESSENTIAL OFFICE CLEANING *Checklist*

Location/Building	Department	Office Number	Week Number

Start Date & Time	Finnish Date & Time	Name	Signature

	Daily/Weekly Office Cleaning Tasks	M	T	W	T	F	S	S	Cleaned By	Date/Time
1	Clean And Sanitize All The Desks And Tables									
2	Clean And Sanitize All The Counter Tops And Surface Areas									
3	Disinfect All Point-Of-Sale Terminals And Touch Screens									
4	Disinfect Touch Points, Light Switches And Other Switches									
5	Clean And Sanitize All Keyboards And Computer Mice									
6	Wipe Down The Walls Wherever There Are Spills And Splashes									
7	Clean And Disinfect All Doors, Door Handles And Doorknobs									
8	Re-Stock Protective Clothing, Face Masks/Shields, Gloves									
9	Clean And Sanitize All The Chairs, Seats And Benches									
10	Clean All The Mirrors, Glass Cabinets/Displays									
11	Replace And Change Burned Out Light Bulbs/Broken Lights									
12	Sweep The Floors To Ensure They're Free From Debris									
13	Mop Tiled And Laminate Floors With Disinfectant Cleaner									
14	Vacuum And Hoover The Carpets, Mats And Rugs									
15	Place Wet Floor Signs If Floors Are Wet After Mopping									
16	Wash & Clean Dirty Cups, Drinking Bottles And Glasses									
17	Clean & Re-Stock Paper Dispensers & Paper Towel Rolls									
18	Wipe Down Equipment & Sanitize Tea And Coffee Makers									
19	Refill Soap Dispensers, Sanitizers And Hand Gels									
20	Clean And Dust Furniture And Office Equipment									
21	Take Out The Rubbish/Trash, Remove Waste And Recycling									
22	Clean & Disinfectant Bins/Waste Disposal Area & Trash Cans									
23	Clean And Wipe Down Windowsills									
24	Vacuum Furnishings, Cushions, Chairs, Sofas And Couches									
25	Spray Air Freshener									
26	Clean And Disinfect Any Cabinets, Shelves And Units									
27	Clean Surfaces And Desk/Work Dividers									
28	Clean And Disinfect Telephones And Headsets									
29	Polish Any Wooden Furniture And Hardwood Surfaces									

	Monthly Office Cleaning Tasks	M	T	W	T	F	S	S	Cleaned By	Date/Time
1	Clean Skirting Boards/Baseboards And Corners									
2	Clean And Disinfect All The Walls From Top To Bottom									
3	Clean Blinds (Take Down And Wash If Possible)									
4	Wash And Clean Windows (Inside And Outside)									
5	Clean And Disinfect Shared Surfaces									
6	Steam Clean Carpets And Rugs									
7	Dust And Clean Ceilings, Ceiling Corners And Ceiling Tiles									
8	Check For Broken Chairs And Tables									
9	Dust And Wash Radiator Covers									
10	Clean And Disinfect Ceiling Wall Vents									
11	Clean And Vacuum Central Heating Units									
12	Wash And Clean Light Covers									
13	Clean Drapes And Curtains (Take Down And Wash if Possible)									
14	Check Cleaning Supplies And Re-Stock As Necessary									
15	Check Ceiling Fans, Fire Sprinklers And Smoke Alarms									
16	Check Hardware, Door Stops And Lock Mechanisms									
17	Fire Exit Lights And Emergency Lights Checked & Functioning									
18	Organize And De-Clutter Office Drawers									
19	Organize And De-Clutter Storeroom									
	Daily/Weekly Toilets/Restroom Cleaning Tasks	M	T	W	T	F	S	S	Cleaned By	Date/Time
1	Clean And Disinfect All Doors, Door Handles And Doorknobs									
2	Disinfect Touch Points, Light Switches And Other Switches									
3	Toilet Roll Holders Cleaned And Disinfected And Re-Stocked									
4	Wipe Down The Walls Wherever There Are Spills And Splashes									
5	Electric Hand Dryers Cleaned, Disinfected & Operating Correctly									
6	Sweep The Floors To Ensure They're Free From Debris									
7	Mop Tiled And Laminate Floors With Disinfectant Cleaner									
8	Paper Dispensers & Paper Towel Rolls Cleaned & Re-Stocked									
9	Take Out The Rubbish/Trash, Remove Waste And Recycling									
10	Clean & Disinfectant Bins/Waste Disposal Area & Trash Cans									
11	Feminine Hygiene Bins/Containers Cleaned And Disinfected									
12	Toilets Cleaned & Disinfected, Outside, Inside And Handles									
13	Urinals & Urinal Screens Cleaned, Disinfected & Blocks Replaced									
14	Wall Mirrors Cleaned With Glass Cleaner									
15	Clean And Re-Stock Paper Dispensers & Paper Towel Rolls									
16	Refill Soap Dispensers, Sanitizers And Hand Gels									
17	Sinks, Taps, Fixtures, Surface Areas Cleaned And Disinfected									

	Daily/Weekly Toilets/Restroom Cleaning Tasks Con	M	T	W	T	F	S	S	Cleaned By	Date/Time
18	Windowsills Clean And Wiped Down									
19	Check Plumbing And Schedule Work If Required									
20	Air Fresheners Checked And Replaced									
21	Fire Exit Lights And Emergency Lights Checked & Functioning									
22	Place Wet Floor Signs If Floors Are Wet After Mopping									
23	Cabinets Cleaned And Disinfected									
	Monthly Toilets/Restroom Cleaning Tasks	M	T	W	T	F	S	S	Cleaned By	Date/Time
1	Toilet/Restroom Service Storeroom/Cupboard Clean And Tidy									
2	Walls Free Of Graffiti, Stickers, Gum And Residue									
3	Wash And Clean Windows (Inside And Outside)									
4	Check Hardware, Door Stops And Lock Mechanisms									
5	All Fittings Securely Fixed (Schedule Maintenance If Not)									
6	Dust And Clean Ceilings, Ceiling Corners And Ceiling Tiles									
7	Clean Skirting Boards/Baseboards And Corners									
8	Thoroughly Clean Grout And Tiles									
9	Ceiling Wall Vents Cleaned And Disinfected									
10	Clean And Vacuum Central Heating Units									
11	Wash And Clean Light Covers									
12	Wash All Toilet And Restroom Mats									
	Daily/Weekly Kitchen Cleaning Tasks	M	T	W	T	F	S	S	Cleaned By	Date/Time
1	Wash And Sanitize All Counter Tops And Prep Area Surfaces									
2	Empty Dishwasher, Run The Dishwasher/Dish Drainer									
3	Disinfect Touch Points, Light Switches And Other Switches									
4	Take Out The Rubbish/Trash, Remove Waste And Recycling									
5	Clean & Disinfectant Bins/Waste Disposal Area & Trash Cans									
6	Wipe Down The Walls Wherever There Are Spills And Splashes									
7	Sweep The Floors To Ensure They're Free From Debris									
8	Mop Tiled And Laminate Floors With Disinfectant Cleaner									
9	Wet Floor Signs In Place If Floors Are Wet After Mopping									
10	Thoroughly Clean And Disinfect The Sinks And Taps									
11	Clean Exterior Of Appliances, Check For Spilled Food									
12	Replace Empty Paper Towel Rolls And Cloth Roller Towels									
13	Refill Soap Dispensers And Hand Sanitizers/Hand Gels									
14	Wipe Down Equipment, Tea And Coffee Makers, Toasters Etc									
15	Fire Exit Lights And Emergency Lights Checked & Functioning									
16	Pour Drain Cleaner Down Floor And Sink Drains									
17	Clean Inside Microwave, Check For Spilled Food									

	Daily/Weekly Kitchen Cleaning Tasks Continued	M	T	W	T	F	S	S	CLEANED BY	DATE/TIME
18	Replace Wash Rags, Cloths And Tea Towels With Clean Ones									
19	Wash Rags, Cloths, Tea Towels And Towels In Washing Machine									
20	Replace And Change Burned Out Light Bulbs/Broken Lights									
21	Clean Inside Of Dishwasher									
22	Sanitise Sponges Or Replace Damaged Sponges With New									
23	Dishes, Pots, Pans, And Utensils To Be Stored Away Properly									
24	Clean Out Refrigerator And Wipe Down Shelves And Drawers									
	Monthly Kitchen Cleaning Tasks	M	T	W	T	F	S	S	Cleaned By	Date/Time
1	Wash And Clean Air Vents									
2	Sort Through And Organize Cooking Utensils, Pans And Pots									
3	Wash And Clean Air Vents									
4	Check Plates, Cups And Glasses And Bin Anything Chipped									
5	Clean And Vacuum Central Heating Units									
6	Wash And Clean Light Covers									
7	Clean And De-Lime Dishwasher									
8	Dust And Clean Ceilings, Ceiling Corners And Ceiling Tiles									
9	Thoroughly Clean Grout And Tiles									
10	Clean Refrigerator Coils To Remove Dust, Unplug First									
11	Run Cleaning & Sanitizing Chemicals Through Coffee Machine									
12	Disinfect And Clean All The Walls From Top To Bottom									
13	Check For Out Of Date Food In Cabinets/Cupboards									
14	Clean Skirting Boards/Baseboards And Corners									
15	Clean Under Refrigerator									
16	Wash And Clean Doors, Door Frames And Glass									
17	Sort Through Leftover Items In The Fridge/Refrigerators									
18	Wash And Clean Windows (Inside And Outside)									
19	Replace Pest Traps									

ESSENTIAL CLEANING NOTES

....

....

....

....

....

....

....

....

ESSENTIAL OFFICE CLEANING *Checklist*

Location/Building	Department	Office Number	Week Number

Start Date & Time	Finnish Date & Time	Name	Signature

	Daily/Weekly Office Cleaning Tasks	M	T	W	T	F	S	S	Cleaned By	Date/Time
1	Clean And Sanitize All The Desks And Tables									
2	Clean And Sanitize All The Counter Tops And Surface Areas									
3	Disinfect All Point-Of-Sale Terminals And Touch Screens									
4	Disinfect Touch Points, Light Switches And Other Switches									
5	Clean And Sanitize All Keyboards And Computer Mice									
6	Wipe Down The Walls Wherever There Are Spills And Splashes									
7	Clean And Disinfect All Doors, Door Handles And Doorknobs									
8	Re-Stock Protective Clothing, Face Masks/Shields, Gloves									
9	Clean And Sanitize All The Chairs, Seats And Benches									
10	Clean All The Mirrors, Glass Cabinets/Displays									
11	Replace And Change Burned Out Light Bulbs/Broken Lights									
12	Sweep The Floors To Ensure They're Free From Debris									
13	Mop Tiled And Laminate Floors With Disinfectant Cleaner									
14	Vacuum And Hoover The Carpets, Mats And Rugs									
15	Place Wet Floor Signs If Floors Are Wet After Mopping									
16	Wash & Clean Dirty Cups, Drinking Bottles And Glasses									
17	Clean & Re-Stock Paper Dispensers & Paper Towel Rolls									
18	Wipe Down Equipment & Sanitize Tea And Coffee Makers									
19	Refill Soap Dispensers, Sanitizers And Hand Gels									
20	Clean And Dust Furniture And Office Equipment									
21	Take Out The Rubbish/Trash, Remove Waste And Recycling									
22	Clean & Disinfectant Bins/Waste Disposal Area & Trash Cans									
23	Clean And Wipe Down Windowsills									
24	Vacuum Furnishings, Cushions, Chairs, Sofas And Couches									
25	Spray Air Freshener									
26	Clean And Disinfect Any Cabinets, Shelves And Units									
27	Clean Surfaces And Desk/Work Dividers									
28	Clean And Disinfect Telephones And Headsets									
29	Polish Any Wooden Furniture And Hardwood Surfaces									

	Monthly Office Cleaning Tasks	M	T	W	T	F	S	S	Cleaned By	Date/Time
1	Clean Skirting Boards/Baseboards And Corners									
2	Clean And Disinfect All The Walls From Top To Bottom									
3	Clean Blinds (Take Down And Wash If Possible)									
4	Wash And Clean Windows (Inside And Outside)									
5	Clean And Disinfect Shared Surfaces									
6	Steam Clean Carpets And Rugs									
7	Dust And Clean Ceilings, Ceiling Corners And Ceiling Tiles									
8	Check For Broken Chairs And Tables									
9	Dust And Wash Radiator Covers									
10	Clean And Disinfect Ceiling Wall Vents									
11	Clean And Vacuum Central Heating Units									
12	Wash And Clean Light Covers									
13	Clean Drapes And Curtains (Take Down And Wash if Possible)									
14	Check Cleaning Supplies And Re-Stock As Necessary									
15	Check Ceiling Fans, Fire Sprinklers And Smoke Alarms									
16	Check Hardware, Door Stops And Lock Mechanisms									
17	Fire Exit Lights And Emergency Lights Checked & Functioning									
18	Organize And De-Clutter Office Drawers									
19	Organize And De-Clutter Storeroom									

	Daily/Weekly Toilets/Restroom Cleaning Tasks	M	T	W	T	F	S	S	Cleaned By	Date/Time
1	Clean And Disinfect All Doors, Door Handles And Doorknobs									
2	Disinfect Touch Points, Light Switches And Other Switches									
3	Toilet Roll Holders Cleaned And Disinfected And Re-Stocked									
4	Wipe Down The Walls Wherever There Are Spills And Splashes									
5	Electric Hand Dryers Cleaned, Disinfected & Operating Correctly									
6	Sweep The Floors To Ensure They're Free From Debris									
7	Mop Tiled And Laminate Floors With Disinfectant Cleaner									
8	Paper Dispensers & Paper Towel Rolls Cleaned & Re-Stocked									
9	Take Out The Rubbish/Trash, Remove Waste And Recycling									
10	Clean & Disinfectant Bins/Waste Disposal Area & Trash Cans									
11	Feminine Hygiene Bins/Containers Cleaned And Disinfected									
12	Toilets Cleaned & Disinfected, Outside, Inside And Handles									
13	Urinals & Urinal Screens Cleaned, Disinfected & Blocks Replaced									
14	Wall Mirrors Cleaned With Glass Cleaner									
15	Clean And Re-Stock Paper Dispensers & Paper Towel Rolls									
16	Refill Soap Dispensers, Sanitizers And Hand Gels									
17	Sinks, Taps, Fixtures, Surface Areas Cleaned And Disinfected									

	Daily/Weekly Toilets/Restroom Cleaning Tasks Con	M	T	W	T	F	S	S	Cleaned By	Date/Time
18	Windowsills Clean And Wiped Down									
19	Check Plumbing And Schedule Work If Required									
20	Air Fresheners Checked And Replaced									
21	Fire Exit Lights And Emergency Lights Checked & Functioning									
22	Place Wet Floor Signs If Floors Are Wet After Mopping									
23	Cabinets Cleaned And Disinfected									
	Monthly Toilets/Restroom Cleaning Tasks	M	T	W	T	F	S	S	Cleaned By	Date/Time
1	Toilet/Restroom Service Storeroom/Cupboard Clean And Tidy									
2	Walls Free Of Graffiti, Stickers, Gum And Residue									
3	Wash And Clean Windows (Inside And Outside)									
4	Check Hardware, Door Stops And Lock Mechanisms									
5	All Fittings Securely Fixed (Schedule Maintenance If Not)									
6	Dust And Clean Ceilings, Ceiling Corners And Ceiling Tiles									
7	Clean Skirting Boards/Baseboards And Corners									
8	Thoroughly Clean Grout And Tiles									
9	Ceiling Wall Vents Cleaned And Disinfected									
10	Clean And Vacuum Central Heating Units									
11	Wash And Clean Light Covers									
12	Wash All Toilet And Restroom Mats									
	Daily/Weekly Kitchen Cleaning Tasks	M	T	W	T	F	S	S	Cleaned By	Date/Time
1	Wash And Sanitize All Counter Tops And Prep Area Surfaces									
2	Empty Dishwasher, Run The Dishwasher/Dish Drainer									
3	Disinfect Touch Points, Light Switches And Other Switches									
4	Take Out The Rubbish/Trash, Remove Waste And Recycling									
5	Clean & Disinfectant Bins/Waste Disposal Area & Trash Cans									
6	Wipe Down The Walls Wherever There Are Spills And Splashes									
7	Sweep The Floors To Ensure They're Free From Debris									
8	Mop Tiled And Laminate Floors With Disinfectant Cleaner									
9	Wet Floor Signs In Place If Floors Are Wet After Mopping									
10	Thoroughly Clean And Disinfect The Sinks And Taps									
11	Clean Exterior Of Appliances, Check For Spilled Food									
12	Replace Empty Paper Towel Rolls And Cloth Roller Towels									
13	Refill Soap Dispensers And Hand Sanitizers/Hand Gels									
14	Wipe Down Equipment, Tea And Coffee Makers, Toasters Etc									
15	Fire Exit Lights And Emergency Lights Checked & Functioning									
16	Pour Drain Cleaner Down Floor And Sink Drains									
17	Clean Inside Microwave, Check For Spilled Food									

	Daily/Weekly Kitchen Cleaning Tasks Continued	M	T	W	T	F	S	S	CLEANED BY	DATE/TIME
18	Replace Wash Rags, Cloths And Tea Towels With Clean Ones									
19	Wash Rags, Cloths, Tea Towels And Towels In Washing Machine									
20	Replace And Change Burned Out Light Bulbs/Broken Lights									
21	Clean Inside Of Dishwasher									
22	Sanitise Sponges Or Replace Damaged Sponges With New									
23	Dishes, Pots, Pans, And Utensils To Be Stored Away Properly									
24	Clean Out Refrigerator And Wipe Down Shelves And Drawers									
	Monthly Kitchen Cleaning Tasks	M	T	W	T	F	S	S	Cleaned By	Date/Time
1	Wash And Clean Air Vents									
2	Sort Through And Organize Cooking Utensils, Pans And Pots									
3	Wash And Clean Air Vents									
4	Check Plates, Cups And Glasses And Bin Anything Chipped									
5	Clean And Vacuum Central Heating Units									
6	Wash And Clean Light Covers									
7	Clean And De-Lime Dishwasher									
8	Dust And Clean Ceilings, Ceiling Corners And Ceiling Tiles									
9	Thoroughly Clean Grout And Tiles									
10	Clean Refrigerator Coils To Remove Dust, Unplug First									
11	Run Cleaning & Sanitizing Chemicals Through Coffee Machine									
12	Disinfect And Clean All The Walls From Top To Bottom									
13	Check For Out Of Date Food In Cabinets/Cupboards									
14	Clean Skirting Boards/Baseboards And Corners									
15	Clean Under Refrigerator									
16	Wash And Clean Doors, Door Frames And Glass									
17	Sort Through Leftover Items In The Fridge/Refrigerators									
18	Wash And Clean Windows (Inside And Outside)									
19	Replace Pest Traps									

ESSENTIAL CLEANING NOTES

....

....

....

....

....

....

....

....

ESSENTIAL OFFICE CLEANING *Checklist*

Location/Building	Department	Office Number	Week Number

Start Date & Time	Finnish Date & Time	Name	Signature

	Daily/Weekly Office Cleaning Tasks	M	T	W	T	F	S	S	Cleaned By	Date/Time
1	Clean And Sanitize All The Desks And Tables									
2	Clean And Sanitize All The Counter Tops And Surface Areas									
3	Disinfect All Point-Of-Sale Terminals And Touch Screens									
4	Disinfect Touch Points, Light Switches And Other Switches									
5	Clean And Sanitize All Keyboards And Computer Mice									
6	Wipe Down The Walls Wherever There Are Spills And Splashes									
7	Clean And Disinfect All Doors, Door Handles And Doorknobs									
8	Re-Stock Protective Clothing, Face Masks/Shields, Gloves									
9	Clean And Sanitize All The Chairs, Seats And Benches									
10	Clean All The Mirrors, Glass Cabinets/Displays									
11	Replace And Change Burned Out Light Bulbs/Broken Lights									
12	Sweep The Floors To Ensure They're Free From Debris									
13	Mop Tiled And Laminate Floors With Disinfectant Cleaner									
14	Vacuum And Hoover The Carpets, Mats And Rugs									
15	Place Wet Floor Signs If Floors Are Wet After Mopping									
16	Wash & Clean Dirty Cups, Drinking Bottles And Glasses									
17	Clean & Re-Stock Paper Dispensers & Paper Towel Rolls									
18	Wipe Down Equipment & Sanitize Tea And Coffee Makers									
19	Refill Soap Dispensers, Sanitizers And Hand Gels									
20	Clean And Dust Furniture And Office Equipment									
21	Take Out The Rubbish/Trash, Remove Waste And Recycling									
22	Clean & Disinfectant Bins/Waste Disposal Area & Trash Cans									
23	Clean And Wipe Down Windowsills									
24	Vacuum Furnishings, Cushions, Chairs, Sofas And Couches									
25	Spray Air Freshener									
26	Clean And Disinfect Any Cabinets, Shelves And Units									
27	Clean Surfaces And Desk/Work Dividers									
28	Clean And Disinfect Telephones And Headsets									
29	Polish Any Wooden Furniture And Hardwood Surfaces									

	Monthly Office Cleaning Tasks	M	T	W	T	F	S	S	Cleaned By	Date/Time
1	Clean Skirting Boards/Baseboards And Corners									
2	Clean And Disinfect All The Walls From Top To Bottom									
3	Clean Blinds (Take Down And Wash If Possible)									
4	Wash And Clean Windows (Inside And Outside)									
5	Clean And Disinfect Shared Surfaces									
6	Steam Clean Carpets And Rugs									
7	Dust And Clean Ceilings, Ceiling Corners And Ceiling Tiles									
8	Check For Broken Chairs And Tables									
9	Dust And Wash Radiator Covers									
10	Clean And Disinfect Ceiling Wall Vents									
11	Clean And Vacuum Central Heating Units									
12	Wash And Clean Light Covers									
13	Clean Drapes And Curtains (Take Down And Wash if Possible)									
14	Check Cleaning Supplies And Re-Stock As Necessary									
15	Check Ceiling Fans, Fire Sprinklers And Smoke Alarms									
16	Check Hardware, Door Stops And Lock Mechanisms									
17	Fire Exit Lights And Emergency Lights Checked & Functioning									
18	Organize And De-Clutter Office Drawers									
19	Organize And De-Clutter Storeroom									
	Daily/Weekly Toilets/Restroom Cleaning Tasks	M	T	W	T	F	S	S	Cleaned By	Date/Time
1	Clean And Disinfect All Doors, Door Handles And Doorknobs									
2	Disinfect Touch Points, Light Switches And Other Switches									
3	Toilet Roll Holders Cleaned And Disinfected And Re-Stocked									
4	Wipe Down The Walls Wherever There Are Spills And Splashes									
5	Electric Hand Dryers Cleaned, Disinfected & Operating Correctly									
6	Sweep The Floors To Ensure They're Free From Debris									
7	Mop Tiled And Laminate Floors With Disinfectant Cleaner									
8	Paper Dispensers & Paper Towel Rolls Cleaned & Re-Stocked									
9	Take Out The Rubbish/Trash, Remove Waste And Recycling									
10	Clean & Disinfectant Bins/Waste Disposal Area & Trash Cans									
11	Feminine Hygiene Bins/Containers Cleaned And Disinfected									
12	Toilets Cleaned & Disinfected, Outside, Inside And Handles									
13	Urinals & Urinal Screens Cleaned, Disinfected & Blocks Replaced									
14	Wall Mirrors Cleaned With Glass Cleaner									
15	Clean And Re-Stock Paper Dispensers & Paper Towel Rolls									
16	Refill Soap Dispensers, Sanitizers And Hand Gels									
17	Sinks, Taps, Fixtures, Surface Areas Cleaned And Disinfected									

	Daily/Weekly Toilets/Restroom Cleaning Tasks Con	M	T	W	T	F	S	S	Cleaned By	Date/Time
18	Windowsills Clean And Wiped Down									
19	Check Plumbing And Schedule Work If Required									
20	Air Fresheners Checked And Replaced									
21	Fire Exit Lights And Emergency Lights Checked & Functioning									
22	Place Wet Floor Signs If Floors Are Wet After Mopping									
23	Cabinets Cleaned And Disinfected									
	Monthly Toilets/Restroom Cleaning Tasks	M	T	W	T	F	S	S	Cleaned By	Date/Time
1	Toilet/Restroom Service Storeroom/Cupboard Clean And Tidy									
2	Walls Free Of Graffiti, Stickers, Gum And Residue									
3	Wash And Clean Windows (Inside And Outside)									
4	Check Hardware, Door Stops And Lock Mechanisms									
5	All Fittings Securely Fixed (Schedule Maintenance If Not)									
6	Dust And Clean Ceilings, Ceiling Corners And Ceiling Tiles									
7	Clean Skirting Boards/Baseboards And Corners									
8	Thoroughly Clean Grout And Tiles									
9	Ceiling Wall Vents Cleaned And Disinfected									
10	Clean And Vacuum Central Heating Units									
11	Wash And Clean Light Covers									
12	Wash All Toilet And Restroom Mats									
	Daily/Weekly Kitchen Cleaning Tasks	M	T	W	T	F	S	S	Cleaned By	Date/Time
1	Wash And Sanitize All Counter Tops And Prep Area Surfaces									
2	Empty Dishwasher, Run The Dishwasher/Dish Drainer									
3	Disinfect Touch Points, Light Switches And Other Switches									
4	Take Out The Rubbish/Trash, Remove Waste And Recycling									
5	Clean & Disinfectant Bins/Waste Disposal Area & Trash Cans									
6	Wipe Down The Walls Wherever There Are Spills And Splashes									
7	Sweep The Floors To Ensure They're Free From Debris									
8	Mop Tiled And Laminate Floors With Disinfectant Cleaner									
9	Wet Floor Signs In Place If Floors Are Wet After Mopping									
10	Thoroughly Clean And Disinfect The Sinks And Taps									
11	Clean Exterior Of Appliances, Check For Spilled Food									
12	Replace Empty Paper Towel Rolls And Cloth Roller Towels									
13	Refill Soap Dispensers And Hand Sanitizers/Hand Gels									
14	Wipe Down Equipment, Tea And Coffee Makers, Toasters Etc									
15	Fire Exit Lights And Emergency Lights Checked & Functioning									
16	Pour Drain Cleaner Down Floor And Sink Drains									
17	Clean Inside Microwave, Check For Spilled Food									

	Daily/Weekly Kitchen Cleaning Tasks Continued	M	T	W	T	F	S	S	CLEANED BY	DATE/TIME
18	Replace Wash Rags, Cloths And Tea Towels With Clean Ones									
19	Wash Rags, Cloths, Tea Towels And Towels In Washing Machine									
20	Replace And Change Burned Out Light Bulbs/Broken Lights									
21	Clean Inside Of Dishwasher									
22	Sanitise Sponges Or Replace Damaged Sponges With New									
23	Dishes, Pots, Pans, And Utensils To Be Stored Away Properly									
24	Clean Out Refrigerator And Wipe Down Shelves And Drawers									
	Monthly Kitchen Cleaning Tasks	M	T	W	T	F	S	S	Cleaned By	Date/Time
1	Wash And Clean Air Vents									
2	Sort Through And Organize Cooking Utensils, Pans And Pots									
3	Wash And Clean Air Vents									
4	Check Plates, Cups And Glasses And Bin Anything Chipped									
5	Clean And Vacuum Central Heating Units									
6	Wash And Clean Light Covers									
7	Clean And De-Lime Dishwasher									
8	Dust And Clean Ceilings, Ceiling Corners And Ceiling Tiles									
9	Thoroughly Clean Grout And Tiles									
10	Clean Refrigerator Coils To Remove Dust, Unplug First									
11	Run Cleaning & Sanitizing Chemicals Through Coffee Machine									
12	Disinfect And Clean All The Walls From Top To Bottom									
13	Check For Out Of Date Food In Cabinets/Cupboards									
14	Clean Skirting Boards/Baseboards And Corners									
15	Clean Under Refrigerator									
16	Wash And Clean Doors, Door Frames And Glass									
17	Sort Through Leftover Items In The Fridge/Refrigerators									
18	Wash And Clean Windows (Inside And Outside)									
19	Replace Pest Traps									

ESSENTIAL CLEANING NOTES

....

....

....

....

....

....

ESSENTIAL OFFICE CLEANING *Checklist*

Location/Building	Department	Office Number	Week Number

Start Date & Time	Finnish Date & Time	Name	Signature

	Daily/Weekly Office Cleaning Tasks	M	T	W	T	F	S	S	Cleaned By	Date/Time
1	Clean And Sanitize All The Desks And Tables									
2	Clean And Sanitize All The Counter Tops And Surface Areas									
3	Disinfect All Point-Of-Sale Terminals And Touch Screens									
4	Disinfect Touch Points, Light Switches And Other Switches									
5	Clean And Sanitize All Keyboards And Computer Mice									
6	Wipe Down The Walls Wherever There Are Spills And Splashes									
7	Clean And Disinfect All Doors, Door Handles And Doorknobs									
8	Re-Stock Protective Clothing, Face Masks/Shields, Gloves									
9	Clean And Sanitize All The Chairs, Seats And Benches									
10	Clean All The Mirrors, Glass Cabinets/Displays									
11	Replace And Change Burned Out Light Bulbs/Broken Lights									
12	Sweep The Floors To Ensure They're Free From Debris									
13	Mop Tiled And Laminate Floors With Disinfectant Cleaner									
14	Vacuum And Hoover The Carpets, Mats And Rugs									
15	Place Wet Floor Signs If Floors Are Wet After Mopping									
16	Wash & Clean Dirty Cups, Drinking Bottles And Glasses									
17	Clean & Re-Stock Paper Dispensers & Paper Towel Rolls									
18	Wipe Down Equipment & Sanitize Tea And Coffee Makers									
19	Refill Soap Dispensers, Sanitizers And Hand Gels									
20	Clean And Dust Furniture And Office Equipment									
21	Take Out The Rubbish/Trash, Remove Waste And Recycling									
22	Clean & Disinfectant Bins/Waste Disposal Area & Trash Cans									
23	Clean And Wipe Down Windowsills									
24	Vacuum Furnishings, Cushions, Chairs, Sofas And Couches									
25	Spray Air Freshener									
26	Clean And Disinfect Any Cabinets, Shelves And Units									
27	Clean Surfaces And Desk/Work Dividers									
28	Clean And Disinfect Telephones And Headsets									
29	Polish Any Wooden Furniture And Hardwood Surfaces									

	Monthly Office Cleaning Tasks	M	T	W	T	F	S	S	Cleaned By	Date/Time
1	Clean Skirting Boards/Baseboards And Corners									
2	Clean And Disinfect All The Walls From Top To Bottom									
3	Clean Blinds (Take Down And Wash If Possible)									
4	Wash And Clean Windows (Inside And Outside)									
5	Clean And Disinfect Shared Surfaces									
6	Steam Clean Carpets And Rugs									
7	Dust And Clean Ceilings, Ceiling Corners And Ceiling Tiles									
8	Check For Broken Chairs And Tables									
9	Dust And Wash Radiator Covers									
10	Clean And Disinfect Ceiling Wall Vents									
11	Clean And Vacuum Central Heating Units									
12	Wash And Clean Light Covers									
13	Clean Drapes And Curtains (Take Down And Wash if Possible)									
14	Check Cleaning Supplies And Re-Stock As Necessary									
15	Check Ceiling Fans, Fire Sprinklers And Smoke Alarms									
16	Check Hardware, Door Stops And Lock Mechanisms									
17	Fire Exit Lights And Emergency Lights Checked & Functioning									
18	Organize And De-Clutter Office Drawers									
19	Organize And De-Clutter Storeroom									

	Daily/Weekly Toilets/Restroom Cleaning Tasks	M	T	W	T	F	S	S	Cleaned By	Date/Time
1	Clean And Disinfect All Doors, Door Handles And Doorknobs									
2	Disinfect Touch Points, Light Switches And Other Switches									
3	Toilet Roll Holders Cleaned And Disinfected And Re-Stocked									
4	Wipe Down The Walls Wherever There Are Spills And Splashes									
5	Electric Hand Dryers Cleaned, Disinfected & Operating Correctly									
6	Sweep The Floors To Ensure They're Free From Debris									
7	Mop Tiled And Laminate Floors With Disinfectant Cleaner									
8	Paper Dispensers & Paper Towel Rolls Cleaned & Re-Stocked									
9	Take Out The Rubbish/Trash, Remove Waste And Recycling									
10	Clean & Disinfectant Bins/Waste Disposal Area & Trash Cans									
11	Feminine Hygiene Bins/Containers Cleaned And Disinfected									
12	Toilets Cleaned & Disinfected, Outside, Inside And Handles									
13	Urinals & Urinal Screens Cleaned, Disinfected & Blocks Replaced									
14	Wall Mirrors Cleaned With Glass Cleaner									
15	Clean And Re-Stock Paper Dispensers & Paper Towel Rolls									
16	Refill Soap Dispensers, Sanitizers And Hand Gels									
17	Sinks, Taps, Fixtures, Surface Areas Cleaned And Disinfected									

	Daily/Weekly Toilets/Restroom Cleaning Tasks Con	M	T	W	T	F	S	S	Cleaned By	Date/Time
18	Windowsills Clean And Wiped Down									
19	Check Plumbing And Schedule Work If Required									
20	Air Fresheners Checked And Replaced									
21	Fire Exit Lights And Emergency Lights Checked & Functioning									
22	Place Wet Floor Signs If Floors Are Wet After Mopping									
23	Cabinets Cleaned And Disinfected									
	Monthly Toilets/Restroom Cleaning Tasks	M	T	W	T	F	S	S	Cleaned By	Date/Time
1	Toilet/Restroom Service Storeroom/Cupboard Clean And Tidy									
2	Walls Free Of Graffiti, Stickers, Gum And Residue									
3	Wash And Clean Windows (Inside And Outside)									
4	Check Hardware, Door Stops And Lock Mechanisms									
5	All Fittings Securely Fixed (Schedule Maintenance If Not)									
6	Dust And Clean Ceilings, Ceiling Corners And Ceiling Tiles									
7	Clean Skirting Boards/Baseboards And Corners									
8	Thoroughly Clean Grout And Tiles									
9	Ceiling Wall Vents Cleaned And Disinfected									
10	Clean And Vacuum Central Heating Units									
11	Wash And Clean Light Covers									
12	Wash All Toilet And Restroom Mats									
	Daily/Weekly Kitchen Cleaning Tasks	M	T	W	T	F	S	S	Cleaned By	Date/Time
1	Wash And Sanitize All Counter Tops And Prep Area Surfaces									
2	Empty Dishwasher, Run The Dishwasher/Dish Drainer									
3	Disinfect Touch Points, Light Switches And Other Switches									
4	Take Out The Rubbish/Trash, Remove Waste And Recycling									
5	Clean & Disinfectant Bins/Waste Disposal Area & Trash Cans									
6	Wipe Down The Walls Wherever There Are Spills And Splashes									
7	Sweep The Floors To Ensure They're Free From Debris									
8	Mop Tiled And Laminate Floors With Disinfectant Cleaner									
9	Wet Floor Signs In Place If Floors Are Wet After Mopping									
10	Thoroughly Clean And Disinfect The Sinks And Taps									
11	Clean Exterior Of Appliances, Check For Spilled Food									
12	Replace Empty Paper Towel Rolls And Cloth Roller Towels									
13	Refill Soap Dispensers And Hand Sanitizers/Hand Gels									
14	Wipe Down Equipment, Tea And Coffee Makers, Toasters Etc									
15	Fire Exit Lights And Emergency Lights Checked & Functioning									
16	Pour Drain Cleaner Down Floor And Sink Drains									
17	Clean Inside Microwave, Check For Spilled Food									

	Daily/Weekly Kitchen Cleaning Tasks Continued	M	T	W	T	F	S	S	CLEANED BY	DATE/TIME
18	Replace Wash Rags, Cloths And Tea Towels With Clean Ones									
19	Wash Rags, Cloths, Tea Towels And Towels In Washing Machine									
20	Replace And Change Burned Out Light Bulbs/Broken Lights									
21	Clean Inside Of Dishwasher									
22	Sanitise Sponges Or Replace Damaged Sponges With New									
23	Dishes, Pots, Pans, And Utensils To Be Stored Away Properly									
24	Clean Out Refrigerator And Wipe Down Shelves And Drawers									
	Monthly Kitchen Cleaning Tasks	M	T	W	T	F	S	S	Cleaned By	Date/Time
1	Wash And Clean Air Vents									
2	Sort Through And Organize Cooking Utensils, Pans And Pots									
3	Wash And Clean Air Vents									
4	Check Plates, Cups And Glasses And Bin Anything Chipped									
5	Clean And Vacuum Central Heating Units									
6	Wash And Clean Light Covers									
7	Clean And De-Lime Dishwasher									
8	Dust And Clean Ceilings, Ceiling Corners And Ceiling Tiles									
9	Thoroughly Clean Grout And Tiles									
10	Clean Refrigerator Coils To Remove Dust, Unplug First									
11	Run Cleaning & Sanitizing Chemicals Through Coffee Machine									
12	Disinfect And Clean All The Walls From Top To Bottom									
13	Check For Out Of Date Food In Cabinets/Cupboards									
14	Clean Skirting Boards/Baseboards And Corners									
15	Clean Under Refrigerator									
16	Wash And Clean Doors, Door Frames And Glass									
17	Sort Through Leftover Items In The Fridge/Refrigerators									
18	Wash And Clean Windows (Inside And Outside)									
19	Replace Pest Traps									

ESSENTIAL CLEANING NOTES

....

....

....

....

....

....

....

....

ESSENTIAL OFFICE CLEANING *Checklist*

Location/Building	Department	Office Number	Week Number

Start Date & Time	Finnish Date & Time	Name	Signature

	Daily/Weekly Office Cleaning Tasks	M	T	W	T	F	S	S	Cleaned By	Date/Time
1	Clean And Sanitize All The Desks And Tables									
2	Clean And Sanitize All The Counter Tops And Surface Areas									
3	Disinfect All Point-Of-Sale Terminals And Touch Screens									
4	Disinfect Touch Points, Light Switches And Other Switches									
5	Clean And Sanitize All Keyboards And Computer Mice									
6	Wipe Down The Walls Wherever There Are Spills And Splashes									
7	Clean And Disinfect All Doors, Door Handles And Doorknobs									
8	Re-Stock Protective Clothing, Face Masks/Shields, Gloves									
9	Clean And Sanitize All The Chairs, Seats And Benches									
10	Clean All The Mirrors, Glass Cabinets/Displays									
11	Replace And Change Burned Out Light Bulbs/Broken Lights									
12	Sweep The Floors To Ensure They're Free From Debris									
13	Mop Tiled And Laminate Floors With Disinfectant Cleaner									
14	Vacuum And Hoover The Carpets, Mats And Rugs									
15	Place Wet Floor Signs If Floors Are Wet After Mopping									
16	Wash & Clean Dirty Cups, Drinking Bottles And Glasses									
17	Clean & Re-Stock Paper Dispensers & Paper Towel Rolls									
18	Wipe Down Equipment & Sanitize Tea And Coffee Makers									
19	Refill Soap Dispensers, Sanitizers And Hand Gels									
20	Clean And Dust Furniture And Office Equipment									
21	Take Out The Rubbish/Trash, Remove Waste And Recycling									
22	Clean & Disinfectant Bins/Waste Disposal Area & Trash Cans									
23	Clean And Wipe Down Windowsills									
24	Vacuum Furnishings, Cushions, Chairs, Sofas And Couches									
25	Spray Air Freshener									
26	Clean And Disinfect Any Cabinets, Shelves And Units									
27	Clean Surfaces And Desk/Work Dividers									
28	Clean And Disinfect Telephones And Headsets									
29	Polish Any Wooden Furniture And Hardwood Surfaces									

	Monthly Office Cleaning Tasks	M	T	W	T	F	S	S	Cleaned By	Date/Time
1	Clean Skirting Boards/Baseboards And Corners									
2	Clean And Disinfect All The Walls From Top To Bottom									
3	Clean Blinds (Take Down And Wash If Possible)									
4	Wash And Clean Windows (Inside And Outside)									
5	Clean And Disinfect Shared Surfaces									
6	Steam Clean Carpets And Rugs									
7	Dust And Clean Ceilings, Ceiling Corners And Ceiling Tiles									
8	Check For Broken Chairs And Tables									
9	Dust And Wash Radiator Covers									
10	Clean And Disinfect Ceiling Wall Vents									
11	Clean And Vacuum Central Heating Units									
12	Wash And Clean Light Covers									
13	Clean Drapes And Curtains (Take Down And Wash if Possible)									
14	Check Cleaning Supplies And Re-Stock As Necessary									
15	Check Ceiling Fans, Fire Sprinklers And Smoke Alarms									
16	Check Hardware, Door Stops And Lock Mechanisms									
17	Fire Exit Lights And Emergency Lights Checked & Functioning									
18	Organize And De-Clutter Office Drawers									
19	Organize And De-Clutter Storeroom									
	Daily/Weekly Toilets/Restroom Cleaning Tasks	M	T	W	T	F	S	S	Cleaned By	Date/Time
1	Clean And Disinfect All Doors, Door Handles And Doorknobs									
2	Disinfect Touch Points, Light Switches And Other Switches									
3	Toilet Roll Holders Cleaned And Disinfected And Re-Stocked									
4	Wipe Down The Walls Wherever There Are Spills And Splashes									
5	Electric Hand Dryers Cleaned, Disinfected & Operating Correctly									
6	Sweep The Floors To Ensure They're Free From Debris									
7	Mop Tiled And Laminate Floors With Disinfectant Cleaner									
8	Paper Dispensers & Paper Towel Rolls Cleaned & Re-Stocked									
9	Take Out The Rubbish/Trash, Remove Waste And Recycling									
10	Clean & Disinfectant Bins/Waste Disposal Area & Trash Cans									
11	Feminine Hygiene Bins/Containers Cleaned And Disinfected									
12	Toilets Cleaned & Disinfected, Outside, Inside And Handles									
13	Urinals & Urinal Screens Cleaned, Disinfected & Blocks Replaced									
14	Wall Mirrors Cleaned With Glass Cleaner									
15	Clean And Re-Stock Paper Dispensers & Paper Towel Rolls									
16	Refill Soap Dispensers, Sanitizers And Hand Gels									
17	Sinks, Taps, Fixtures, Surface Areas Cleaned And Disinfected									

	Daily/Weekly Toilets/Restroom Cleaning Tasks Con	M	T	W	T	F	S	S	Cleaned By	Date/Time
18	Windowsills Clean And Wiped Down									
19	Check Plumbing And Schedule Work If Required									
20	Air Fresheners Checked And Replaced									
21	Fire Exit Lights And Emergency Lights Checked & Functioning									
22	Place Wet Floor Signs If Floors Are Wet After Mopping									
23	Cabinets Cleaned And Disinfected									
	Monthly Toilets/Restroom Cleaning Tasks	M	T	W	T	F	S	S	Cleaned By	Date/Time
1	Toilet/Restroom Service Storeroom/Cupboard Clean And Tidy									
2	Walls Free Of Graffiti, Stickers, Gum And Residue									
3	Wash And Clean Windows (Inside And Outside)									
4	Check Hardware, Door Stops And Lock Mechanisms									
5	All Fittings Securely Fixed (Schedule Maintenance If Not)									
6	Dust And Clean Ceilings, Ceiling Corners And Ceiling Tiles									
7	Clean Skirting Boards/Baseboards And Corners									
8	Thoroughly Clean Grout And Tiles									
9	Ceiling Wall Vents Cleaned And Disinfected									
10	Clean And Vacuum Central Heating Units									
11	Wash And Clean Light Covers									
12	Wash All Toilet And Restroom Mats									
	Daily/Weekly Kitchen Cleaning Tasks	M	T	W	T	F	S	S	Cleaned By	Date/Time
1	Wash And Sanitize All Counter Tops And Prep Area Surfaces									
2	Empty Dishwasher, Run The Dishwasher/Dish Drainer									
3	Disinfect Touch Points, Light Switches And Other Switches									
4	Take Out The Rubbish/Trash, Remove Waste And Recycling									
5	Clean & Disinfectant Bins/Waste Disposal Area & Trash Cans									
6	Wipe Down The Walls Wherever There Are Spills And Splashes									
7	Sweep The Floors To Ensure They're Free From Debris									
8	Mop Tiled And Laminate Floors With Disinfectant Cleaner									
9	Wet Floor Signs In Place If Floors Are Wet After Mopping									
10	Thoroughly Clean And Disinfect The Sinks And Taps									
11	Clean Exterior Of Appliances, Check For Spilled Food									
12	Replace Empty Paper Towel Rolls And Cloth Roller Towels									
13	Refill Soap Dispensers And Hand Sanitizers/Hand Gels									
14	Wipe Down Equipment, Tea And Coffee Makers, Toasters Etc									
15	Fire Exit Lights And Emergency Lights Checked & Functioning									
16	Pour Drain Cleaner Down Floor And Sink Drains									
17	Clean Inside Microwave, Check For Spilled Food									

	Daily/Weekly Kitchen Cleaning Tasks Continued	M	T	W	T	F	S	S	CLEANED BY	DATE/TIME
18	Replace Wash Rags, Cloths And Tea Towels With Clean Ones									
19	Wash Rags, Cloths, Tea Towels And Towels In Washing Machine									
20	Replace And Change Burned Out Light Bulbs/Broken Lights									
21	Clean Inside Of Dishwasher									
22	Sanitise Sponges Or Replace Damaged Sponges With New									
23	Dishes, Pots, Pans, And Utensils To Be Stored Away Properly									
24	Clean Out Refrigerator And Wipe Down Shelves And Drawers									
	Monthly Kitchen Cleaning Tasks	M	T	W	T	F	S	S	Cleaned By	Date/Time
1	Wash And Clean Air Vents									
2	Sort Through And Organize Cooking Utensils, Pans And Pots									
3	Wash And Clean Air Vents									
4	Check Plates, Cups And Glasses And Bin Anything Chipped									
5	Clean And Vacuum Central Heating Units									
6	Wash And Clean Light Covers									
7	Clean And De-Lime Dishwasher									
8	Dust And Clean Ceilings, Ceiling Corners And Ceiling Tiles									
9	Thoroughly Clean Grout And Tiles									
10	Clean Refrigerator Coils To Remove Dust, Unplug First									
11	Run Cleaning & Sanitizing Chemicals Through Coffee Machine									
12	Disinfect And Clean All The Walls From Top To Bottom									
13	Check For Out Of Date Food In Cabinets/Cupboards									
14	Clean Skirting Boards/Baseboards And Corners									
15	Clean Under Refrigerator									
16	Wash And Clean Doors, Door Frames And Glass									
17	Sort Through Leftover Items In The Fridge/Refrigerators									
18	Wash And Clean Windows (Inside And Outside)									
19	Replace Pest Traps									

ESSENTIAL CLEANING NOTES

....

....

....

....

....

....

....

ESSENTIAL OFFICE CLEANING *Checklist*

Location/Building	Department	Office Number	Week Number

Start Date & Time	Finnish Date & Time	Name	Signature

	Daily/Weekly Office Cleaning Tasks	M	T	W	T	F	S	S	Cleaned By	Date/Time
1	Clean And Sanitize All The Desks And Tables									
2	Clean And Sanitize All The Counter Tops And Surface Areas									
3	Disinfect All Point-Of-Sale Terminals And Touch Screens									
4	Disinfect Touch Points, Light Switches And Other Switches									
5	Clean And Sanitize All Keyboards And Computer Mice									
6	Wipe Down The Walls Wherever There Are Spills And Splashes									
7	Clean And Disinfect All Doors, Door Handles And Doorknobs									
8	Re-Stock Protective Clothing, Face Masks/Shields, Gloves									
9	Clean And Sanitize All The Chairs, Seats And Benches									
10	Clean All The Mirrors, Glass Cabinets/Displays									
11	Replace And Change Burned Out Light Bulbs/Broken Lights									
12	Sweep The Floors To Ensure They're Free From Debris									
13	Mop Tiled And Laminate Floors With Disinfectant Cleaner									
14	Vacuum And Hoover The Carpets, Mats And Rugs									
15	Place Wet Floor Signs If Floors Are Wet After Mopping									
16	Wash & Clean Dirty Cups, Drinking Bottles And Glasses									
17	Clean & Re-Stock Paper Dispensers & Paper Towel Rolls									
18	Wipe Down Equipment & Sanitize Tea And Coffee Makers									
19	Refill Soap Dispensers, Sanitizers And Hand Gels									
20	Clean And Dust Furniture And Office Equipment									
21	Take Out The Rubbish/Trash, Remove Waste And Recycling									
22	Clean & Disinfectant Bins/Waste Disposal Area & Trash Cans									
23	Clean And Wipe Down Windowsills									
24	Vacuum Furnishings, Cushions, Chairs, Sofas And Couches									
25	Spray Air Freshener									
26	Clean And Disinfect Any Cabinets, Shelves And Units									
27	Clean Surfaces And Desk/Work Dividers									
28	Clean And Disinfect Telephones And Headsets									
29	Polish Any Wooden Furniture And Hardwood Surfaces									

	Monthly Office Cleaning Tasks	M	T	W	T	F	S	S	Cleaned By	Date/Time
1	Clean Skirting Boards/Baseboards And Corners									
2	Clean And Disinfect All The Walls From Top To Bottom									
3	Clean Blinds (Take Down And Wash If Possible)									
4	Wash And Clean Windows (Inside And Outside)									
5	Clean And Disinfect Shared Surfaces									
6	Steam Clean Carpets And Rugs									
7	Dust And Clean Ceilings, Ceiling Corners And Ceiling Tiles									
8	Check For Broken Chairs And Tables									
9	Dust And Wash Radiator Covers									
10	Clean And Disinfect Ceiling Wall Vents									
11	Clean And Vacuum Central Heating Units									
12	Wash And Clean Light Covers									
13	Clean Drapes And Curtains (Take Down And Wash if Possible)									
14	Check Cleaning Supplies And Re-Stock As Necessary									
15	Check Ceiling Fans, Fire Sprinklers And Smoke Alarms									
16	Check Hardware, Door Stops And Lock Mechanisms									
17	Fire Exit Lights And Emergency Lights Checked & Functioning									
18	Organize And De-Clutter Office Drawers									
19	Organize And De-Clutter Storeroom									
	Daily/Weekly Toilets/Restroom Cleaning Tasks	M	T	W	T	F	S	S	Cleaned By	Date/Time
1	Clean And Disinfect All Doors, Door Handles And Doorknobs									
2	Disinfect Touch Points, Light Switches And Other Switches									
3	Toilet Roll Holders Cleaned And Disinfected And Re-Stocked									
4	Wipe Down The Walls Wherever There Are Spills And Splashes									
5	Electric Hand Dryers Cleaned, Disinfected & Operating Correctly									
6	Sweep The Floors To Ensure They're Free From Debris									
7	Mop Tiled And Laminate Floors With Disinfectant Cleaner									
8	Paper Dispensers & Paper Towel Rolls Cleaned & Re-Stocked									
9	Take Out The Rubbish/Trash, Remove Waste And Recycling									
10	Clean & Disinfectant Bins/Waste Disposal Area & Trash Cans									
11	Feminine Hygiene Bins/Containers Cleaned And Disinfected									
12	Toilets Cleaned & Disinfected, Outside, Inside And Handles									
13	Urinals & Urinal Screens Cleaned, Disinfected & Blocks Replaced									
14	Wall Mirrors Cleaned With Glass Cleaner									
15	Clean And Re-Stock Paper Dispensers & Paper Towel Rolls									
16	Refill Soap Dispensers, Sanitizers And Hand Gels									
17	Sinks, Taps, Fixtures, Surface Areas Cleaned And Disinfected									

	Daily/Weekly Toilets/Restroom Cleaning Tasks Con	M	T	W	T	F	S	S	Cleaned By	Date/Time
18	Windowsills Clean And Wiped Down									
19	Check Plumbing And Schedule Work If Required									
20	Air Fresheners Checked And Replaced									
21	Fire Exit Lights And Emergency Lights Checked & Functioning									
22	Place Wet Floor Signs If Floors Are Wet After Mopping									
23	Cabinets Cleaned And Disinfected									
	Monthly Toilets/Restroom Cleaning Tasks	M	T	W	T	F	S	S	Cleaned By	Date/Time
1	Toilet/Restroom Service Storeroom/Cupboard Clean And Tidy									
2	Walls Free Of Graffiti, Stickers, Gum And Residue									
3	Wash And Clean Windows (Inside And Outside)									
4	Check Hardware, Door Stops And Lock Mechanisms									
5	All Fittings Securely Fixed (Schedule Maintenance If Not)									
6	Dust And Clean Ceilings, Ceiling Corners And Ceiling Tiles									
7	Clean Skirting Boards/Baseboards And Corners									
8	Thoroughly Clean Grout And Tiles									
9	Ceiling Wall Vents Cleaned And Disinfected									
10	Clean And Vacuum Central Heating Units									
11	Wash And Clean Light Covers									
12	Wash All Toilet And Restroom Mats									
	Daily/Weekly Kitchen Cleaning Tasks	M	T	W	T	F	S	S	Cleaned By	Date/Time
1	Wash And Sanitize All Counter Tops And Prep Area Surfaces									
2	Empty Dishwasher, Run The Dishwasher/Dish Drainer									
3	Disinfect Touch Points, Light Switches And Other Switches									
4	Take Out The Rubbish/Trash, Remove Waste And Recycling									
5	Clean & Disinfectant Bins/Waste Disposal Area & Trash Cans									
6	Wipe Down The Walls Wherever There Are Spills And Splashes									
7	Sweep The Floors To Ensure They're Free From Debris									
8	Mop Tiled And Laminate Floors With Disinfectant Cleaner									
9	Wet Floor Signs In Place If Floors Are Wet After Mopping									
10	Thoroughly Clean And Disinfect The Sinks And Taps									
11	Clean Exterior Of Appliances, Check For Spilled Food									
12	Replace Empty Paper Towel Rolls And Cloth Roller Towels									
13	Refill Soap Dispensers And Hand Sanitizers/Hand Gels									
14	Wipe Down Equipment, Tea And Coffee Makers, Toasters Etc									
15	Fire Exit Lights And Emergency Lights Checked & Functioning									
16	Pour Drain Cleaner Down Floor And Sink Drains									
17	Clean Inside Microwave, Check For Spilled Food									

	Daily/Weekly Kitchen Cleaning Tasks Continued	M	T	W	T	F	S	S	CLEANED BY	DATE/TIME
18	Replace Wash Rags, Cloths And Tea Towels With Clean Ones									
19	Wash Rags, Cloths, Tea Towels And Towels In Washing Machine									
20	Replace And Change Burned Out Light Bulbs/Broken Lights									
21	Clean Inside Of Dishwasher									
22	Sanitise Sponges Or Replace Damaged Sponges With New									
23	Dishes, Pots, Pans, And Utensils To Be Stored Away Properly									
24	Clean Out Refrigerator And Wipe Down Shelves And Drawers									
	Monthly Kitchen Cleaning Tasks	M	T	W	T	F	S	S	Cleaned By	Date/Time
1	Wash And Clean Air Vents									
2	Sort Through And Organize Cooking Utensils, Pans And Pots									
3	Wash And Clean Air Vents									
4	Check Plates, Cups And Glasses And Bin Anything Chipped									
5	Clean And Vacuum Central Heating Units									
6	Wash And Clean Light Covers									
7	Clean And De-Lime Dishwasher									
8	Dust And Clean Ceilings, Ceiling Corners And Ceiling Tiles									
9	Thoroughly Clean Grout And Tiles									
10	Clean Refrigerator Coils To Remove Dust, Unplug First									
11	Run Cleaning & Sanitizing Chemicals Through Coffee Machine									
12	Disinfect And Clean All The Walls From Top To Bottom									
13	Check For Out Of Date Food In Cabinets/Cupboards									
14	Clean Skirting Boards/Baseboards And Corners									
15	Clean Under Refrigerator									
16	Wash And Clean Doors, Door Frames And Glass									
17	Sort Through Leftover Items In The Fridge/Refrigerators									
18	Wash And Clean Windows (Inside And Outside)									
19	Replace Pest Traps									

ESSENTIAL CLEANING NOTES

....

....

....

....

....

....

....

....

ESSENTIAL OFFICE CLEANING *Checklist*

Location/Building	Department	Office Number	Week Number

Start Date & Time	Finnish Date & Time	Name	Signature

	Daily/Weekly Office Cleaning Tasks	M	T	W	T	F	S	S	Cleaned By	Date/Time
1	Clean And Sanitize All The Desks And Tables									
2	Clean And Sanitize All The Counter Tops And Surface Areas									
3	Disinfect All Point-Of-Sale Terminals And Touch Screens									
4	Disinfect Touch Points, Light Switches And Other Switches									
5	Clean And Sanitize All Keyboards And Computer Mice									
6	Wipe Down The Walls Wherever There Are Spills And Splashes									
7	Clean And Disinfect All Doors, Door Handles And Doorknobs									
8	Re-Stock Protective Clothing, Face Masks/Shields, Gloves									
9	Clean And Sanitize All The Chairs, Seats And Benches									
10	Clean All The Mirrors, Glass Cabinets/Displays									
11	Replace And Change Burned Out Light Bulbs/Broken Lights									
12	Sweep The Floors To Ensure They're Free From Debris									
13	Mop Tiled And Laminate Floors With Disinfectant Cleaner									
14	Vacuum And Hoover The Carpets, Mats And Rugs									
15	Place Wet Floor Signs If Floors Are Wet After Mopping									
16	Wash & Clean Dirty Cups, Drinking Bottles And Glasses									
17	Clean & Re-Stock Paper Dispensers & Paper Towel Rolls									
18	Wipe Down Equipment & Sanitize Tea And Coffee Makers									
19	Refill Soap Dispensers, Sanitizers And Hand Gels									
20	Clean And Dust Furniture And Office Equipment									
21	Take Out The Rubbish/Trash, Remove Waste And Recycling									
22	Clean & Disinfectant Bins/Waste Disposal Area & Trash Cans									
23	Clean And Wipe Down Windowsills									
24	Vacuum Furnishings, Cushions, Chairs, Sofas And Couches									
25	Spray Air Freshener									
26	Clean And Disinfect Any Cabinets, Shelves And Units									
27	Clean Surfaces And Desk/Work Dividers									
28	Clean And Disinfect Telephones And Headsets									
29	Polish Any Wooden Furniture And Hardwood Surfaces									

	Monthly Office Cleaning Tasks	M	T	W	T	F	S	S	Cleaned By	Date/Time
1	Clean Skirting Boards/Baseboards And Corners									
2	Clean And Disinfect All The Walls From Top To Bottom									
3	Clean Blinds (Take Down And Wash If Possible)									
4	Wash And Clean Windows (Inside And Outside)									
5	Clean And Disinfect Shared Surfaces									
6	Steam Clean Carpets And Rugs									
7	Dust And Clean Ceilings, Ceiling Corners And Ceiling Tiles									
8	Check For Broken Chairs And Tables									
9	Dust And Wash Radiator Covers									
10	Clean And Disinfect Ceiling Wall Vents									
11	Clean And Vacuum Central Heating Units									
12	Wash And Clean Light Covers									
13	Clean Drapes And Curtains (Take Down And Wash if Possible)									
14	Check Cleaning Supplies And Re-Stock As Necessary									
15	Check Ceiling Fans, Fire Sprinklers And Smoke Alarms									
16	Check Hardware, Door Stops And Lock Mechanisms									
17	Fire Exit Lights And Emergency Lights Checked & Functioning									
18	Organize And De-Clutter Office Drawers									
19	Organize And De-Clutter Storeroom									
	Daily/Weekly Toilets/Restroom Cleaning Tasks	M	T	W	T	F	S	S	Cleaned By	Date/Time
1	Clean And Disinfect All Doors, Door Handles And Doorknobs									
2	Disinfect Touch Points, Light Switches And Other Switches									
3	Toilet Roll Holders Cleaned And Disinfected And Re-Stocked									
4	Wipe Down The Walls Wherever There Are Spills And Splashes									
5	Electric Hand Dryers Cleaned, Disinfected & Operating Correctly									
6	Sweep The Floors To Ensure They're Free From Debris									
7	Mop Tiled And Laminate Floors With Disinfectant Cleaner									
8	Paper Dispensers & Paper Towel Rolls Cleaned & Re-Stocked									
9	Take Out The Rubbish/Trash, Remove Waste And Recycling									
10	Clean & Disinfectant Bins/Waste Disposal Area & Trash Cans									
11	Feminine Hygiene Bins/Containers Cleaned And Disinfected									
12	Toilets Cleaned & Disinfected, Outside, Inside And Handles									
13	Urinals & Urinal Screens Cleaned, Disinfected & Blocks Replaced									
14	Wall Mirrors Cleaned With Glass Cleaner									
15	Clean And Re-Stock Paper Dispensers & Paper Towel Rolls									
16	Refill Soap Dispensers, Sanitizers And Hand Gels									
17	Sinks, Taps, Fixtures, Surface Areas Cleaned And Disinfected									

	Daily/Weekly Toilets/Restroom Cleaning Tasks Con	M	T	W	T	F	S	S	Cleaned By	Date/Time
18	Windowsills Clean And Wiped Down									
19	Check Plumbing And Schedule Work If Required									
20	Air Fresheners Checked And Replaced									
21	Fire Exit Lights And Emergency Lights Checked & Functioning									
22	Place Wet Floor Signs If Floors Are Wet After Mopping									
23	Cabinets Cleaned And Disinfected									
	Monthly Toilets/Restroom Cleaning Tasks	M	T	W	T	F	S	S	Cleaned By	Date/Time
1	Toilet/Restroom Service Storeroom/Cupboard Clean And Tidy									
2	Walls Free Of Graffiti, Stickers, Gum And Residue									
3	Wash And Clean Windows (Inside And Outside)									
4	Check Hardware, Door Stops And Lock Mechanisms									
5	All Fittings Securely Fixed (Schedule Maintenance If Not)									
6	Dust And Clean Ceilings, Ceiling Corners And Ceiling Tiles									
7	Clean Skirting Boards/Baseboards And Corners									
8	Thoroughly Clean Grout And Tiles									
9	Ceiling Wall Vents Cleaned And Disinfected									
10	Clean And Vacuum Central Heating Units									
11	Wash And Clean Light Covers									
12	Wash All Toilet And Restroom Mats									
	Daily/Weekly Kitchen Cleaning Tasks	M	T	W	T	F	S	S	Cleaned By	Date/Time
1	Wash And Sanitize All Counter Tops And Prep Area Surfaces									
2	Empty Dishwasher, Run The Dishwasher/Dish Drainer									
3	Disinfect Touch Points, Light Switches And Other Switches									
4	Take Out The Rubbish/Trash, Remove Waste And Recycling									
5	Clean & Disinfectant Bins/Waste Disposal Area & Trash Cans									
6	Wipe Down The Walls Wherever There Are Spills And Splashes									
7	Sweep The Floors To Ensure They're Free From Debris									
8	Mop Tiled And Laminate Floors With Disinfectant Cleaner									
9	Wet Floor Signs In Place If Floors Are Wet After Mopping									
10	Thoroughly Clean And Disinfect The Sinks And Taps									
11	Clean Exterior Of Appliances, Check For Spilled Food									
12	Replace Empty Paper Towel Rolls And Cloth Roller Towels									
13	Refill Soap Dispensers And Hand Sanitizers/Hand Gels									
14	Wipe Down Equipment, Tea And Coffee Makers, Toasters Etc									
15	Fire Exit Lights And Emergency Lights Checked & Functioning									
16	Pour Drain Cleaner Down Floor And Sink Drains									
17	Clean Inside Microwave, Check For Spilled Food									

	Daily/Weekly Kitchen Cleaning Tasks Continued	M	T	W	T	F	S	S	CLEANED BY	DATE/TIME
18	Replace Wash Rags, Cloths And Tea Towels With Clean Ones									
19	Wash Rags, Cloths, Tea Towels And Towels In Washing Machine									
20	Replace And Change Burned Out Light Bulbs/Broken Lights									
21	Clean Inside Of Dishwasher									
22	Sanitise Sponges Or Replace Damaged Sponges With New									
23	Dishes, Pots, Pans, And Utensils To Be Stored Away Properly									
24	Clean Out Refrigerator And Wipe Down Shelves And Drawers									
	Monthly Kitchen Cleaning Tasks	M	T	W	T	F	S	S	Cleaned By	Date/Time
1	Wash And Clean Air Vents									
2	Sort Through And Organize Cooking Utensils, Pans And Pots									
3	Wash And Clean Air Vents									
4	Check Plates, Cups And Glasses And Bin Anything Chipped									
5	Clean And Vacuum Central Heating Units									
6	Wash And Clean Light Covers									
7	Clean And De-Lime Dishwasher									
8	Dust And Clean Ceilings, Ceiling Corners And Ceiling Tiles									
9	Thoroughly Clean Grout And Tiles									
10	Clean Refrigerator Coils To Remove Dust, Unplug First									
11	Run Cleaning & Sanitizing Chemicals Through Coffee Machine									
12	Disinfect And Clean All The Walls From Top To Bottom									
13	Check For Out Of Date Food In Cabinets/Cupboards									
14	Clean Skirting Boards/Baseboards And Corners									
15	Clean Under Refrigerator									
16	Wash And Clean Doors, Door Frames And Glass									
17	Sort Through Leftover Items In The Fridge/Refrigerators									
18	Wash And Clean Windows (Inside And Outside)									
19	Replace Pest Traps									

ESSENTIAL CLEANING NOTES

....

....

....

....

....

....

....

ESSENTIAL OFFICE CLEANING *Checklist*

Location/Building	Department	Office Number	Week Number

Start Date & Time	Finnish Date & Time	Name	Signature

	Daily/Weekly Office Cleaning Tasks	M	T	W	T	F	S	S	Cleaned By	Date/Time
1	Clean And Sanitize All The Desks And Tables									
2	Clean And Sanitize All The Counter Tops And Surface Areas									
3	Disinfect All Point-Of-Sale Terminals And Touch Screens									
4	Disinfect Touch Points, Light Switches And Other Switches									
5	Clean And Sanitize All Keyboards And Computer Mice									
6	Wipe Down The Walls Wherever There Are Spills And Splashes									
7	Clean And Disinfect All Doors, Door Handles And Doorknobs									
8	Re-Stock Protective Clothing, Face Masks/Shields, Gloves									
9	Clean And Sanitize All The Chairs, Seats And Benches									
10	Clean All The Mirrors, Glass Cabinets/Displays									
11	Replace And Change Burned Out Light Bulbs/Broken Lights									
12	Sweep The Floors To Ensure They're Free From Debris									
13	Mop Tiled And Laminate Floors With Disinfectant Cleaner									
14	Vacuum And Hoover The Carpets, Mats And Rugs									
15	Place Wet Floor Signs If Floors Are Wet After Mopping									
16	Wash & Clean Dirty Cups, Drinking Bottles And Glasses									
17	Clean & Re-Stock Paper Dispensers & Paper Towel Rolls									
18	Wipe Down Equipment & Sanitize Tea And Coffee Makers									
19	Refill Soap Dispensers, Sanitizers And Hand Gels									
20	Clean And Dust Furniture And Office Equipment									
21	Take Out The Rubbish/Trash, Remove Waste And Recycling									
22	Clean & Disinfectant Bins/Waste Disposal Area & Trash Cans									
23	Clean And Wipe Down Windowsills									
24	Vacuum Furnishings, Cushions, Chairs, Sofas And Couches									
25	Spray Air Freshener									
26	Clean And Disinfect Any Cabinets, Shelves And Units									
27	Clean Surfaces And Desk/Work Dividers									
28	Clean And Disinfect Telephones And Headsets									
29	Polish Any Wooden Furniture And Hardwood Surfaces									

	Monthly Office Cleaning Tasks	M	T	W	T	F	S	S	Cleaned By	Date/Time
1	Clean Skirting Boards/Baseboards And Corners									
2	Clean And Disinfect All The Walls From Top To Bottom									
3	Clean Blinds (Take Down And Wash If Possible)									
4	Wash And Clean Windows (Inside And Outside)									
5	Clean And Disinfect Shared Surfaces									
6	Steam Clean Carpets And Rugs									
7	Dust And Clean Ceilings, Ceiling Corners And Ceiling Tiles									
8	Check For Broken Chairs And Tables									
9	Dust And Wash Radiator Covers									
10	Clean And Disinfect Ceiling Wall Vents									
11	Clean And Vacuum Central Heating Units									
12	Wash And Clean Light Covers									
13	Clean Drapes And Curtains (Take Down And Wash if Possible)									
14	Check Cleaning Supplies And Re-Stock As Necessary									
15	Check Ceiling Fans, Fire Sprinklers And Smoke Alarms									
16	Check Hardware, Door Stops And Lock Mechanisms									
17	Fire Exit Lights And Emergency Lights Checked & Functioning									
18	Organize And De-Clutter Office Drawers									
19	Organize And De-Clutter Storeroom									
	Daily/Weekly Toilets/Restroom Cleaning Tasks	M	T	W	T	F	S	S	Cleaned By	Date/Time
1	Clean And Disinfect All Doors, Door Handles And Doorknobs									
2	Disinfect Touch Points, Light Switches And Other Switches									
3	Toilet Roll Holders Cleaned And Disinfected And Re-Stocked									
4	Wipe Down The Walls Wherever There Are Spills And Splashes									
5	Electric Hand Dryers Cleaned, Disinfected & Operating Correctly									
6	Sweep The Floors To Ensure They're Free From Debris									
7	Mop Tiled And Laminate Floors With Disinfectant Cleaner									
8	Paper Dispensers & Paper Towel Rolls Cleaned & Re-Stocked									
9	Take Out The Rubbish/Trash, Remove Waste And Recycling									
10	Clean & Disinfectant Bins/Waste Disposal Area & Trash Cans									
11	Feminine Hygiene Bins/Containers Cleaned And Disinfected									
12	Toilets Cleaned & Disinfected, Outside, Inside And Handles									
13	Urinals & Urinal Screens Cleaned, Disinfected & Blocks Replaced									
14	Wall Mirrors Cleaned With Glass Cleaner									
15	Clean And Re-Stock Paper Dispensers & Paper Towel Rolls									
16	Refill Soap Dispensers, Sanitizers And Hand Gels									
17	Sinks, Taps, Fixtures, Surface Areas Cleaned And Disinfected									

	Daily/Weekly Toilets/Restroom Cleaning Tasks Con	M	T	W	T	F	S	S	Cleaned By	Date/Time
18	Windowsills Clean And Wiped Down									
19	Check Plumbing And Schedule Work If Required									
20	Air Fresheners Checked And Replaced									
21	Fire Exit Lights And Emergency Lights Checked & Functioning									
22	Place Wet Floor Signs If Floors Are Wet After Mopping									
23	Cabinets Cleaned And Disinfected									
	Monthly Toilets/Restroom Cleaning Tasks	M	T	W	T	F	S	S	Cleaned By	Date/Time
1	Toilet/Restroom Service Storeroom/Cupboard Clean And Tidy									
2	Walls Free Of Graffiti, Stickers, Gum And Residue									
3	Wash And Clean Windows (Inside And Outside)									
4	Check Hardware, Door Stops And Lock Mechanisms									
5	All Fittings Securely Fixed (Schedule Maintenance If Not)									
6	Dust And Clean Ceilings, Ceiling Corners And Ceiling Tiles									
7	Clean Skirting Boards/Baseboards And Corners									
8	Thoroughly Clean Grout And Tiles									
9	Ceiling Wall Vents Cleaned And Disinfected									
10	Clean And Vacuum Central Heating Units									
11	Wash And Clean Light Covers									
12	Wash All Toilet And Restroom Mats									
	Daily/Weekly Kitchen Cleaning Tasks	M	T	W	T	F	S	S	Cleaned By	Date/Time
1	Wash And Sanitize All Counter Tops And Prep Area Surfaces									
2	Empty Dishwasher, Run The Dishwasher/Dish Drainer									
3	Disinfect Touch Points, Light Switches And Other Switches									
4	Take Out The Rubbish/Trash, Remove Waste And Recycling									
5	Clean & Disinfectant Bins/Waste Disposal Area & Trash Cans									
6	Wipe Down The Walls Wherever There Are Spills And Splashes									
7	Sweep The Floors To Ensure They're Free From Debris									
8	Mop Tiled And Laminate Floors With Disinfectant Cleaner									
9	Wet Floor Signs In Place If Floors Are Wet After Mopping									
10	Thoroughly Clean And Disinfect The Sinks And Taps									
11	Clean Exterior Of Appliances, Check For Spilled Food									
12	Replace Empty Paper Towel Rolls And Cloth Roller Towels									
13	Refill Soap Dispensers And Hand Sanitizers/Hand Gels									
14	Wipe Down Equipment, Tea And Coffee Makers, Toasters Etc									
15	Fire Exit Lights And Emergency Lights Checked & Functioning									
16	Pour Drain Cleaner Down Floor And Sink Drains									
17	Clean Inside Microwave, Check For Spilled Food									

	Daily/Weekly Kitchen Cleaning Tasks Continued	M	T	W	T	F	S	S	CLEANED BY	DATE/TIME
18	Replace Wash Rags, Cloths And Tea Towels With Clean Ones									
19	Wash Rags, Cloths, Tea Towels And Towels In Washing Machine									
20	Replace And Change Burned Out Light Bulbs/Broken Lights									
21	Clean Inside Of Dishwasher									
22	Sanitise Sponges Or Replace Damaged Sponges With New									
23	Dishes, Pots, Pans, And Utensils To Be Stored Away Properly									
24	Clean Out Refrigerator And Wipe Down Shelves And Drawers									
	Monthly Kitchen Cleaning Tasks	M	T	W	T	F	S	S	Cleaned By	Date/Time
1	Wash And Clean Air Vents									
2	Sort Through And Organize Cooking Utensils, Pans And Pots									
3	Wash And Clean Air Vents									
4	Check Plates, Cups And Glasses And Bin Anything Chipped									
5	Clean And Vacuum Central Heating Units									
6	Wash And Clean Light Covers									
7	Clean And De-Lime Dishwasher									
8	Dust And Clean Ceilings, Ceiling Corners And Ceiling Tiles									
9	Thoroughly Clean Grout And Tiles									
10	Clean Refrigerator Coils To Remove Dust, Unplug First									
11	Run Cleaning & Sanitizing Chemicals Through Coffee Machine									
12	Disinfect And Clean All The Walls From Top To Bottom									
13	Check For Out Of Date Food In Cabinets/Cupboards									
14	Clean Skirting Boards/Baseboards And Corners									
15	Clean Under Refrigerator									
16	Wash And Clean Doors, Door Frames And Glass									
17	Sort Through Leftover Items In The Fridge/Refrigerators									
18	Wash And Clean Windows (Inside And Outside)									
19	Replace Pest Traps									

ESSENTIAL CLEANING NOTES

....

....

....

....

....

....

....

ESSENTIAL OFFICE CLEANING *Checklist*

Location/Building	Department	Office Number	Week Number

Start Date & Time	Finnish Date & Time	Name	Signature

	Daily/Weekly Office Cleaning Tasks	M	T	W	T	F	S	S	Cleaned By	Date/Time
1	Clean And Sanitize All The Desks And Tables									
2	Clean And Sanitize All The Counter Tops And Surface Areas									
3	Disinfect All Point-Of-Sale Terminals And Touch Screens									
4	Disinfect Touch Points, Light Switches And Other Switches									
5	Clean And Sanitize All Keyboards And Computer Mice									
6	Wipe Down The Walls Wherever There Are Spills And Splashes									
7	Clean And Disinfect All Doors, Door Handles And Doorknobs									
8	Re-Stock Protective Clothing, Face Masks/Shields, Gloves									
9	Clean And Sanitize All The Chairs, Seats And Benches									
10	Clean All The Mirrors, Glass Cabinets/Displays									
11	Replace And Change Burned Out Light Bulbs/Broken Lights									
12	Sweep The Floors To Ensure They're Free From Debris									
13	Mop Tiled And Laminate Floors With Disinfectant Cleaner									
14	Vacuum And Hoover The Carpets, Mats And Rugs									
15	Place Wet Floor Signs If Floors Are Wet After Mopping									
16	Wash & Clean Dirty Cups, Drinking Bottles And Glasses									
17	Clean & Re-Stock Paper Dispensers & Paper Towel Rolls									
18	Wipe Down Equipment & Sanitize Tea And Coffee Makers									
19	Refill Soap Dispensers, Sanitizers And Hand Gels									
20	Clean And Dust Furniture And Office Equipment									
21	Take Out The Rubbish/Trash, Remove Waste And Recycling									
22	Clean & Disinfectant Bins/Waste Disposal Area & Trash Cans									
23	Clean And Wipe Down Windowsills									
24	Vacuum Furnishings, Cushions, Chairs, Sofas And Couches									
25	Spray Air Freshener									
26	Clean And Disinfect Any Cabinets, Shelves And Units									
27	Clean Surfaces And Desk/Work Dividers									
28	Clean And Disinfect Telephones And Headsets									
29	Polish Any Wooden Furniture And Hardwood Surfaces									

	Monthly Office Cleaning Tasks	M	T	W	T	F	S	S	Cleaned By	Date/Time
1	Clean Skirting Boards/Baseboards And Corners									
2	Clean And Disinfect All The Walls From Top To Bottom									
3	Clean Blinds (Take Down And Wash If Possible)									
4	Wash And Clean Windows (Inside And Outside)									
5	Clean And Disinfect Shared Surfaces									
6	Steam Clean Carpets And Rugs									
7	Dust And Clean Ceilings, Ceiling Corners And Ceiling Tiles									
8	Check For Broken Chairs And Tables									
9	Dust And Wash Radiator Covers									
10	Clean And Disinfect Ceiling Wall Vents									
11	Clean And Vacuum Central Heating Units									
12	Wash And Clean Light Covers									
13	Clean Drapes And Curtains (Take Down And Wash if Possible)									
14	Check Cleaning Supplies And Re-Stock As Necessary									
15	Check Ceiling Fans, Fire Sprinklers And Smoke Alarms									
16	Check Hardware, Door Stops And Lock Mechanisms									
17	Fire Exit Lights And Emergency Lights Checked & Functioning									
18	Organize And De-Clutter Office Drawers									
19	Organize And De-Clutter Storeroom									
	Daily/Weekly Toilets/Restroom Cleaning Tasks	M	T	W	T	F	S	S	Cleaned By	Date/Time
1	Clean And Disinfect All Doors, Door Handles And Doorknobs									
2	Disinfect Touch Points, Light Switches And Other Switches									
3	Toilet Roll Holders Cleaned And Disinfected And Re-Stocked									
4	Wipe Down The Walls Wherever There Are Spills And Splashes									
5	Electric Hand Dryers Cleaned, Disinfected & Operating Correctly									
6	Sweep The Floors To Ensure They're Free From Debris									
7	Mop Tiled And Laminate Floors With Disinfectant Cleaner									
8	Paper Dispensers & Paper Towel Rolls Cleaned & Re-Stocked									
9	Take Out The Rubbish/Trash, Remove Waste And Recycling									
10	Clean & Disinfectant Bins/Waste Disposal Area & Trash Cans									
11	Feminine Hygiene Bins/Containers Cleaned And Disinfected									
12	Toilets Cleaned & Disinfected, Outside, Inside And Handles									
13	Urinals & Urinal Screens Cleaned, Disinfected & Blocks Replaced									
14	Wall Mirrors Cleaned With Glass Cleaner									
15	Clean And Re-Stock Paper Dispensers & Paper Towel Rolls									
16	Refill Soap Dispensers, Sanitizers And Hand Gels									
17	Sinks, Taps, Fixtures, Surface Areas Cleaned And Disinfected									

	Daily/Weekly Toilets/Restroom Cleaning Tasks Con	M	T	W	T	F	S	S	Cleaned By	Date/Time
18	Windowsills Clean And Wiped Down									
19	Check Plumbing And Schedule Work If Required									
20	Air Fresheners Checked And Replaced									
21	Fire Exit Lights And Emergency Lights Checked & Functioning									
22	Place Wet Floor Signs If Floors Are Wet After Mopping									
23	Cabinets Cleaned And Disinfected									
	Monthly Toilets/Restroom Cleaning Tasks	M	T	W	T	F	S	S	Cleaned By	Date/Time
1	Toilet/Restroom Service Storeroom/Cupboard Clean And Tidy									
2	Walls Free Of Graffiti, Stickers, Gum And Residue									
3	Wash And Clean Windows (Inside And Outside)									
4	Check Hardware, Door Stops And Lock Mechanisms									
5	All Fittings Securely Fixed (Schedule Maintenance If Not)									
6	Dust And Clean Ceilings, Ceiling Corners And Ceiling Tiles									
7	Clean Skirting Boards/Baseboards And Corners									
8	Thoroughly Clean Grout And Tiles									
9	Ceiling Wall Vents Cleaned And Disinfected									
10	Clean And Vacuum Central Heating Units									
11	Wash And Clean Light Covers									
12	Wash All Toilet And Restroom Mats									
	Daily/Weekly Kitchen Cleaning Tasks	M	T	W	T	F	S	S	Cleaned By	Date/Time
1	Wash And Sanitize All Counter Tops And Prep Area Surfaces									
2	Empty Dishwasher, Run The Dishwasher/Dish Drainer									
3	Disinfect Touch Points, Light Switches And Other Switches									
4	Take Out The Rubbish/Trash, Remove Waste And Recycling									
5	Clean & Disinfectant Bins/Waste Disposal Area & Trash Cans									
6	Wipe Down The Walls Wherever There Are Spills And Splashes									
7	Sweep The Floors To Ensure They're Free From Debris									
8	Mop Tiled And Laminate Floors With Disinfectant Cleaner									
9	Wet Floor Signs In Place If Floors Are Wet After Mopping									
10	Thoroughly Clean And Disinfect The Sinks And Taps									
11	Clean Exterior Of Appliances, Check For Spilled Food									
12	Replace Empty Paper Towel Rolls And Cloth Roller Towels									
13	Refill Soap Dispensers And Hand Sanitizers/Hand Gels									
14	Wipe Down Equipment, Tea And Coffee Makers, Toasters Etc									
15	Fire Exit Lights And Emergency Lights Checked & Functioning									
16	Pour Drain Cleaner Down Floor And Sink Drains									
17	Clean Inside Microwave, Check For Spilled Food									

	Daily/Weekly Kitchen Cleaning Tasks Continued	M	T	W	T	F	S	S	CLEANED BY	DATE/TIME
18	Replace Wash Rags, Cloths And Tea Towels With Clean Ones									
19	Wash Rags, Cloths, Tea Towels And Towels In Washing Machine									
20	Replace And Change Burned Out Light Bulbs/Broken Lights									
21	Clean Inside Of Dishwasher									
22	Sanitise Sponges Or Replace Damaged Sponges With New									
23	Dishes, Pots, Pans, And Utensils To Be Stored Away Properly									
24	Clean Out Refrigerator And Wipe Down Shelves And Drawers									
	Monthly Kitchen Cleaning Tasks	M	T	W	T	F	S	S	Cleaned By	Date/Time
1	Wash And Clean Air Vents									
2	Sort Through And Organize Cooking Utensils, Pans And Pots									
3	Wash And Clean Air Vents									
4	Check Plates, Cups And Glasses And Bin Anything Chipped									
5	Clean And Vacuum Central Heating Units									
6	Wash And Clean Light Covers									
7	Clean And De-Lime Dishwasher									
8	Dust And Clean Ceilings, Ceiling Corners And Ceiling Tiles									
9	Thoroughly Clean Grout And Tiles									
10	Clean Refrigerator Coils To Remove Dust, Unplug First									
11	Run Cleaning & Sanitizing Chemicals Through Coffee Machine									
12	Disinfect And Clean All The Walls From Top To Bottom									
13	Check For Out Of Date Food In Cabinets/Cupboards									
14	Clean Skirting Boards/Baseboards And Corners									
15	Clean Under Refrigerator									
16	Wash And Clean Doors, Door Frames And Glass									
17	Sort Through Leftover Items In The Fridge/Refrigerators									
18	Wash And Clean Windows (Inside And Outside)									
19	Replace Pest Traps									

ESSENTIAL CLEANING NOTES

....

....

....

....

....

....

....

....

ESSENTIAL OFFICE CLEANING *Checklist*

Location/Building	Department	Office Number	Week Number

Start Date & Time	Finnish Date & Time	Name	Signature

	Daily/Weekly Office Cleaning Tasks	M	T	W	T	F	S	S	Cleaned By	Date/Time
1	Clean And Sanitize All The Desks And Tables									
2	Clean And Sanitize All The Counter Tops And Surface Areas									
3	Disinfect All Point-Of-Sale Terminals And Touch Screens									
4	Disinfect Touch Points, Light Switches And Other Switches									
5	Clean And Sanitize All Keyboards And Computer Mice									
6	Wipe Down The Walls Wherever There Are Spills And Splashes									
7	Clean And Disinfect All Doors, Door Handles And Doorknobs									
8	Re-Stock Protective Clothing, Face Masks/Shields, Gloves									
9	Clean And Sanitize All The Chairs, Seats And Benches									
10	Clean All The Mirrors, Glass Cabinets/Displays									
11	Replace And Change Burned Out Light Bulbs/Broken Lights									
12	Sweep The Floors To Ensure They're Free From Debris									
13	Mop Tiled And Laminate Floors With Disinfectant Cleaner									
14	Vacuum And Hoover The Carpets, Mats And Rugs									
15	Place Wet Floor Signs If Floors Are Wet After Mopping									
16	Wash & Clean Dirty Cups, Drinking Bottles And Glasses									
17	Clean & Re-Stock Paper Dispensers & Paper Towel Rolls									
18	Wipe Down Equipment & Sanitize Tea And Coffee Makers									
19	Refill Soap Dispensers, Sanitizers And Hand Gels									
20	Clean And Dust Furniture And Office Equipment									
21	Take Out The Rubbish/Trash, Remove Waste And Recycling									
22	Clean & Disinfectant Bins/Waste Disposal Area & Trash Cans									
23	Clean And Wipe Down Windowsills									
24	Vacuum Furnishings, Cushions, Chairs, Sofas And Couches									
25	Spray Air Freshener									
26	Clean And Disinfect Any Cabinets, Shelves And Units									
27	Clean Surfaces And Desk/Work Dividers									
28	Clean And Disinfect Telephones And Headsets									
29	Polish Any Wooden Furniture And Hardwood Surfaces									

	Monthly Office Cleaning Tasks	M	T	W	T	F	S	S	Cleaned By	Date/Time
1	Clean Skirting Boards/Baseboards And Corners									
2	Clean And Disinfect All The Walls From Top To Bottom									
3	Clean Blinds (Take Down And Wash If Possible)									
4	Wash And Clean Windows (Inside And Outside)									
5	Clean And Disinfect Shared Surfaces									
6	Steam Clean Carpets And Rugs									
7	Dust And Clean Ceilings, Ceiling Corners And Ceiling Tiles									
8	Check For Broken Chairs And Tables									
9	Dust And Wash Radiator Covers									
10	Clean And Disinfect Ceiling Wall Vents									
11	Clean And Vacuum Central Heating Units									
12	Wash And Clean Light Covers									
13	Clean Drapes And Curtains (Take Down And Wash if Possible)									
14	Check Cleaning Supplies And Re-Stock As Necessary									
15	Check Ceiling Fans, Fire Sprinklers And Smoke Alarms									
16	Check Hardware, Door Stops And Lock Mechanisms									
17	Fire Exit Lights And Emergency Lights Checked & Functioning									
18	Organize And De-Clutter Office Drawers									
19	Organize And De-Clutter Storeroom									
	Daily/Weekly Toilets/Restroom Cleaning Tasks	M	T	W	T	F	S	S	Cleaned By	Date/Time
1	Clean And Disinfect All Doors, Door Handles And Doorknobs									
2	Disinfect Touch Points, Light Switches And Other Switches									
3	Toilet Roll Holders Cleaned And Disinfected And Re-Stocked									
4	Wipe Down The Walls Wherever There Are Spills And Splashes									
5	Electric Hand Dryers Cleaned, Disinfected & Operating Correctly									
6	Sweep The Floors To Ensure They're Free From Debris									
7	Mop Tiled And Laminate Floors With Disinfectant Cleaner									
8	Paper Dispensers & Paper Towel Rolls Cleaned & Re-Stocked									
9	Take Out The Rubbish/Trash, Remove Waste And Recycling									
10	Clean & Disinfectant Bins/Waste Disposal Area & Trash Cans									
11	Feminine Hygiene Bins/Containers Cleaned And Disinfected									
12	Toilets Cleaned & Disinfected, Outside, Inside And Handles									
13	Urinals & Urinal Screens Cleaned, Disinfected & Blocks Replaced									
14	Wall Mirrors Cleaned With Glass Cleaner									
15	Clean And Re-Stock Paper Dispensers & Paper Towel Rolls									
16	Refill Soap Dispensers, Sanitizers And Hand Gels									
17	Sinks, Taps, Fixtures, Surface Areas Cleaned And Disinfected									

Daily/Weekly Toilets/Restroom Cleaning Tasks Con	M	T	W	T	F	S	S	Cleaned By	Date/Time
18 Windowsills Clean And Wiped Down									
19 Check Plumbing And Schedule Work If Required									
20 Air Fresheners Checked And Replaced									
21 Fire Exit Lights And Emergency Lights Checked & Functioning									
22 Place Wet Floor Signs If Floors Are Wet After Mopping									
23 Cabinets Cleaned And Disinfected									
Monthly Toilets/Restroom Cleaning Tasks	M	T	W	T	F	S	S	Cleaned By	Date/Time
1 Toilet/Restroom Service Storeroom/Cupboard Clean And Tidy									
2 Walls Free Of Graffiti, Stickers, Gum And Residue									
3 Wash And Clean Windows (Inside And Outside)									
4 Check Hardware, Door Stops And Lock Mechanisms									
5 All Fittings Securely Fixed (Schedule Maintenance If Not)									
6 Dust And Clean Ceilings, Ceiling Corners And Ceiling Tiles									
7 Clean Skirting Boards/Baseboards And Corners									
8 Thoroughly Clean Grout And Tiles									
9 Ceiling Wall Vents Cleaned And Disinfected									
10 Clean And Vacuum Central Heating Units									
11 Wash And Clean Light Covers									
12 Wash All Toilet And Restroom Mats									
Daily/Weekly Kitchen Cleaning Tasks	M	T	W	T	F	S	S	Cleaned By	Date/Time
1 Wash And Sanitize All Counter Tops And Prep Area Surfaces									
2 Empty Dishwasher, Run The Dishwasher/Dish Drainer									
3 Disinfect Touch Points, Light Switches And Other Switches									
4 Take Out The Rubbish/Trash, Remove Waste And Recycling									
5 Clean & Disinfectant Bins/Waste Disposal Area & Trash Cans									
6 Wipe Down The Walls Wherever There Are Spills And Splashes									
7 Sweep The Floors To Ensure They're Free From Debris									
8 Mop Tiled And Laminate Floors With Disinfectant Cleaner									
9 Wet Floor Signs In Place If Floors Are Wet After Mopping									
10 Thoroughly Clean And Disinfect The Sinks And Taps									
11 Clean Exterior Of Appliances, Check For Spilled Food									
12 Replace Empty Paper Towel Rolls And Cloth Roller Towels									
13 Refill Soap Dispensers And Hand Sanitizers/Hand Gels									
14 Wipe Down Equipment, Tea And Coffee Makers, Toasters Etc									
15 Fire Exit Lights And Emergency Lights Checked & Functioning									
16 Pour Drain Cleaner Down Floor And Sink Drains									
17 Clean Inside Microwave, Check For Spilled Food									

	Daily/Weekly Kitchen Cleaning Tasks Continued	M	T	W	T	F	S	S	CLEANED BY	DATE/TIME
18	Replace Wash Rags, Cloths And Tea Towels With Clean Ones									
19	Wash Rags, Cloths, Tea Towels And Towels In Washing Machine									
20	Replace And Change Burned Out Light Bulbs/Broken Lights									
21	Clean Inside Of Dishwasher									
22	Sanitise Sponges Or Replace Damaged Sponges With New									
23	Dishes, Pots, Pans, And Utensils To Be Stored Away Properly									
24	Clean Out Refrigerator And Wipe Down Shelves And Drawers									
	Monthly Kitchen Cleaning Tasks	M	T	W	T	F	S	S	Cleaned By	Date/Time
1	Wash And Clean Air Vents									
2	Sort Through And Organize Cooking Utensils, Pans And Pots									
3	Wash And Clean Air Vents									
4	Check Plates, Cups And Glasses And Bin Anything Chipped									
5	Clean And Vacuum Central Heating Units									
6	Wash And Clean Light Covers									
7	Clean And De-Lime Dishwasher									
8	Dust And Clean Ceilings, Ceiling Corners And Ceiling Tiles									
9	Thoroughly Clean Grout And Tiles									
10	Clean Refrigerator Coils To Remove Dust, Unplug First									
11	Run Cleaning & Sanitizing Chemicals Through Coffee Machine									
12	Disinfect And Clean All The Walls From Top To Bottom									
13	Check For Out Of Date Food In Cabinets/Cupboards									
14	Clean Skirting Boards/Baseboards And Corners									
15	Clean Under Refrigerator									
16	Wash And Clean Doors, Door Frames And Glass									
17	Sort Through Leftover Items In The Fridge/Refrigerators									
18	Wash And Clean Windows (Inside And Outside)									
19	Replace Pest Traps									

ESSENTIAL CLEANING NOTES

....

....

....

....

....

....

....

....

....

....

ESSENTIAL OFFICE CLEANING *Checklist*

Location/Building	Department	Office Number	Week Number

Start Date & Time	Finnish Date & Time	Name	Signature

	Daily/Weekly Office Cleaning Tasks	M	T	W	T	F	S	S	Cleaned By	Date/Time
1	Clean And Sanitize All The Desks And Tables									
2	Clean And Sanitize All The Counter Tops And Surface Areas									
3	Disinfect All Point-Of-Sale Terminals And Touch Screens									
4	Disinfect Touch Points, Light Switches And Other Switches									
5	Clean And Sanitize All Keyboards And Computer Mice									
6	Wipe Down The Walls Wherever There Are Spills And Splashes									
7	Clean And Disinfect All Doors, Door Handles And Doorknobs									
8	Re-Stock Protective Clothing, Face Masks/Shields, Gloves									
9	Clean And Sanitize All The Chairs, Seats And Benches									
10	Clean All The Mirrors, Glass Cabinets/Displays									
11	Replace And Change Burned Out Light Bulbs/Broken Lights									
12	Sweep The Floors To Ensure They're Free From Debris									
13	Mop Tiled And Laminate Floors With Disinfectant Cleaner									
14	Vacuum And Hoover The Carpets, Mats And Rugs									
15	Place Wet Floor Signs If Floors Are Wet After Mopping									
16	Wash & Clean Dirty Cups, Drinking Bottles And Glasses									
17	Clean & Re-Stock Paper Dispensers & Paper Towel Rolls									
18	Wipe Down Equipment & Sanitize Tea And Coffee Makers									
19	Refill Soap Dispensers, Sanitizers And Hand Gels									
20	Clean And Dust Furniture And Office Equipment									
21	Take Out The Rubbish/Trash, Remove Waste And Recycling									
22	Clean & Disinfectant Bins/Waste Disposal Area & Trash Cans									
23	Clean And Wipe Down Windowsills									
24	Vacuum Furnishings, Cushions, Chairs, Sofas And Couches									
25	Spray Air Freshener									
26	Clean And Disinfect Any Cabinets, Shelves And Units									
27	Clean Surfaces And Desk/Work Dividers									
28	Clean And Disinfect Telephones And Headsets									
29	Polish Any Wooden Furniture And Hardwood Surfaces									

	Monthly Office Cleaning Tasks	M	T	W	T	F	S	S	Cleaned By	Date/Time
1	Clean Skirting Boards/Baseboards And Corners									
2	Clean And Disinfect All The Walls From Top To Bottom									
3	Clean Blinds (Take Down And Wash If Possible)									
4	Wash And Clean Windows (Inside And Outside)									
5	Clean And Disinfect Shared Surfaces									
6	Steam Clean Carpets And Rugs									
7	Dust And Clean Ceilings, Ceiling Corners And Ceiling Tiles									
8	Check For Broken Chairs And Tables									
9	Dust And Wash Radiator Covers									
10	Clean And Disinfect Ceiling Wall Vents									
11	Clean And Vacuum Central Heating Units									
12	Wash And Clean Light Covers									
13	Clean Drapes And Curtains (Take Down And Wash if Possible)									
14	Check Cleaning Supplies And Re-Stock As Necessary									
15	Check Ceiling Fans, Fire Sprinklers And Smoke Alarms									
16	Check Hardware, Door Stops And Lock Mechanisms									
17	Fire Exit Lights And Emergency Lights Checked & Functioning									
18	Organize And De-Clutter Office Drawers									
19	Organize And De-Clutter Storeroom									
	Daily/Weekly Toilets/Restroom Cleaning Tasks	M	T	W	T	F	S	S	Cleaned By	Date/Time
1	Clean And Disinfect All Doors, Door Handles And Doorknobs									
2	Disinfect Touch Points, Light Switches And Other Switches									
3	Toilet Roll Holders Cleaned And Disinfected And Re-Stocked									
4	Wipe Down The Walls Wherever There Are Spills And Splashes									
5	Electric Hand Dryers Cleaned, Disinfected & Operating Correctly									
6	Sweep The Floors To Ensure They're Free From Debris									
7	Mop Tiled And Laminate Floors With Disinfectant Cleaner									
8	Paper Dispensers & Paper Towel Rolls Cleaned & Re-Stocked									
9	Take Out The Rubbish/Trash, Remove Waste And Recycling									
10	Clean & Disinfectant Bins/Waste Disposal Area & Trash Cans									
11	Feminine Hygiene Bins/Containers Cleaned And Disinfected									
12	Toilets Cleaned & Disinfected, Outside, Inside And Handles									
13	Urinals & Urinal Screens Cleaned, Disinfected & Blocks Replaced									
14	Wall Mirrors Cleaned With Glass Cleaner									
15	Clean And Re-Stock Paper Dispensers & Paper Towel Rolls									
16	Refill Soap Dispensers, Sanitizers And Hand Gels									
17	Sinks, Taps, Fixtures, Surface Areas Cleaned And Disinfected									

	Daily/Weekly Toilets/Restroom Cleaning Tasks Con	M	T	W	T	F	S	S	Cleaned By	Date/Time
18	Windowsills Clean And Wiped Down									
19	Check Plumbing And Schedule Work If Required									
20	Air Fresheners Checked And Replaced									
21	Fire Exit Lights And Emergency Lights Checked & Functioning									
22	Place Wet Floor Signs If Floors Are Wet After Mopping									
23	Cabinets Cleaned And Disinfected									
	Monthly Toilets/Restroom Cleaning Tasks	M	T	W	T	F	S	S	Cleaned By	Date/Time
1	Toilet/Restroom Service Storeroom/Cupboard Clean And Tidy									
2	Walls Free Of Graffiti, Stickers, Gum And Residue									
3	Wash And Clean Windows (Inside And Outside)									
4	Check Hardware, Door Stops And Lock Mechanisms									
5	All Fittings Securely Fixed (Schedule Maintenance If Not)									
6	Dust And Clean Ceilings, Ceiling Corners And Ceiling Tiles									
7	Clean Skirting Boards/Baseboards And Corners									
8	Thoroughly Clean Grout And Tiles									
9	Ceiling Wall Vents Cleaned And Disinfected									
10	Clean And Vacuum Central Heating Units									
11	Wash And Clean Light Covers									
12	Wash All Toilet And Restroom Mats									
	Daily/Weekly Kitchen Cleaning Tasks	M	T	W	T	F	S	S	Cleaned By	Date/Time
1	Wash And Sanitize All Counter Tops And Prep Area Surfaces									
2	Empty Dishwasher, Run The Dishwasher/Dish Drainer									
3	Disinfect Touch Points, Light Switches And Other Switches									
4	Take Out The Rubbish/Trash, Remove Waste And Recycling									
5	Clean & Disinfectant Bins/Waste Disposal Area & Trash Cans									
6	Wipe Down The Walls Wherever There Are Spills And Splashes									
7	Sweep The Floors To Ensure They're Free From Debris									
8	Mop Tiled And Laminate Floors With Disinfectant Cleaner									
9	Wet Floor Signs In Place If Floors Are Wet After Mopping									
10	Thoroughly Clean And Disinfect The Sinks And Taps									
11	Clean Exterior Of Appliances, Check For Spilled Food									
12	Replace Empty Paper Towel Rolls And Cloth Roller Towels									
13	Refill Soap Dispensers And Hand Sanitizers/Hand Gels									
14	Wipe Down Equipment, Tea And Coffee Makers, Toasters Etc									
15	Fire Exit Lights And Emergency Lights Checked & Functioning									
16	Pour Drain Cleaner Down Floor And Sink Drains									
17	Clean Inside Microwave, Check For Spilled Food									

	Daily/Weekly Kitchen Cleaning Tasks Continued	M	T	W	T	F	S	S	CLEANED BY	DATE/TIME
18	Replace Wash Rags, Cloths And Tea Towels With Clean Ones									
19	Wash Rags, Cloths, Tea Towels And Towels In Washing Machine									
20	Replace And Change Burned Out Light Bulbs/Broken Lights									
21	Clean Inside Of Dishwasher									
22	Sanitise Sponges Or Replace Damaged Sponges With New									
23	Dishes, Pots, Pans, And Utensils To Be Stored Away Properly									
24	Clean Out Refrigerator And Wipe Down Shelves And Drawers									
	Monthly Kitchen Cleaning Tasks	M	T	W	T	F	S	S	Cleaned By	Date/Time
1	Wash And Clean Air Vents									
2	Sort Through And Organize Cooking Utensils, Pans And Pots									
3	Wash And Clean Air Vents									
4	Check Plates, Cups And Glasses And Bin Anything Chipped									
5	Clean And Vacuum Central Heating Units									
6	Wash And Clean Light Covers									
7	Clean And De-Lime Dishwasher									
8	Dust And Clean Ceilings, Ceiling Corners And Ceiling Tiles									
9	Thoroughly Clean Grout And Tiles									
10	Clean Refrigerator Coils To Remove Dust, Unplug First									
11	Run Cleaning & Sanitizing Chemicals Through Coffee Machine									
12	Disinfect And Clean All The Walls From Top To Bottom									
13	Check For Out Of Date Food In Cabinets/Cupboards									
14	Clean Skirting Boards/Baseboards And Corners									
15	Clean Under Refrigerator									
16	Wash And Clean Doors, Door Frames And Glass									
17	Sort Through Leftover Items In The Fridge/Refrigerators									
18	Wash And Clean Windows (Inside And Outside)									
19	Replace Pest Traps									

ESSENTIAL CLEANING NOTES

....
....
....
....
....
....
....
....

ESSENTIAL OFFICE CLEANING *Checklist*

Location/Building	Department	Office Number	Week Number

Start Date & Time	Finnish Date & Time	Name	Signature

	Daily/Weekly Office Cleaning Tasks	M	T	W	T	F	S	S	Cleaned By	Date/Time
1	Clean And Sanitize All The Desks And Tables									
2	Clean And Sanitize All The Counter Tops And Surface Areas									
3	Disinfect All Point-Of-Sale Terminals And Touch Screens									
4	Disinfect Touch Points, Light Switches And Other Switches									
5	Clean And Sanitize All Keyboards And Computer Mice									
6	Wipe Down The Walls Wherever There Are Spills And Splashes									
7	Clean And Disinfect All Doors, Door Handles And Doorknobs									
8	Re-Stock Protective Clothing, Face Masks/Shields, Gloves									
9	Clean And Sanitize All The Chairs, Seats And Benches									
10	Clean All The Mirrors, Glass Cabinets/Displays									
11	Replace And Change Burned Out Light Bulbs/Broken Lights									
12	Sweep The Floors To Ensure They're Free From Debris									
13	Mop Tiled And Laminate Floors With Disinfectant Cleaner									
14	Vacuum And Hoover The Carpets, Mats And Rugs									
15	Place Wet Floor Signs If Floors Are Wet After Mopping									
16	Wash & Clean Dirty Cups, Drinking Bottles And Glasses									
17	Clean & Re-Stock Paper Dispensers & Paper Towel Rolls									
18	Wipe Down Equipment & Sanitize Tea And Coffee Makers									
19	Refill Soap Dispensers, Sanitizers And Hand Gels									
20	Clean And Dust Furniture And Office Equipment									
21	Take Out The Rubbish/Trash, Remove Waste And Recycling									
22	Clean & Disinfectant Bins/Waste Disposal Area & Trash Cans									
23	Clean And Wipe Down Windowsills									
24	Vacuum Furnishings, Cushions, Chairs, Sofas And Couches									
25	Spray Air Freshener									
26	Clean And Disinfect Any Cabinets, Shelves And Units									
27	Clean Surfaces And Desk/Work Dividers									
28	Clean And Disinfect Telephones And Headsets									
29	Polish Any Wooden Furniture And Hardwood Surfaces									

	Monthly Office Cleaning Tasks	M	T	W	T	F	S	S	Cleaned By	Date/Time
1	Clean Skirting Boards/Baseboards And Corners									
2	Clean And Disinfect All The Walls From Top To Bottom									
3	Clean Blinds (Take Down And Wash If Possible)									
4	Wash And Clean Windows (Inside And Outside)									
5	Clean And Disinfect Shared Surfaces									
6	Steam Clean Carpets And Rugs									
7	Dust And Clean Ceilings, Ceiling Corners And Ceiling Tiles									
8	Check For Broken Chairs And Tables									
9	Dust And Wash Radiator Covers									
10	Clean And Disinfect Ceiling Wall Vents									
11	Clean And Vacuum Central Heating Units									
12	Wash And Clean Light Covers									
13	Clean Drapes And Curtains (Take Down And Wash if Possible)									
14	Check Cleaning Supplies And Re-Stock As Necessary									
15	Check Ceiling Fans, Fire Sprinklers And Smoke Alarms									
16	Check Hardware, Door Stops And Lock Mechanisms									
17	Fire Exit Lights And Emergency Lights Checked & Functioning									
18	Organize And De-Clutter Office Drawers									
19	Organize And De-Clutter Storeroom									
	Daily/Weekly Toilets/Restroom Cleaning Tasks	M	T	W	T	F	S	S	Cleaned By	Date/Time
1	Clean And Disinfect All Doors, Door Handles And Doorknobs									
2	Disinfect Touch Points, Light Switches And Other Switches									
3	Toilet Roll Holders Cleaned And Disinfected And Re-Stocked									
4	Wipe Down The Walls Wherever There Are Spills And Splashes									
5	Electric Hand Dryers Cleaned, Disinfected & Operating Correctly									
6	Sweep The Floors To Ensure They're Free From Debris									
7	Mop Tiled And Laminate Floors With Disinfectant Cleaner									
8	Paper Dispensers & Paper Towel Rolls Cleaned & Re-Stocked									
9	Take Out The Rubbish/Trash, Remove Waste And Recycling									
10	Clean & Disinfectant Bins/Waste Disposal Area & Trash Cans									
11	Feminine Hygiene Bins/Containers Cleaned And Disinfected									
12	Toilets Cleaned & Disinfected, Outside, Inside And Handles									
13	Urinals & Urinal Screens Cleaned, Disinfected & Blocks Replaced									
14	Wall Mirrors Cleaned With Glass Cleaner									
15	Clean And Re-Stock Paper Dispensers & Paper Towel Rolls									
16	Refill Soap Dispensers, Sanitizers And Hand Gels									
17	Sinks, Taps, Fixtures, Surface Areas Cleaned And Disinfected									

	Daily/Weekly Toilets/Restroom Cleaning Tasks Con	M	T	W	T	F	S	S	Cleaned By	Date/Time
18	Windowsills Clean And Wiped Down									
19	Check Plumbing And Schedule Work If Required									
20	Air Fresheners Checked And Replaced									
21	Fire Exit Lights And Emergency Lights Checked & Functioning									
22	Place Wet Floor Signs If Floors Are Wet After Mopping									
23	Cabinets Cleaned And Disinfected									
	Monthly Toilets/Restroom Cleaning Tasks	M	T	W	T	F	S	S	Cleaned By	Date/Time
1	Toilet/Restroom Service Storeroom/Cupboard Clean And Tidy									
2	Walls Free Of Graffiti, Stickers, Gum And Residue									
3	Wash And Clean Windows (Inside And Outside)									
4	Check Hardware, Door Stops And Lock Mechanisms									
5	All Fittings Securely Fixed (Schedule Maintenance If Not)									
6	Dust And Clean Ceilings, Ceiling Corners And Ceiling Tiles									
7	Clean Skirting Boards/Baseboards And Corners									
8	Thoroughly Clean Grout And Tiles									
9	Ceiling Wall Vents Cleaned And Disinfected									
10	Clean And Vacuum Central Heating Units									
11	Wash And Clean Light Covers									
12	Wash All Toilet And Restroom Mats									
	Daily/Weekly Kitchen Cleaning Tasks	M	T	W	T	F	S	S	Cleaned By	Date/Time
1	Wash And Sanitize All Counter Tops And Prep Area Surfaces									
2	Empty Dishwasher, Run The Dishwasher/Dish Drainer									
3	Disinfect Touch Points, Light Switches And Other Switches									
4	Take Out The Rubbish/Trash, Remove Waste And Recycling									
5	Clean & Disinfectant Bins/Waste Disposal Area & Trash Cans									
6	Wipe Down The Walls Wherever There Are Spills And Splashes									
7	Sweep The Floors To Ensure They're Free From Debris									
8	Mop Tiled And Laminate Floors With Disinfectant Cleaner									
9	Wet Floor Signs In Place If Floors Are Wet After Mopping									
10	Thoroughly Clean And Disinfect The Sinks And Taps									
11	Clean Exterior Of Appliances, Check For Spilled Food									
12	Replace Empty Paper Towel Rolls And Cloth Roller Towels									
13	Refill Soap Dispensers And Hand Sanitizers/Hand Gels									
14	Wipe Down Equipment, Tea And Coffee Makers, Toasters Etc									
15	Fire Exit Lights And Emergency Lights Checked & Functioning									
16	Pour Drain Cleaner Down Floor And Sink Drains									
17	Clean Inside Microwave, Check For Spilled Food									

	Daily/Weekly Kitchen Cleaning Tasks Continued	M	T	W	T	F	S	S	CLEANED BY	DATE/TIME
18	Replace Wash Rags, Cloths And Tea Towels With Clean Ones									
19	Wash Rags, Cloths, Tea Towels And Towels In Washing Machine									
20	Replace And Change Burned Out Light Bulbs/Broken Lights									
21	Clean Inside Of Dishwasher									
22	Sanitise Sponges Or Replace Damaged Sponges With New									
23	Dishes, Pots, Pans, And Utensils To Be Stored Away Properly									
24	Clean Out Refrigerator And Wipe Down Shelves And Drawers									
	Monthly Kitchen Cleaning Tasks	M	T	W	T	F	S	S	Cleaned By	Date/Time
1	Wash And Clean Air Vents									
2	Sort Through And Organize Cooking Utensils, Pans And Pots									
3	Wash And Clean Air Vents									
4	Check Plates, Cups And Glasses And Bin Anything Chipped									
5	Clean And Vacuum Central Heating Units									
6	Wash And Clean Light Covers									
7	Clean And De-Lime Dishwasher									
8	Dust And Clean Ceilings, Ceiling Corners And Ceiling Tiles									
9	Thoroughly Clean Grout And Tiles									
10	Clean Refrigerator Coils To Remove Dust, Unplug First									
11	Run Cleaning & Sanitizing Chemicals Through Coffee Machine									
12	Disinfect And Clean All The Walls From Top To Bottom									
13	Check For Out Of Date Food In Cabinets/Cupboards									
14	Clean Skirting Boards/Baseboards And Corners									
15	Clean Under Refrigerator									
16	Wash And Clean Doors, Door Frames And Glass									
17	Sort Through Leftover Items In The Fridge/Refrigerators									
18	Wash And Clean Windows (Inside And Outside)									
19	Replace Pest Traps									

ESSENTIAL CLEANING NOTES

....

....

....

....

....

....

....

....

ESSENTIAL OFFICE CLEANING *Checklist*

Location/Building	Department	Office Number	Week Number

Start Date & Time	Finnish Date & Time	Name	Signature

	Daily/Weekly Office Cleaning Tasks	M	T	W	T	F	S	S	Cleaned By	Date/Time
1	Clean And Sanitize All The Desks And Tables									
2	Clean And Sanitize All The Counter Tops And Surface Areas									
3	Disinfect All Point-Of-Sale Terminals And Touch Screens									
4	Disinfect Touch Points, Light Switches And Other Switches									
5	Clean And Sanitize All Keyboards And Computer Mice									
6	Wipe Down The Walls Wherever There Are Spills And Splashes									
7	Clean And Disinfect All Doors, Door Handles And Doorknobs									
8	Re-Stock Protective Clothing, Face Masks/Shields, Gloves									
9	Clean And Sanitize All The Chairs, Seats And Benches									
10	Clean All The Mirrors, Glass Cabinets/Displays									
11	Replace And Change Burned Out Light Bulbs/Broken Lights									
12	Sweep The Floors To Ensure They're Free From Debris									
13	Mop Tiled And Laminate Floors With Disinfectant Cleaner									
14	Vacuum And Hoover The Carpets, Mats And Rugs									
15	Place Wet Floor Signs If Floors Are Wet After Mopping									
16	Wash & Clean Dirty Cups, Drinking Bottles And Glasses									
17	Clean & Re-Stock Paper Dispensers & Paper Towel Rolls									
18	Wipe Down Equipment & Sanitize Tea And Coffee Makers									
19	Refill Soap Dispensers, Sanitizers And Hand Gels									
20	Clean And Dust Furniture And Office Equipment									
21	Take Out The Rubbish/Trash, Remove Waste And Recycling									
22	Clean & Disinfectant Bins/Waste Disposal Area & Trash Cans									
23	Clean And Wipe Down Windowsills									
24	Vacuum Furnishings, Cushions, Chairs, Sofas And Couches									
25	Spray Air Freshener									
26	Clean And Disinfect Any Cabinets, Shelves And Units									
27	Clean Surfaces And Desk/Work Dividers									
28	Clean And Disinfect Telephones And Headsets									
29	Polish Any Wooden Furniture And Hardwood Surfaces									

	Monthly Office Cleaning Tasks	M	T	W	T	F	S	S	Cleaned By	Date/Time
1	Clean Skirting Boards/Baseboards And Corners									
2	Clean And Disinfect All The Walls From Top To Bottom									
3	Clean Blinds (Take Down And Wash If Possible)									
4	Wash And Clean Windows (Inside And Outside)									
5	Clean And Disinfect Shared Surfaces									
6	Steam Clean Carpets And Rugs									
7	Dust And Clean Ceilings, Ceiling Corners And Ceiling Tiles									
8	Check For Broken Chairs And Tables									
9	Dust And Wash Radiator Covers									
10	Clean And Disinfect Ceiling Wall Vents									
11	Clean And Vacuum Central Heating Units									
12	Wash And Clean Light Covers									
13	Clean Drapes And Curtains (Take Down And Wash if Possible)									
14	Check Cleaning Supplies And Re-Stock As Necessary									
15	Check Ceiling Fans, Fire Sprinklers And Smoke Alarms									
16	Check Hardware, Door Stops And Lock Mechanisms									
17	Fire Exit Lights And Emergency Lights Checked & Functioning									
18	Organize And De-Clutter Office Drawers									
19	Organize And De-Clutter Storeroom									
	Daily/Weekly Toilets/Restroom Cleaning Tasks	M	T	W	T	F	S	S	Cleaned By	Date/Time
1	Clean And Disinfect All Doors, Door Handles And Doorknobs									
2	Disinfect Touch Points, Light Switches And Other Switches									
3	Toilet Roll Holders Cleaned And Disinfected And Re-Stocked									
4	Wipe Down The Walls Wherever There Are Spills And Splashes									
5	Electric Hand Dryers Cleaned, Disinfected & Operating Correctly									
6	Sweep The Floors To Ensure They're Free From Debris									
7	Mop Tiled And Laminate Floors With Disinfectant Cleaner									
8	Paper Dispensers & Paper Towel Rolls Cleaned & Re-Stocked									
9	Take Out The Rubbish/Trash, Remove Waste And Recycling									
10	Clean & Disinfectant Bins/Waste Disposal Area & Trash Cans									
11	Feminine Hygiene Bins/Containers Cleaned And Disinfected									
12	Toilets Cleaned & Disinfected, Outside, Inside And Handles									
13	Urinals & Urinal Screens Cleaned, Disinfected & Blocks Replaced									
14	Wall Mirrors Cleaned With Glass Cleaner									
15	Clean And Re-Stock Paper Dispensers & Paper Towel Rolls									
16	Refill Soap Dispensers, Sanitizers And Hand Gels									
17	Sinks, Taps, Fixtures, Surface Areas Cleaned And Disinfected									

	Daily/Weekly Toilets/Restroom Cleaning Tasks Con	M	T	W	T	F	S	S	Cleaned By	Date/Time
18	Windowsills Clean And Wiped Down									
19	Check Plumbing And Schedule Work If Required									
20	Air Fresheners Checked And Replaced									
21	Fire Exit Lights And Emergency Lights Checked & Functioning									
22	Place Wet Floor Signs If Floors Are Wet After Mopping									
23	Cabinets Cleaned And Disinfected									
	Monthly Toilets/Restroom Cleaning Tasks	M	T	W	T	F	S	S	Cleaned By	Date/Time
1	Toilet/Restroom Service Storeroom/Cupboard Clean And Tidy									
2	Walls Free Of Graffiti, Stickers, Gum And Residue									
3	Wash And Clean Windows (Inside And Outside)									
4	Check Hardware, Door Stops And Lock Mechanisms									
5	All Fittings Securely Fixed (Schedule Maintenance If Not)									
6	Dust And Clean Ceilings, Ceiling Corners And Ceiling Tiles									
7	Clean Skirting Boards/Baseboards And Corners									
8	Thoroughly Clean Grout And Tiles									
9	Ceiling Wall Vents Cleaned And Disinfected									
10	Clean And Vacuum Central Heating Units									
11	Wash And Clean Light Covers									
12	Wash All Toilet And Restroom Mats									
	Daily/Weekly Kitchen Cleaning Tasks	M	T	W	T	F	S	S	Cleaned By	Date/Time
1	Wash And Sanitize All Counter Tops And Prep Area Surfaces									
2	Empty Dishwasher, Run The Dishwasher/Dish Drainer									
3	Disinfect Touch Points, Light Switches And Other Switches									
4	Take Out The Rubbish/Trash, Remove Waste And Recycling									
5	Clean & Disinfectant Bins/Waste Disposal Area & Trash Cans									
6	Wipe Down The Walls Wherever There Are Spills And Splashes									
7	Sweep The Floors To Ensure They're Free From Debris									
8	Mop Tiled And Laminate Floors With Disinfectant Cleaner									
9	Wet Floor Signs In Place If Floors Are Wet After Mopping									
10	Thoroughly Clean And Disinfect The Sinks And Taps									
11	Clean Exterior Of Appliances, Check For Spilled Food									
12	Replace Empty Paper Towel Rolls And Cloth Roller Towels									
13	Refill Soap Dispensers And Hand Sanitizers/Hand Gels									
14	Wipe Down Equipment, Tea And Coffee Makers, Toasters Etc									
15	Fire Exit Lights And Emergency Lights Checked & Functioning									
16	Pour Drain Cleaner Down Floor And Sink Drains									
17	Clean Inside Microwave, Check For Spilled Food									

	Daily/Weekly Kitchen Cleaning Tasks Continued	M	T	W	T	F	S	S	CLEANED BY	DATE/TIME
18	Replace Wash Rags, Cloths And Tea Towels With Clean Ones									
19	Wash Rags, Cloths, Tea Towels And Towels In Washing Machine									
20	Replace And Change Burned Out Light Bulbs/Broken Lights									
21	Clean Inside Of Dishwasher									
22	Sanitise Sponges Or Replace Damaged Sponges With New									
23	Dishes, Pots, Pans, And Utensils To Be Stored Away Properly									
24	Clean Out Refrigerator And Wipe Down Shelves And Drawers									
	Monthly Kitchen Cleaning Tasks	M	T	W	T	F	S	S	Cleaned By	Date/Time
1	Wash And Clean Air Vents									
2	Sort Through And Organize Cooking Utensils, Pans And Pots									
3	Wash And Clean Air Vents									
4	Check Plates, Cups And Glasses And Bin Anything Chipped									
5	Clean And Vacuum Central Heating Units									
6	Wash And Clean Light Covers									
7	Clean And De-Lime Dishwasher									
8	Dust And Clean Ceilings, Ceiling Corners And Ceiling Tiles									
9	Thoroughly Clean Grout And Tiles									
10	Clean Refrigerator Coils To Remove Dust, Unplug First									
11	Run Cleaning & Sanitizing Chemicals Through Coffee Machine									
12	Disinfect And Clean All The Walls From Top To Bottom									
13	Check For Out Of Date Food In Cabinets/Cupboards									
14	Clean Skirting Boards/Baseboards And Corners									
15	Clean Under Refrigerator									
16	Wash And Clean Doors, Door Frames And Glass									
17	Sort Through Leftover Items In The Fridge/Refrigerators									
18	Wash And Clean Windows (Inside And Outside)									
19	Replace Pest Traps									

ESSENTIAL CLEANING NOTES

....

....

....

....

....

....

....

....

ESSENTIAL OFFICE CLEANING *Checklist*

Location/Building	Department	Office Number	Week Number

Start Date & Time	Finnish Date & Time	Name	Signature

	Daily/Weekly Office Cleaning Tasks	M	T	W	T	F	S	S	Cleaned By	Date/Time
1	Clean And Sanitize All The Desks And Tables									
2	Clean And Sanitize All The Counter Tops And Surface Areas									
3	Disinfect All Point-Of-Sale Terminals And Touch Screens									
4	Disinfect Touch Points, Light Switches And Other Switches									
5	Clean And Sanitize All Keyboards And Computer Mice									
6	Wipe Down The Walls Wherever There Are Spills And Splashes									
7	Clean And Disinfect All Doors, Door Handles And Doorknobs									
8	Re-Stock Protective Clothing, Face Masks/Shields, Gloves									
9	Clean And Sanitize All The Chairs, Seats And Benches									
10	Clean All The Mirrors, Glass Cabinets/Displays									
11	Replace And Change Burned Out Light Bulbs/Broken Lights									
12	Sweep The Floors To Ensure They're Free From Debris									
13	Mop Tiled And Laminate Floors With Disinfectant Cleaner									
14	Vacuum And Hoover The Carpets, Mats And Rugs									
15	Place Wet Floor Signs If Floors Are Wet After Mopping									
16	Wash & Clean Dirty Cups, Drinking Bottles And Glasses									
17	Clean & Re-Stock Paper Dispensers & Paper Towel Rolls									
18	Wipe Down Equipment & Sanitize Tea And Coffee Makers									
19	Refill Soap Dispensers, Sanitizers And Hand Gels									
20	Clean And Dust Furniture And Office Equipment									
21	Take Out The Rubbish/Trash, Remove Waste And Recycling									
22	Clean & Disinfectant Bins/Waste Disposal Area & Trash Cans									
23	Clean And Wipe Down Windowsills									
24	Vacuum Furnishings, Cushions, Chairs, Sofas And Couches									
25	Spray Air Freshener									
26	Clean And Disinfect Any Cabinets, Shelves And Units									
27	Clean Surfaces And Desk/Work Dividers									
28	Clean And Disinfect Telephones And Headsets									
29	Polish Any Wooden Furniture And Hardwood Surfaces									

	Monthly Office Cleaning Tasks	M	T	W	T	F	S	S	Cleaned By	Date/Time
1	Clean Skirting Boards/Baseboards And Corners									
2	Clean And Disinfect All The Walls From Top To Bottom									
3	Clean Blinds (Take Down And Wash If Possible)									
4	Wash And Clean Windows (Inside And Outside)									
5	Clean And Disinfect Shared Surfaces									
6	Steam Clean Carpets And Rugs									
7	Dust And Clean Ceilings, Ceiling Corners And Ceiling Tiles									
8	Check For Broken Chairs And Tables									
9	Dust And Wash Radiator Covers									
10	Clean And Disinfect Ceiling Wall Vents									
11	Clean And Vacuum Central Heating Units									
12	Wash And Clean Light Covers									
13	Clean Drapes And Curtains (Take Down And Wash if Possible)									
14	Check Cleaning Supplies And Re-Stock As Necessary									
15	Check Ceiling Fans, Fire Sprinklers And Smoke Alarms									
16	Check Hardware, Door Stops And Lock Mechanisms									
17	Fire Exit Lights And Emergency Lights Checked & Functioning									
18	Organize And De-Clutter Office Drawers									
19	Organize And De-Clutter Storeroom									

	Daily/Weekly Toilets/Restroom Cleaning Tasks	M	T	W	T	F	S	S	Cleaned By	Date/Time
1	Clean And Disinfect All Doors, Door Handles And Doorknobs									
2	Disinfect Touch Points, Light Switches And Other Switches									
3	Toilet Roll Holders Cleaned And Disinfected And Re-Stocked									
4	Wipe Down The Walls Wherever There Are Spills And Splashes									
5	Electric Hand Dryers Cleaned, Disinfected & Operating Correctly									
6	Sweep The Floors To Ensure They're Free From Debris									
7	Mop Tiled And Laminate Floors With Disinfectant Cleaner									
8	Paper Dispensers & Paper Towel Rolls Cleaned & Re-Stocked									
9	Take Out The Rubbish/Trash, Remove Waste And Recycling									
10	Clean & Disinfectant Bins/Waste Disposal Area & Trash Cans									
11	Feminine Hygiene Bins/Containers Cleaned And Disinfected									
12	Toilets Cleaned & Disinfected, Outside, Inside And Handles									
13	Urinals & Urinal Screens Cleaned, Disinfected & Blocks Replaced									
14	Wall Mirrors Cleaned With Glass Cleaner									
15	Clean And Re-Stock Paper Dispensers & Paper Towel Rolls									
16	Refill Soap Dispensers, Sanitizers And Hand Gels									
17	Sinks, Taps, Fixtures, Surface Areas Cleaned And Disinfected									

	Daily/Weekly Toilets/Restroom Cleaning Tasks Con	M	T	W	T	F	S	S	Cleaned By	Date/Time
18	Windowsills Clean And Wiped Down									
19	Check Plumbing And Schedule Work If Required									
20	Air Fresheners Checked And Replaced									
21	Fire Exit Lights And Emergency Lights Checked & Functioning									
22	Place Wet Floor Signs If Floors Are Wet After Mopping									
23	Cabinets Cleaned And Disinfected									
	Monthly Toilets/Restroom Cleaning Tasks	M	T	W	T	F	S	S	Cleaned By	Date/Time
1	Toilet/Restroom Service Storeroom/Cupboard Clean And Tidy									
2	Walls Free Of Graffiti, Stickers, Gum And Residue									
3	Wash And Clean Windows (Inside And Outside)									
4	Check Hardware, Door Stops And Lock Mechanisms									
5	All Fittings Securely Fixed (Schedule Maintenance If Not)									
6	Dust And Clean Ceilings, Ceiling Corners And Ceiling Tiles									
7	Clean Skirting Boards/Baseboards And Corners									
8	Thoroughly Clean Grout And Tiles									
9	Ceiling Wall Vents Cleaned And Disinfected									
10	Clean And Vacuum Central Heating Units									
11	Wash And Clean Light Covers									
12	Wash All Toilet And Restroom Mats									
	Daily/Weekly Kitchen Cleaning Tasks	M	T	W	T	F	S	S	Cleaned By	Date/Time
1	Wash And Sanitize All Counter Tops And Prep Area Surfaces									
2	Empty Dishwasher, Run The Dishwasher/Dish Drainer									
3	Disinfect Touch Points, Light Switches And Other Switches									
4	Take Out The Rubbish/Trash, Remove Waste And Recycling									
5	Clean & Disinfectant Bins/Waste Disposal Area & Trash Cans									
6	Wipe Down The Walls Wherever There Are Spills And Splashes									
7	Sweep The Floors To Ensure They're Free From Debris									
8	Mop Tiled And Laminate Floors With Disinfectant Cleaner									
9	Wet Floor Signs In Place If Floors Are Wet After Mopping									
10	Thoroughly Clean And Disinfect The Sinks And Taps									
11	Clean Exterior Of Appliances, Check For Spilled Food									
12	Replace Empty Paper Towel Rolls And Cloth Roller Towels									
13	Refill Soap Dispensers And Hand Sanitizers/Hand Gels									
14	Wipe Down Equipment, Tea And Coffee Makers, Toasters Etc									
15	Fire Exit Lights And Emergency Lights Checked & Functioning									
16	Pour Drain Cleaner Down Floor And Sink Drains									
17	Clean Inside Microwave, Check For Spilled Food									

	Daily/Weekly Kitchen Cleaning Tasks Continued	M	T	W	T	F	S	S	CLEANED BY	DATE/TIME
18	Replace Wash Rags, Cloths And Tea Towels With Clean Ones									
19	Wash Rags, Cloths, Tea Towels And Towels In Washing Machine									
20	Replace And Change Burned Out Light Bulbs/Broken Lights									
21	Clean Inside Of Dishwasher									
22	Sanitise Sponges Or Replace Damaged Sponges With New									
23	Dishes, Pots, Pans, And Utensils To Be Stored Away Properly									
24	Clean Out Refrigerator And Wipe Down Shelves And Drawers									
	Monthly Kitchen Cleaning Tasks	M	T	W	T	F	S	S	Cleaned By	Date/Time
1	Wash And Clean Air Vents									
2	Sort Through And Organize Cooking Utensils, Pans And Pots									
3	Wash And Clean Air Vents									
4	Check Plates, Cups And Glasses And Bin Anything Chipped									
5	Clean And Vacuum Central Heating Units									
6	Wash And Clean Light Covers									
7	Clean And De-Lime Dishwasher									
8	Dust And Clean Ceilings, Ceiling Corners And Ceiling Tiles									
9	Thoroughly Clean Grout And Tiles									
10	Clean Refrigerator Coils To Remove Dust, Unplug First									
11	Run Cleaning & Sanitizing Chemicals Through Coffee Machine									
12	Disinfect And Clean All The Walls From Top To Bottom									
13	Check For Out Of Date Food In Cabinets/Cupboards									
14	Clean Skirting Boards/Baseboards And Corners									
15	Clean Under Refrigerator									
16	Wash And Clean Doors, Door Frames And Glass									
17	Sort Through Leftover Items In The Fridge/Refrigerators									
18	Wash And Clean Windows (Inside And Outside)									
19	Replace Pest Traps									

ESSENTIAL CLEANING NOTES

....

....

....

....

....

....

ESSENTIAL OFFICE CLEANING *Checklist*

Location/Building	Department	Office Number	Week Number

Start Date & Time	Finnish Date & Time	Name	Signature

	Daily/Weekly Office Cleaning Tasks	M	T	W	T	F	S	S	Cleaned By	Date/Time
1	Clean And Sanitize All The Desks And Tables									
2	Clean And Sanitize All The Counter Tops And Surface Areas									
3	Disinfect All Point-Of-Sale Terminals And Touch Screens									
4	Disinfect Touch Points, Light Switches And Other Switches									
5	Clean And Sanitize All Keyboards And Computer Mice									
6	Wipe Down The Walls Wherever There Are Spills And Splashes									
7	Clean And Disinfect All Doors, Door Handles And Doorknobs									
8	Re-Stock Protective Clothing, Face Masks/Shields, Gloves									
9	Clean And Sanitize All The Chairs, Seats And Benches									
10	Clean All The Mirrors, Glass Cabinets/Displays									
11	Replace And Change Burned Out Light Bulbs/Broken Lights									
12	Sweep The Floors To Ensure They're Free From Debris									
13	Mop Tiled And Laminate Floors With Disinfectant Cleaner									
14	Vacuum And Hoover The Carpets, Mats And Rugs									
15	Place Wet Floor Signs If Floors Are Wet After Mopping									
16	Wash & Clean Dirty Cups, Drinking Bottles And Glasses									
17	Clean & Re-Stock Paper Dispensers & Paper Towel Rolls									
18	Wipe Down Equipment & Sanitize Tea And Coffee Makers									
19	Refill Soap Dispensers, Sanitizers And Hand Gels									
20	Clean And Dust Furniture And Office Equipment									
21	Take Out The Rubbish/Trash, Remove Waste And Recycling									
22	Clean & Disinfectant Bins/Waste Disposal Area & Trash Cans									
23	Clean And Wipe Down Windowsills									
24	Vacuum Furnishings, Cushions, Chairs, Sofas And Couches									
25	Spray Air Freshener									
26	Clean And Disinfect Any Cabinets, Shelves And Units									
27	Clean Surfaces And Desk/Work Dividers									
28	Clean And Disinfect Telephones And Headsets									
29	Polish Any Wooden Furniture And Hardwood Surfaces									

	Monthly Office Cleaning Tasks	M	T	W	T	F	S	S	Cleaned By	Date/Time
1	Clean Skirting Boards/Baseboards And Corners									
2	Clean And Disinfect All The Walls From Top To Bottom									
3	Clean Blinds (Take Down And Wash If Possible)									
4	Wash And Clean Windows (Inside And Outside)									
5	Clean And Disinfect Shared Surfaces									
6	Steam Clean Carpets And Rugs									
7	Dust And Clean Ceilings, Ceiling Corners And Ceiling Tiles									
8	Check For Broken Chairs And Tables									
9	Dust And Wash Radiator Covers									
10	Clean And Disinfect Ceiling Wall Vents									
11	Clean And Vacuum Central Heating Units									
12	Wash And Clean Light Covers									
13	Clean Drapes And Curtains (Take Down And Wash if Possible)									
14	Check Cleaning Supplies And Re-Stock As Necessary									
15	Check Ceiling Fans, Fire Sprinklers And Smoke Alarms									
16	Check Hardware, Door Stops And Lock Mechanisms									
17	Fire Exit Lights And Emergency Lights Checked & Functioning									
18	Organize And De-Clutter Office Drawers									
19	Organize And De-Clutter Storeroom									
	Daily/Weekly Toilets/Restroom Cleaning Tasks	M	T	W	T	F	S	S	Cleaned By	Date/Time
1	Clean And Disinfect All Doors, Door Handles And Doorknobs									
2	Disinfect Touch Points, Light Switches And Other Switches									
3	Toilet Roll Holders Cleaned And Disinfected And Re-Stocked									
4	Wipe Down The Walls Wherever There Are Spills And Splashes									
5	Electric Hand Dryers Cleaned, Disinfected & Operating Correctly									
6	Sweep The Floors To Ensure They're Free From Debris									
7	Mop Tiled And Laminate Floors With Disinfectant Cleaner									
8	Paper Dispensers & Paper Towel Rolls Cleaned & Re-Stocked									
9	Take Out The Rubbish/Trash, Remove Waste And Recycling									
10	Clean & Disinfectant Bins/Waste Disposal Area & Trash Cans									
11	Feminine Hygiene Bins/Containers Cleaned And Disinfected									
12	Toilets Cleaned & Disinfected, Outside, Inside And Handles									
13	Urinals & Urinal Screens Cleaned, Disinfected & Blocks Replaced									
14	Wall Mirrors Cleaned With Glass Cleaner									
15	Clean And Re-Stock Paper Dispensers & Paper Towel Rolls									
16	Refill Soap Dispensers, Sanitizers And Hand Gels									
17	Sinks, Taps, Fixtures, Surface Areas Cleaned And Disinfected									

	Daily/Weekly Toilets/Restroom Cleaning Tasks Con	M	T	W	T	F	S	S	Cleaned By	Date/Time
18	Windowsills Clean And Wiped Down									
19	Check Plumbing And Schedule Work If Required									
20	Air Fresheners Checked And Replaced									
21	Fire Exit Lights And Emergency Lights Checked & Functioning									
22	Place Wet Floor Signs If Floors Are Wet After Mopping									
23	Cabinets Cleaned And Disinfected									
	Monthly Toilets/Restroom Cleaning Tasks	M	T	W	T	F	S	S	Cleaned By	Date/Time
1	Toilet/Restroom Service Storeroom/Cupboard Clean And Tidy									
2	Walls Free Of Graffiti, Stickers, Gum And Residue									
3	Wash And Clean Windows (Inside And Outside)									
4	Check Hardware, Door Stops And Lock Mechanisms									
5	All Fittings Securely Fixed (Schedule Maintenance If Not)									
6	Dust And Clean Ceilings, Ceiling Corners And Ceiling Tiles									
7	Clean Skirting Boards/Baseboards And Corners									
8	Thoroughly Clean Grout And Tiles									
9	Ceiling Wall Vents Cleaned And Disinfected									
10	Clean And Vacuum Central Heating Units									
11	Wash And Clean Light Covers									
12	Wash All Toilet And Restroom Mats									
	Daily/Weekly Kitchen Cleaning Tasks	M	T	W	T	F	S	S	Cleaned By	Date/Time
1	Wash And Sanitize All Counter Tops And Prep Area Surfaces									
2	Empty Dishwasher, Run The Dishwasher/Dish Drainer									
3	Disinfect Touch Points, Light Switches And Other Switches									
4	Take Out The Rubbish/Trash, Remove Waste And Recycling									
5	Clean & Disinfectant Bins/Waste Disposal Area & Trash Cans									
6	Wipe Down The Walls Wherever There Are Spills And Splashes									
7	Sweep The Floors To Ensure They're Free From Debris									
8	Mop Tiled And Laminate Floors With Disinfectant Cleaner									
9	Wet Floor Signs In Place If Floors Are Wet After Mopping									
10	Thoroughly Clean And Disinfect The Sinks And Taps									
11	Clean Exterior Of Appliances, Check For Spilled Food									
12	Replace Empty Paper Towel Rolls And Cloth Roller Towels									
13	Refill Soap Dispensers And Hand Sanitizers/Hand Gels									
14	Wipe Down Equipment, Tea And Coffee Makers, Toasters Etc									
15	Fire Exit Lights And Emergency Lights Checked & Functioning									
16	Pour Drain Cleaner Down Floor And Sink Drains									
17	Clean Inside Microwave, Check For Spilled Food									

	Daily/Weekly Kitchen Cleaning Tasks Continued	M	T	W	T	F	S	S	CLEANED BY	DATE/TIME
18	Replace Wash Rags, Cloths And Tea Towels With Clean Ones									
19	Wash Rags, Cloths, Tea Towels And Towels In Washing Machine									
20	Replace And Change Burned Out Light Bulbs/Broken Lights									
21	Clean Inside Of Dishwasher									
22	Sanitise Sponges Or Replace Damaged Sponges With New									
23	Dishes, Pots, Pans, And Utensils To Be Stored Away Properly									
24	Clean Out Refrigerator And Wipe Down Shelves And Drawers									
	Monthly Kitchen Cleaning Tasks	M	T	W	T	F	S	S	Cleaned By	Date/Time
1	Wash And Clean Air Vents									
2	Sort Through And Organize Cooking Utensils, Pans And Pots									
3	Wash And Clean Air Vents									
4	Check Plates, Cups And Glasses And Bin Anything Chipped									
5	Clean And Vacuum Central Heating Units									
6	Wash And Clean Light Covers									
7	Clean And De-Lime Dishwasher									
8	Dust And Clean Ceilings, Ceiling Corners And Ceiling Tiles									
9	Thoroughly Clean Grout And Tiles									
10	Clean Refrigerator Coils To Remove Dust, Unplug First									
11	Run Cleaning & Sanitizing Chemicals Through Coffee Machine									
12	Disinfect And Clean All The Walls From Top To Bottom									
13	Check For Out Of Date Food In Cabinets/Cupboards									
14	Clean Skirting Boards/Baseboards And Corners									
15	Clean Under Refrigerator									
16	Wash And Clean Doors, Door Frames And Glass									
17	Sort Through Leftover Items In The Fridge/Refrigerators									
18	Wash And Clean Windows (Inside And Outside)									
19	Replace Pest Traps									

ESSENTIAL CLEANING NOTES

....

....

....

....

....

....

....

ESSENTIAL OFFICE CLEANING *Checklist*

Location/Building	Department	Office Number	Week Number

Start Date & Time	Finnish Date & Time	Name	Signature

	Daily/Weekly Office Cleaning Tasks	M	T	W	T	F	S	S	Cleaned By	Date/Time
1	Clean And Sanitize All The Desks And Tables									
2	Clean And Sanitize All The Counter Tops And Surface Areas									
3	Disinfect All Point-Of-Sale Terminals And Touch Screens									
4	Disinfect Touch Points, Light Switches And Other Switches									
5	Clean And Sanitize All Keyboards And Computer Mice									
6	Wipe Down The Walls Wherever There Are Spills And Splashes									
7	Clean And Disinfect All Doors, Door Handles And Doorknobs									
8	Re-Stock Protective Clothing, Face Masks/Shields, Gloves									
9	Clean And Sanitize All The Chairs, Seats And Benches									
10	Clean All The Mirrors, Glass Cabinets/Displays									
11	Replace And Change Burned Out Light Bulbs/Broken Lights									
12	Sweep The Floors To Ensure They're Free From Debris									
13	Mop Tiled And Laminate Floors With Disinfectant Cleaner									
14	Vacuum And Hoover The Carpets, Mats And Rugs									
15	Place Wet Floor Signs If Floors Are Wet After Mopping									
16	Wash & Clean Dirty Cups, Drinking Bottles And Glasses									
17	Clean & Re-Stock Paper Dispensers & Paper Towel Rolls									
18	Wipe Down Equipment & Sanitize Tea And Coffee Makers									
19	Refill Soap Dispensers, Sanitizers And Hand Gels									
20	Clean And Dust Furniture And Office Equipment									
21	Take Out The Rubbish/Trash, Remove Waste And Recycling									
22	Clean & Disinfectant Bins/Waste Disposal Area & Trash Cans									
23	Clean And Wipe Down Windowsills									
24	Vacuum Furnishings, Cushions, Chairs, Sofas And Couches									
25	Spray Air Freshener									
26	Clean And Disinfect Any Cabinets, Shelves And Units									
27	Clean Surfaces And Desk/Work Dividers									
28	Clean And Disinfect Telephones And Headsets									
29	Polish Any Wooden Furniture And Hardwood Surfaces									

	Monthly Office Cleaning Tasks	M	T	W	T	F	S	S	Cleaned By	Date/Time
1	Clean Skirting Boards/Baseboards And Corners									
2	Clean And Disinfect All The Walls From Top To Bottom									
3	Clean Blinds (Take Down And Wash If Possible)									
4	Wash And Clean Windows (Inside And Outside)									
5	Clean And Disinfect Shared Surfaces									
6	Steam Clean Carpets And Rugs									
7	Dust And Clean Ceilings, Ceiling Corners And Ceiling Tiles									
8	Check For Broken Chairs And Tables									
9	Dust And Wash Radiator Covers									
10	Clean And Disinfect Ceiling Wall Vents									
11	Clean And Vacuum Central Heating Units									
12	Wash And Clean Light Covers									
13	Clean Drapes And Curtains (Take Down And Wash if Possible)									
14	Check Cleaning Supplies And Re-Stock As Necessary									
15	Check Ceiling Fans, Fire Sprinklers And Smoke Alarms									
16	Check Hardware, Door Stops And Lock Mechanisms									
17	Fire Exit Lights And Emergency Lights Checked & Functioning									
18	Organize And De-Clutter Office Drawers									
19	Organize And De-Clutter Storeroom									
	Daily/Weekly Toilets/Restroom Cleaning Tasks	M	T	W	T	F	S	S	Cleaned By	Date/Time
1	Clean And Disinfect All Doors, Door Handles And Doorknobs									
2	Disinfect Touch Points, Light Switches And Other Switches									
3	Toilet Roll Holders Cleaned And Disinfected And Re-Stocked									
4	Wipe Down The Walls Wherever There Are Spills And Splashes									
5	Electric Hand Dryers Cleaned, Disinfected & Operating Correctly									
6	Sweep The Floors To Ensure They're Free From Debris									
7	Mop Tiled And Laminate Floors With Disinfectant Cleaner									
8	Paper Dispensers & Paper Towel Rolls Cleaned & Re-Stocked									
9	Take Out The Rubbish/Trash, Remove Waste And Recycling									
10	Clean & Disinfectant Bins/Waste Disposal Area & Trash Cans									
11	Feminine Hygiene Bins/Containers Cleaned And Disinfected									
12	Toilets Cleaned & Disinfected, Outside, Inside And Handles									
13	Urinals & Urinal Screens Cleaned, Disinfected & Blocks Replaced									
14	Wall Mirrors Cleaned With Glass Cleaner									
15	Clean And Re-Stock Paper Dispensers & Paper Towel Rolls									
16	Refill Soap Dispensers, Sanitizers And Hand Gels									
17	Sinks, Taps, Fixtures, Surface Areas Cleaned And Disinfected									

	Daily/Weekly Toilets/Restroom Cleaning Tasks Con	M	T	W	T	F	S	S	Cleaned By	Date/Time
18	Windowsills Clean And Wiped Down									
19	Check Plumbing And Schedule Work If Required									
20	Air Fresheners Checked And Replaced									
21	Fire Exit Lights And Emergency Lights Checked & Functioning									
22	Place Wet Floor Signs If Floors Are Wet After Mopping									
23	Cabinets Cleaned And Disinfected									
	Monthly Toilets/Restroom Cleaning Tasks	M	T	W	T	F	S	S	Cleaned By	Date/Time
1	Toilet/Restroom Service Storeroom/Cupboard Clean And Tidy									
2	Walls Free Of Graffiti, Stickers, Gum And Residue									
3	Wash And Clean Windows (Inside And Outside)									
4	Check Hardware, Door Stops And Lock Mechanisms									
5	All Fittings Securely Fixed (Schedule Maintenance If Not)									
6	Dust And Clean Ceilings, Ceiling Corners And Ceiling Tiles									
7	Clean Skirting Boards/Baseboards And Corners									
8	Thoroughly Clean Grout And Tiles									
9	Ceiling Wall Vents Cleaned And Disinfected									
10	Clean And Vacuum Central Heating Units									
11	Wash And Clean Light Covers									
12	Wash All Toilet And Restroom Mats									
	Daily/Weekly Kitchen Cleaning Tasks	M	T	W	T	F	S	S	Cleaned By	Date/Time
1	Wash And Sanitize All Counter Tops And Prep Area Surfaces									
2	Empty Dishwasher, Run The Dishwasher/Dish Drainer									
3	Disinfect Touch Points, Light Switches And Other Switches									
4	Take Out The Rubbish/Trash, Remove Waste And Recycling									
5	Clean & Disinfectant Bins/Waste Disposal Area & Trash Cans									
6	Wipe Down The Walls Wherever There Are Spills And Splashes									
7	Sweep The Floors To Ensure They're Free From Debris									
8	Mop Tiled And Laminate Floors With Disinfectant Cleaner									
9	Wet Floor Signs In Place If Floors Are Wet After Mopping									
10	Thoroughly Clean And Disinfect The Sinks And Taps									
11	Clean Exterior Of Appliances, Check For Spilled Food									
12	Replace Empty Paper Towel Rolls And Cloth Roller Towels									
13	Refill Soap Dispensers And Hand Sanitizers/Hand Gels									
14	Wipe Down Equipment, Tea And Coffee Makers, Toasters Etc									
15	Fire Exit Lights And Emergency Lights Checked & Functioning									
16	Pour Drain Cleaner Down Floor And Sink Drains									
17	Clean Inside Microwave, Check For Spilled Food									

	Daily/Weekly Kitchen Cleaning Tasks Continued	M	T	W	T	F	S	S	CLEANED BY	DATE/TIME
18	Replace Wash Rags, Cloths And Tea Towels With Clean Ones									
19	Wash Rags, Cloths, Tea Towels And Towels In Washing Machine									
20	Replace And Change Burned Out Light Bulbs/Broken Lights									
21	Clean Inside Of Dishwasher									
22	Sanitise Sponges Or Replace Damaged Sponges With New									
23	Dishes, Pots, Pans, And Utensils To Be Stored Away Properly									
24	Clean Out Refrigerator And Wipe Down Shelves And Drawers									
	Monthly Kitchen Cleaning Tasks	M	T	W	T	F	S	S	Cleaned By	Date/Time
1	Wash And Clean Air Vents									
2	Sort Through And Organize Cooking Utensils, Pans And Pots									
3	Wash And Clean Air Vents									
4	Check Plates, Cups And Glasses And Bin Anything Chipped									
5	Clean And Vacuum Central Heating Units									
6	Wash And Clean Light Covers									
7	Clean And De-Lime Dishwasher									
8	Dust And Clean Ceilings, Ceiling Corners And Ceiling Tiles									
9	Thoroughly Clean Grout And Tiles									
10	Clean Refrigerator Coils To Remove Dust, Unplug First									
11	Run Cleaning & Sanitizing Chemicals Through Coffee Machine									
12	Disinfect And Clean All The Walls From Top To Bottom									
13	Check For Out Of Date Food In Cabinets/Cupboards									
14	Clean Skirting Boards/Baseboards And Corners									
15	Clean Under Refrigerator									
16	Wash And Clean Doors, Door Frames And Glass									
17	Sort Through Leftover Items In The Fridge/Refrigerators									
18	Wash And Clean Windows (Inside And Outside)									
19	Replace Pest Traps									

ESSENTIAL CLEANING NOTES

....

....

....

....

....

....

....

....

ESSENTIAL OFFICE CLEANING *Checklist*

Location/Building	Department	Office Number	Week Number

Start Date & Time	Finnish Date & Time	Name	Signature

	Daily/Weekly Office Cleaning Tasks	M	T	W	T	F	S	S	Cleaned By	Date/Time
1	Clean And Sanitize All The Desks And Tables									
2	Clean And Sanitize All The Counter Tops And Surface Areas									
3	Disinfect All Point-Of-Sale Terminals And Touch Screens									
4	Disinfect Touch Points, Light Switches And Other Switches									
5	Clean And Sanitize All Keyboards And Computer Mice									
6	Wipe Down The Walls Wherever There Are Spills And Splashes									
7	Clean And Disinfect All Doors, Door Handles And Doorknobs									
8	Re-Stock Protective Clothing, Face Masks/Shields, Gloves									
9	Clean And Sanitize All The Chairs, Seats And Benches									
10	Clean All The Mirrors, Glass Cabinets/Displays									
11	Replace And Change Burned Out Light Bulbs/Broken Lights									
12	Sweep The Floors To Ensure They're Free From Debris									
13	Mop Tiled And Laminate Floors With Disinfectant Cleaner									
14	Vacuum And Hoover The Carpets, Mats And Rugs									
15	Place Wet Floor Signs If Floors Are Wet After Mopping									
16	Wash & Clean Dirty Cups, Drinking Bottles And Glasses									
17	Clean & Re-Stock Paper Dispensers & Paper Towel Rolls									
18	Wipe Down Equipment & Sanitize Tea And Coffee Makers									
19	Refill Soap Dispensers, Sanitizers And Hand Gels									
20	Clean And Dust Furniture And Office Equipment									
21	Take Out The Rubbish/Trash, Remove Waste And Recycling									
22	Clean & Disinfectant Bins/Waste Disposal Area & Trash Cans									
23	Clean And Wipe Down Windowsills									
24	Vacuum Furnishings, Cushions, Chairs, Sofas And Couches									
25	Spray Air Freshener									
26	Clean And Disinfect Any Cabinets, Shelves And Units									
27	Clean Surfaces And Desk/Work Dividers									
28	Clean And Disinfect Telephones And Headsets									
29	Polish Any Wooden Furniture And Hardwood Surfaces									

	Monthly Office Cleaning Tasks	M	T	W	T	F	S	S	Cleaned By	Date/Time
1	Clean Skirting Boards/Baseboards And Corners									
2	Clean And Disinfect All The Walls From Top To Bottom									
3	Clean Blinds (Take Down And Wash If Possible)									
4	Wash And Clean Windows (Inside And Outside)									
5	Clean And Disinfect Shared Surfaces									
6	Steam Clean Carpets And Rugs									
7	Dust And Clean Ceilings, Ceiling Corners And Ceiling Tiles									
8	Check For Broken Chairs And Tables									
9	Dust And Wash Radiator Covers									
10	Clean And Disinfect Ceiling Wall Vents									
11	Clean And Vacuum Central Heating Units									
12	Wash And Clean Light Covers									
13	Clean Drapes And Curtains (Take Down And Wash if Possible)									
14	Check Cleaning Supplies And Re-Stock As Necessary									
15	Check Ceiling Fans, Fire Sprinklers And Smoke Alarms									
16	Check Hardware, Door Stops And Lock Mechanisms									
17	Fire Exit Lights And Emergency Lights Checked & Functioning									
18	Organize And De-Clutter Office Drawers									
19	Organize And De-Clutter Storeroom									
	Daily/Weekly Toilets/Restroom Cleaning Tasks	M	T	W	T	F	S	S	Cleaned By	Date/Time
1	Clean And Disinfect All Doors, Door Handles And Doorknobs									
2	Disinfect Touch Points, Light Switches And Other Switches									
3	Toilet Roll Holders Cleaned And Disinfected And Re-Stocked									
4	Wipe Down The Walls Wherever There Are Spills And Splashes									
5	Electric Hand Dryers Cleaned, Disinfected & Operating Correctly									
6	Sweep The Floors To Ensure They're Free From Debris									
7	Mop Tiled And Laminate Floors With Disinfectant Cleaner									
8	Paper Dispensers & Paper Towel Rolls Cleaned & Re-Stocked									
9	Take Out The Rubbish/Trash, Remove Waste And Recycling									
10	Clean & Disinfectant Bins/Waste Disposal Area & Trash Cans									
11	Feminine Hygiene Bins/Containers Cleaned And Disinfected									
12	Toilets Cleaned & Disinfected, Outside, Inside And Handles									
13	Urinals & Urinal Screens Cleaned, Disinfected & Blocks Replaced									
14	Wall Mirrors Cleaned With Glass Cleaner									
15	Clean And Re-Stock Paper Dispensers & Paper Towel Rolls									
16	Refill Soap Dispensers, Sanitizers And Hand Gels									
17	Sinks, Taps, Fixtures, Surface Areas Cleaned And Disinfected									

	Daily/Weekly Toilets/Restroom Cleaning Tasks Con	M	T	W	T	F	S	S	Cleaned By	Date/Time
18	Windowsills Clean And Wiped Down									
19	Check Plumbing And Schedule Work If Required									
20	Air Fresheners Checked And Replaced									
21	Fire Exit Lights And Emergency Lights Checked & Functioning									
22	Place Wet Floor Signs If Floors Are Wet After Mopping									
23	Cabinets Cleaned And Disinfected									
	Monthly Toilets/Restroom Cleaning Tasks	M	T	W	T	F	S	S	Cleaned By	Date/Time
1	Toilet/Restroom Service Storeroom/Cupboard Clean And Tidy									
2	Walls Free Of Graffiti, Stickers, Gum And Residue									
3	Wash And Clean Windows (Inside And Outside)									
4	Check Hardware, Door Stops And Lock Mechanisms									
5	All Fittings Securely Fixed (Schedule Maintenance If Not)									
6	Dust And Clean Ceilings, Ceiling Corners And Ceiling Tiles									
7	Clean Skirting Boards/Baseboards And Corners									
8	Thoroughly Clean Grout And Tiles									
9	Ceiling Wall Vents Cleaned And Disinfected									
10	Clean And Vacuum Central Heating Units									
11	Wash And Clean Light Covers									
12	Wash All Toilet And Restroom Mats									
	Daily/Weekly Kitchen Cleaning Tasks	M	T	W	T	F	S	S	Cleaned By	Date/Time
1	Wash And Sanitize All Counter Tops And Prep Area Surfaces									
2	Empty Dishwasher, Run The Dishwasher/Dish Drainer									
3	Disinfect Touch Points, Light Switches And Other Switches									
4	Take Out The Rubbish/Trash, Remove Waste And Recycling									
5	Clean & Disinfectant Bins/Waste Disposal Area & Trash Cans									
6	Wipe Down The Walls Wherever There Are Spills And Splashes									
7	Sweep The Floors To Ensure They're Free From Debris									
8	Mop Tiled And Laminate Floors With Disinfectant Cleaner									
9	Wet Floor Signs In Place If Floors Are Wet After Mopping									
10	Thoroughly Clean And Disinfect The Sinks And Taps									
11	Clean Exterior Of Appliances, Check For Spilled Food									
12	Replace Empty Paper Towel Rolls And Cloth Roller Towels									
13	Refill Soap Dispensers And Hand Sanitizers/Hand Gels									
14	Wipe Down Equipment, Tea And Coffee Makers, Toasters Etc									
15	Fire Exit Lights And Emergency Lights Checked & Functioning									
16	Pour Drain Cleaner Down Floor And Sink Drains									
17	Clean Inside Microwave, Check For Spilled Food									

	Daily/Weekly Kitchen Cleaning Tasks Continued	M	T	W	T	F	S	S	CLEANED BY	DATE/TIME
18	Replace Wash Rags, Cloths And Tea Towels With Clean Ones									
19	Wash Rags, Cloths, Tea Towels And Towels In Washing Machine									
20	Replace And Change Burned Out Light Bulbs/Broken Lights									
21	Clean Inside Of Dishwasher									
22	Sanitise Sponges Or Replace Damaged Sponges With New									
23	Dishes, Pots, Pans, And Utensils To Be Stored Away Properly									
24	Clean Out Refrigerator And Wipe Down Shelves And Drawers									
	Monthly Kitchen Cleaning Tasks	M	T	W	T	F	S	S	Cleaned By	Date/Time
1	Wash And Clean Air Vents									
2	Sort Through And Organize Cooking Utensils, Pans And Pots									
3	Wash And Clean Air Vents									
4	Check Plates, Cups And Glasses And Bin Anything Chipped									
5	Clean And Vacuum Central Heating Units									
6	Wash And Clean Light Covers									
7	Clean And De-Lime Dishwasher									
8	Dust And Clean Ceilings, Ceiling Corners And Ceiling Tiles									
9	Thoroughly Clean Grout And Tiles									
10	Clean Refrigerator Coils To Remove Dust, Unplug First									
11	Run Cleaning & Sanitizing Chemicals Through Coffee Machine									
12	Disinfect And Clean All The Walls From Top To Bottom									
13	Check For Out Of Date Food In Cabinets/Cupboards									
14	Clean Skirting Boards/Baseboards And Corners									
15	Clean Under Refrigerator									
16	Wash And Clean Doors, Door Frames And Glass									
17	Sort Through Leftover Items In The Fridge/Refrigerators									
18	Wash And Clean Windows (Inside And Outside)									
19	Replace Pest Traps									

ESSENTIAL CLEANING NOTES

....

....

....

....

....

....

....

....

ESSENTIAL OFFICE CLEANING *Checklist*

Location/Building	Department	Office Number	Week Number

Start Date & Time	Finnish Date & Time	Name	Signature

	Daily/Weekly Office Cleaning Tasks	M	T	W	T	F	S	S	Cleaned By	Date/Time
1	Clean And Sanitize All The Desks And Tables									
2	Clean And Sanitize All The Counter Tops And Surface Areas									
3	Disinfect All Point-Of-Sale Terminals And Touch Screens									
4	Disinfect Touch Points, Light Switches And Other Switches									
5	Clean And Sanitize All Keyboards And Computer Mice									
6	Wipe Down The Walls Wherever There Are Spills And Splashes									
7	Clean And Disinfect All Doors, Door Handles And Doorknobs									
8	Re-Stock Protective Clothing, Face Masks/Shields, Gloves									
9	Clean And Sanitize All The Chairs, Seats And Benches									
10	Clean All The Mirrors, Glass Cabinets/Displays									
11	Replace And Change Burned Out Light Bulbs/Broken Lights									
12	Sweep The Floors To Ensure They're Free From Debris									
13	Mop Tiled And Laminate Floors With Disinfectant Cleaner									
14	Vacuum And Hoover The Carpets, Mats And Rugs									
15	Place Wet Floor Signs If Floors Are Wet After Mopping									
16	Wash & Clean Dirty Cups, Drinking Bottles And Glasses									
17	Clean & Re-Stock Paper Dispensers & Paper Towel Rolls									
18	Wipe Down Equipment & Sanitize Tea And Coffee Makers									
19	Refill Soap Dispensers, Sanitizers And Hand Gels									
20	Clean And Dust Furniture And Office Equipment									
21	Take Out The Rubbish/Trash, Remove Waste And Recycling									
22	Clean & Disinfectant Bins/Waste Disposal Area & Trash Cans									
23	Clean And Wipe Down Windowsills									
24	Vacuum Furnishings, Cushions, Chairs, Sofas And Couches									
25	Spray Air Freshener									
26	Clean And Disinfect Any Cabinets, Shelves And Units									
27	Clean Surfaces And Desk/Work Dividers									
28	Clean And Disinfect Telephones And Headsets									
29	Polish Any Wooden Furniture And Hardwood Surfaces									

	Monthly Office Cleaning Tasks	M	T	W	T	F	S	S	Cleaned By	Date/Time
1	Clean Skirting Boards/Baseboards And Corners									
2	Clean And Disinfect All The Walls From Top To Bottom									
3	Clean Blinds (Take Down And Wash If Possible)									
4	Wash And Clean Windows (Inside And Outside)									
5	Clean And Disinfect Shared Surfaces									
6	Steam Clean Carpets And Rugs									
7	Dust And Clean Ceilings, Ceiling Corners And Ceiling Tiles									
8	Check For Broken Chairs And Tables									
9	Dust And Wash Radiator Covers									
10	Clean And Disinfect Ceiling Wall Vents									
11	Clean And Vacuum Central Heating Units									
12	Wash And Clean Light Covers									
13	Clean Drapes And Curtains (Take Down And Wash if Possible)									
14	Check Cleaning Supplies And Re-Stock As Necessary									
15	Check Ceiling Fans, Fire Sprinklers And Smoke Alarms									
16	Check Hardware, Door Stops And Lock Mechanisms									
17	Fire Exit Lights And Emergency Lights Checked & Functioning									
18	Organize And De-Clutter Office Drawers									
19	Organize And De-Clutter Storeroom									

	Daily/Weekly Toilets/Restroom Cleaning Tasks	M	T	W	T	F	S	S	Cleaned By	Date/Time
1	Clean And Disinfect All Doors, Door Handles And Doorknobs									
2	Disinfect Touch Points, Light Switches And Other Switches									
3	Toilet Roll Holders Cleaned And Disinfected And Re-Stocked									
4	Wipe Down The Walls Wherever There Are Spills And Splashes									
5	Electric Hand Dryers Cleaned, Disinfected & Operating Correctly									
6	Sweep The Floors To Ensure They're Free From Debris									
7	Mop Tiled And Laminate Floors With Disinfectant Cleaner									
8	Paper Dispensers & Paper Towel Rolls Cleaned & Re-Stocked									
9	Take Out The Rubbish/Trash, Remove Waste And Recycling									
10	Clean & Disinfectant Bins/Waste Disposal Area & Trash Cans									
11	Feminine Hygiene Bins/Containers Cleaned And Disinfected									
12	Toilets Cleaned & Disinfected, Outside, Inside And Handles									
13	Urinals & Urinal Screens Cleaned, Disinfected & Blocks Replaced									
14	Wall Mirrors Cleaned With Glass Cleaner									
15	Clean And Re-Stock Paper Dispensers & Paper Towel Rolls									
16	Refill Soap Dispensers, Sanitizers And Hand Gels									
17	Sinks, Taps, Fixtures, Surface Areas Cleaned And Disinfected									

	Daily/Weekly Toilets/Restroom Cleaning Tasks Con	M	T	W	T	F	S	S	Cleaned By	Date/Time
18	Windowsills Clean And Wiped Down									
19	Check Plumbing And Schedule Work If Required									
20	Air Fresheners Checked And Replaced									
21	Fire Exit Lights And Emergency Lights Checked & Functioning									
22	Place Wet Floor Signs If Floors Are Wet After Mopping									
23	Cabinets Cleaned And Disinfected									
	Monthly Toilets/Restroom Cleaning Tasks	M	T	W	T	F	S	S	Cleaned By	Date/Time
1	Toilet/Restroom Service Storeroom/Cupboard Clean And Tidy									
2	Walls Free Of Graffiti, Stickers, Gum And Residue									
3	Wash And Clean Windows (Inside And Outside)									
4	Check Hardware, Door Stops And Lock Mechanisms									
5	All Fittings Securely Fixed (Schedule Maintenance If Not)									
6	Dust And Clean Ceilings, Ceiling Corners And Ceiling Tiles									
7	Clean Skirting Boards/Baseboards And Corners									
8	Thoroughly Clean Grout And Tiles									
9	Ceiling Wall Vents Cleaned And Disinfected									
10	Clean And Vacuum Central Heating Units									
11	Wash And Clean Light Covers									
12	Wash All Toilet And Restroom Mats									
	Daily/Weekly Kitchen Cleaning Tasks	M	T	W	T	F	S	S	Cleaned By	Date/Time
1	Wash And Sanitize All Counter Tops And Prep Area Surfaces									
2	Empty Dishwasher, Run The Dishwasher/Dish Drainer									
3	Disinfect Touch Points, Light Switches And Other Switches									
4	Take Out The Rubbish/Trash, Remove Waste And Recycling									
5	Clean & Disinfectant Bins/Waste Disposal Area & Trash Cans									
6	Wipe Down The Walls Wherever There Are Spills And Splashes									
7	Sweep The Floors To Ensure They're Free From Debris									
8	Mop Tiled And Laminate Floors With Disinfectant Cleaner									
9	Wet Floor Signs In Place If Floors Are Wet After Mopping									
10	Thoroughly Clean And Disinfect The Sinks And Taps									
11	Clean Exterior Of Appliances, Check For Spilled Food									
12	Replace Empty Paper Towel Rolls And Cloth Roller Towels									
13	Refill Soap Dispensers And Hand Sanitizers/Hand Gels									
14	Wipe Down Equipment, Tea And Coffee Makers, Toasters Etc									
15	Fire Exit Lights And Emergency Lights Checked & Functioning									
16	Pour Drain Cleaner Down Floor And Sink Drains									
17	Clean Inside Microwave, Check For Spilled Food									

	Daily/Weekly Kitchen Cleaning Tasks Continued	M	T	W	T	F	S	S	CLEANED BY	DATE/TIME
18	Replace Wash Rags, Cloths And Tea Towels With Clean Ones									
19	Wash Rags, Cloths, Tea Towels And Towels In Washing Machine									
20	Replace And Change Burned Out Light Bulbs/Broken Lights									
21	Clean Inside Of Dishwasher									
22	Sanitise Sponges Or Replace Damaged Sponges With New									
23	Dishes, Pots, Pans, And Utensils To Be Stored Away Properly									
24	Clean Out Refrigerator And Wipe Down Shelves And Drawers									
	Monthly Kitchen Cleaning Tasks	M	T	W	T	F	S	S	Cleaned By	Date/Time
1	Wash And Clean Air Vents									
2	Sort Through And Organize Cooking Utensils, Pans And Pots									
3	Wash And Clean Air Vents									
4	Check Plates, Cups And Glasses And Bin Anything Chipped									
5	Clean And Vacuum Central Heating Units									
6	Wash And Clean Light Covers									
7	Clean And De-Lime Dishwasher									
8	Dust And Clean Ceilings, Ceiling Corners And Ceiling Tiles									
9	Thoroughly Clean Grout And Tiles									
10	Clean Refrigerator Coils To Remove Dust, Unplug First									
11	Run Cleaning & Sanitizing Chemicals Through Coffee Machine									
12	Disinfect And Clean All The Walls From Top To Bottom									
13	Check For Out Of Date Food In Cabinets/Cupboards									
14	Clean Skirting Boards/Baseboards And Corners									
15	Clean Under Refrigerator									
16	Wash And Clean Doors, Door Frames And Glass									
17	Sort Through Leftover Items In The Fridge/Refrigerators									
18	Wash And Clean Windows (Inside And Outside)									
19	Replace Pest Traps									

ESSENTIAL CLEANING NOTES

....

....

....

....

....

....

ESSENTIAL OFFICE CLEANING *Checklist*

Location/Building	Department	Office Number	Week Number

Start Date & Time	Finnish Date & Time	Name	Signature

	Daily/Weekly Office Cleaning Tasks	M	T	W	T	F	S	S	Cleaned By	Date/Time
1	Clean And Sanitize All The Desks And Tables									
2	Clean And Sanitize All The Counter Tops And Surface Areas									
3	Disinfect All Point-Of-Sale Terminals And Touch Screens									
4	Disinfect Touch Points, Light Switches And Other Switches									
5	Clean And Sanitize All Keyboards And Computer Mice									
6	Wipe Down The Walls Wherever There Are Spills And Splashes									
7	Clean And Disinfect All Doors, Door Handles And Doorknobs									
8	Re-Stock Protective Clothing, Face Masks/Shields, Gloves									
9	Clean And Sanitize All The Chairs, Seats And Benches									
10	Clean All The Mirrors, Glass Cabinets/Displays									
11	Replace And Change Burned Out Light Bulbs/Broken Lights									
12	Sweep The Floors To Ensure They're Free From Debris									
13	Mop Tiled And Laminate Floors With Disinfectant Cleaner									
14	Vacuum And Hoover The Carpets, Mats And Rugs									
15	Place Wet Floor Signs If Floors Are Wet After Mopping									
16	Wash & Clean Dirty Cups, Drinking Bottles And Glasses									
17	Clean & Re-Stock Paper Dispensers & Paper Towel Rolls									
18	Wipe Down Equipment & Sanitize Tea And Coffee Makers									
19	Refill Soap Dispensers, Sanitizers And Hand Gels									
20	Clean And Dust Furniture And Office Equipment									
21	Take Out The Rubbish/Trash, Remove Waste And Recycling									
22	Clean & Disinfectant Bins/Waste Disposal Area & Trash Cans									
23	Clean And Wipe Down Windowsills									
24	Vacuum Furnishings, Cushions, Chairs, Sofas And Couches									
25	Spray Air Freshener									
26	Clean And Disinfect Any Cabinets, Shelves And Units									
27	Clean Surfaces And Desk/Work Dividers									
28	Clean And Disinfect Telephones And Headsets									
29	Polish Any Wooden Furniture And Hardwood Surfaces									

	Monthly Office Cleaning Tasks	M	T	W	T	F	S	S	Cleaned By	Date/Time
1	Clean Skirting Boards/Baseboards And Corners									
2	Clean And Disinfect All The Walls From Top To Bottom									
3	Clean Blinds (Take Down And Wash If Possible)									
4	Wash And Clean Windows (Inside And Outside)									
5	Clean And Disinfect Shared Surfaces									
6	Steam Clean Carpets And Rugs									
7	Dust And Clean Ceilings, Ceiling Corners And Ceiling Tiles									
8	Check For Broken Chairs And Tables									
9	Dust And Wash Radiator Covers									
10	Clean And Disinfect Ceiling Wall Vents									
11	Clean And Vacuum Central Heating Units									
12	Wash And Clean Light Covers									
13	Clean Drapes And Curtains (Take Down And Wash if Possible)									
14	Check Cleaning Supplies And Re-Stock As Necessary									
15	Check Ceiling Fans, Fire Sprinklers And Smoke Alarms									
16	Check Hardware, Door Stops And Lock Mechanisms									
17	Fire Exit Lights And Emergency Lights Checked & Functioning									
18	Organize And De-Clutter Office Drawers									
19	Organize And De-Clutter Storeroom									

	Daily/Weekly Toilets/Restroom Cleaning Tasks	M	T	W	T	F	S	S	Cleaned By	Date/Time
1	Clean And Disinfect All Doors, Door Handles And Doorknobs									
2	Disinfect Touch Points, Light Switches And Other Switches									
3	Toilet Roll Holders Cleaned And Disinfected And Re-Stocked									
4	Wipe Down The Walls Wherever There Are Spills And Splashes									
5	Electric Hand Dryers Cleaned, Disinfected & Operating Correctly									
6	Sweep The Floors To Ensure They're Free From Debris									
7	Mop Tiled And Laminate Floors With Disinfectant Cleaner									
8	Paper Dispensers & Paper Towel Rolls Cleaned & Re-Stocked									
9	Take Out The Rubbish/Trash, Remove Waste And Recycling									
10	Clean & Disinfectant Bins/Waste Disposal Area & Trash Cans									
11	Feminine Hygiene Bins/Containers Cleaned And Disinfected									
12	Toilets Cleaned & Disinfected, Outside, Inside And Handles									
13	Urinals & Urinal Screens Cleaned, Disinfected & Blocks Replaced									
14	Wall Mirrors Cleaned With Glass Cleaner									
15	Clean And Re-Stock Paper Dispensers & Paper Towel Rolls									
16	Refill Soap Dispensers, Sanitizers And Hand Gels									
17	Sinks, Taps, Fixtures, Surface Areas Cleaned And Disinfected									

	Daily/Weekly Toilets/Restroom Cleaning Tasks Con	M	T	W	T	F	S	S	Cleaned By	Date/Time
18	Windowsills Clean And Wiped Down									
19	Check Plumbing And Schedule Work If Required									
20	Air Fresheners Checked And Replaced									
21	Fire Exit Lights And Emergency Lights Checked & Functioning									
22	Place Wet Floor Signs If Floors Are Wet After Mopping									
23	Cabinets Cleaned And Disinfected									
	Monthly Toilets/Restroom Cleaning Tasks	M	T	W	T	F	S	S	Cleaned By	Date/Time
1	Toilet/Restroom Service Storeroom/Cupboard Clean And Tidy									
2	Walls Free Of Graffiti, Stickers, Gum And Residue									
3	Wash And Clean Windows (Inside And Outside)									
4	Check Hardware, Door Stops And Lock Mechanisms									
5	All Fittings Securely Fixed (Schedule Maintenance If Not)									
6	Dust And Clean Ceilings, Ceiling Corners And Ceiling Tiles									
7	Clean Skirting Boards/Baseboards And Corners									
8	Thoroughly Clean Grout And Tiles									
9	Ceiling Wall Vents Cleaned And Disinfected									
10	Clean And Vacuum Central Heating Units									
11	Wash And Clean Light Covers									
12	Wash All Toilet And Restroom Mats									
	Daily/Weekly Kitchen Cleaning Tasks	M	T	W	T	F	S	S	Cleaned By	Date/Time
1	Wash And Sanitize All Counter Tops And Prep Area Surfaces									
2	Empty Dishwasher, Run The Dishwasher/Dish Drainer									
3	Disinfect Touch Points, Light Switches And Other Switches									
4	Take Out The Rubbish/Trash, Remove Waste And Recycling									
5	Clean & Disinfectant Bins/Waste Disposal Area & Trash Cans									
6	Wipe Down The Walls Wherever There Are Spills And Splashes									
7	Sweep The Floors To Ensure They're Free From Debris									
8	Mop Tiled And Laminate Floors With Disinfectant Cleaner									
9	Wet Floor Signs In Place If Floors Are Wet After Mopping									
10	Thoroughly Clean And Disinfect The Sinks And Taps									
11	Clean Exterior Of Appliances, Check For Spilled Food									
12	Replace Empty Paper Towel Rolls And Cloth Roller Towels									
13	Refill Soap Dispensers And Hand Sanitizers/Hand Gels									
14	Wipe Down Equipment, Tea And Coffee Makers, Toasters Etc									
15	Fire Exit Lights And Emergency Lights Checked & Functioning									
16	Pour Drain Cleaner Down Floor And Sink Drains									
17	Clean Inside Microwave, Check For Spilled Food									

	Daily/Weekly Kitchen Cleaning Tasks Continued	M	T	W	T	F	S	S	CLEANED BY	DATE/TIME
18	Replace Wash Rags, Cloths And Tea Towels With Clean Ones									
19	Wash Rags, Cloths, Tea Towels And Towels In Washing Machine									
20	Replace And Change Burned Out Light Bulbs/Broken Lights									
21	Clean Inside Of Dishwasher									
22	Sanitise Sponges Or Replace Damaged Sponges With New									
23	Dishes, Pots, Pans, And Utensils To Be Stored Away Properly									
24	Clean Out Refrigerator And Wipe Down Shelves And Drawers									
	Monthly Kitchen Cleaning Tasks	M	T	W	T	F	S	S	Cleaned By	Date/Time
1	Wash And Clean Air Vents									
2	Sort Through And Organize Cooking Utensils, Pans And Pots									
3	Wash And Clean Air Vents									
4	Check Plates, Cups And Glasses And Bin Anything Chipped									
5	Clean And Vacuum Central Heating Units									
6	Wash And Clean Light Covers									
7	Clean And De-Lime Dishwasher									
8	Dust And Clean Ceilings, Ceiling Corners And Ceiling Tiles									
9	Thoroughly Clean Grout And Tiles									
10	Clean Refrigerator Coils To Remove Dust, Unplug First									
11	Run Cleaning & Sanitizing Chemicals Through Coffee Machine									
12	Disinfect And Clean All The Walls From Top To Bottom									
13	Check For Out Of Date Food In Cabinets/Cupboards									
14	Clean Skirting Boards/Baseboards And Corners									
15	Clean Under Refrigerator									
16	Wash And Clean Doors, Door Frames And Glass									
17	Sort Through Leftover Items In The Fridge/Refrigerators									
18	Wash And Clean Windows (Inside And Outside)									
19	Replace Pest Traps									

ESSENTIAL CLEANING NOTES

....

....

....

....

....

....

....

....

ESSENTIAL OFFICE CLEANING *Checklist*

Location/Building	Department	Office Number	Week Number

Start Date & Time	Finnish Date & Time	Name	Signature

	Daily/Weekly Office Cleaning Tasks	M	T	W	T	F	S	S	Cleaned By	Date/Time
1	Clean And Sanitize All The Desks And Tables									
2	Clean And Sanitize All The Counter Tops And Surface Areas									
3	Disinfect All Point-Of-Sale Terminals And Touch Screens									
4	Disinfect Touch Points, Light Switches And Other Switches									
5	Clean And Sanitize All Keyboards And Computer Mice									
6	Wipe Down The Walls Wherever There Are Spills And Splashes									
7	Clean And Disinfect All Doors, Door Handles And Doorknobs									
8	Re-Stock Protective Clothing, Face Masks/Shields, Gloves									
9	Clean And Sanitize All The Chairs, Seats And Benches									
10	Clean All The Mirrors, Glass Cabinets/Displays									
11	Replace And Change Burned Out Light Bulbs/Broken Lights									
12	Sweep The Floors To Ensure They're Free From Debris									
13	Mop Tiled And Laminate Floors With Disinfectant Cleaner									
14	Vacuum And Hoover The Carpets, Mats And Rugs									
15	Place Wet Floor Signs If Floors Are Wet After Mopping									
16	Wash & Clean Dirty Cups, Drinking Bottles And Glasses									
17	Clean & Re-Stock Paper Dispensers & Paper Towel Rolls									
18	Wipe Down Equipment & Sanitize Tea And Coffee Makers									
19	Refill Soap Dispensers, Sanitizers And Hand Gels									
20	Clean And Dust Furniture And Office Equipment									
21	Take Out The Rubbish/Trash, Remove Waste And Recycling									
22	Clean & Disinfectant Bins/Waste Disposal Area & Trash Cans									
23	Clean And Wipe Down Windowsills									
24	Vacuum Furnishings, Cushions, Chairs, Sofas And Couches									
25	Spray Air Freshener									
26	Clean And Disinfect Any Cabinets, Shelves And Units									
27	Clean Surfaces And Desk/Work Dividers									
28	Clean And Disinfect Telephones And Headsets									
29	Polish Any Wooden Furniture And Hardwood Surfaces									

	Monthly Office Cleaning Tasks	M	T	W	T	F	S	S	Cleaned By	Date/Time
1	Clean Skirting Boards/Baseboards And Corners									
2	Clean And Disinfect All The Walls From Top To Bottom									
3	Clean Blinds (Take Down And Wash If Possible)									
4	Wash And Clean Windows (Inside And Outside)									
5	Clean And Disinfect Shared Surfaces									
6	Steam Clean Carpets And Rugs									
7	Dust And Clean Ceilings, Ceiling Corners And Ceiling Tiles									
8	Check For Broken Chairs And Tables									
9	Dust And Wash Radiator Covers									
10	Clean And Disinfect Ceiling Wall Vents									
11	Clean And Vacuum Central Heating Units									
12	Wash And Clean Light Covers									
13	Clean Drapes And Curtains (Take Down And Wash if Possible)									
14	Check Cleaning Supplies And Re-Stock As Necessary									
15	Check Ceiling Fans, Fire Sprinklers And Smoke Alarms									
16	Check Hardware, Door Stops And Lock Mechanisms									
17	Fire Exit Lights And Emergency Lights Checked & Functioning									
18	Organize And De-Clutter Office Drawers									
19	Organize And De-Clutter Storeroom									

	Daily/Weekly Toilets/Restroom Cleaning Tasks	M	T	W	T	F	S	S	Cleaned By	Date/Time
1	Clean And Disinfect All Doors, Door Handles And Doorknobs									
2	Disinfect Touch Points, Light Switches And Other Switches									
3	Toilet Roll Holders Cleaned And Disinfected And Re-Stocked									
4	Wipe Down The Walls Wherever There Are Spills And Splashes									
5	Electric Hand Dryers Cleaned, Disinfected & Operating Correctly									
6	Sweep The Floors To Ensure They're Free From Debris									
7	Mop Tiled And Laminate Floors With Disinfectant Cleaner									
8	Paper Dispensers & Paper Towel Rolls Cleaned & Re-Stocked									
9	Take Out The Rubbish/Trash, Remove Waste And Recycling									
10	Clean & Disinfectant Bins/Waste Disposal Area & Trash Cans									
11	Feminine Hygiene Bins/Containers Cleaned And Disinfected									
12	Toilets Cleaned & Disinfected, Outside, Inside And Handles									
13	Urinals & Urinal Screens Cleaned, Disinfected & Blocks Replaced									
14	Wall Mirrors Cleaned With Glass Cleaner									
15	Clean And Re-Stock Paper Dispensers & Paper Towel Rolls									
16	Refill Soap Dispensers, Sanitizers And Hand Gels									
17	Sinks, Taps, Fixtures, Surface Areas Cleaned And Disinfected									

	Daily/Weekly Toilets/Restroom Cleaning Tasks Con	M	T	W	T	F	S	S	Cleaned By	Date/Time
18	Windowsills Clean And Wiped Down									
19	Check Plumbing And Schedule Work If Required									
20	Air Fresheners Checked And Replaced									
21	Fire Exit Lights And Emergency Lights Checked & Functioning									
22	Place Wet Floor Signs If Floors Are Wet After Mopping									
23	Cabinets Cleaned And Disinfected									
	Monthly Toilets/Restroom Cleaning Tasks	M	T	W	T	F	S	S	Cleaned By	Date/Time
1	Toilet/Restroom Service Storeroom/Cupboard Clean And Tidy									
2	Walls Free Of Graffiti, Stickers, Gum And Residue									
3	Wash And Clean Windows (Inside And Outside)									
4	Check Hardware, Door Stops And Lock Mechanisms									
5	All Fittings Securely Fixed (Schedule Maintenance If Not)									
6	Dust And Clean Ceilings, Ceiling Corners And Ceiling Tiles									
7	Clean Skirting Boards/Baseboards And Corners									
8	Thoroughly Clean Grout And Tiles									
9	Ceiling Wall Vents Cleaned And Disinfected									
10	Clean And Vacuum Central Heating Units									
11	Wash And Clean Light Covers									
12	Wash All Toilet And Restroom Mats									
	Daily/Weekly Kitchen Cleaning Tasks	M	T	W	T	F	S	S	Cleaned By	Date/Time
1	Wash And Sanitize All Counter Tops And Prep Area Surfaces									
2	Empty Dishwasher, Run The Dishwasher/Dish Drainer									
3	Disinfect Touch Points, Light Switches And Other Switches									
4	Take Out The Rubbish/Trash, Remove Waste And Recycling									
5	Clean & Disinfectant Bins/Waste Disposal Area & Trash Cans									
6	Wipe Down The Walls Wherever There Are Spills And Splashes									
7	Sweep The Floors To Ensure They're Free From Debris									
8	Mop Tiled And Laminate Floors With Disinfectant Cleaner									
9	Wet Floor Signs In Place If Floors Are Wet After Mopping									
10	Thoroughly Clean And Disinfect The Sinks And Taps									
11	Clean Exterior Of Appliances, Check For Spilled Food									
12	Replace Empty Paper Towel Rolls And Cloth Roller Towels									
13	Refill Soap Dispensers And Hand Sanitizers/Hand Gels									
14	Wipe Down Equipment, Tea And Coffee Makers, Toasters Etc									
15	Fire Exit Lights And Emergency Lights Checked & Functioning									
16	Pour Drain Cleaner Down Floor And Sink Drains									
17	Clean Inside Microwave, Check For Spilled Food									

	Daily/Weekly Kitchen Cleaning Tasks Continued	M	T	W	T	F	S	S	CLEANED BY	DATE/TIME
18	Replace Wash Rags, Cloths And Tea Towels With Clean Ones									
19	Wash Rags, Cloths, Tea Towels And Towels In Washing Machine									
20	Replace And Change Burned Out Light Bulbs/Broken Lights									
21	Clean Inside Of Dishwasher									
22	Sanitise Sponges Or Replace Damaged Sponges With New									
23	Dishes, Pots, Pans, And Utensils To Be Stored Away Properly									
24	Clean Out Refrigerator And Wipe Down Shelves And Drawers									
	Monthly Kitchen Cleaning Tasks	M	T	W	T	F	S	S	Cleaned By	Date/Time
1	Wash And Clean Air Vents									
2	Sort Through And Organize Cooking Utensils, Pans And Pots									
3	Wash And Clean Air Vents									
4	Check Plates, Cups And Glasses And Bin Anything Chipped									
5	Clean And Vacuum Central Heating Units									
6	Wash And Clean Light Covers									
7	Clean And De-Lime Dishwasher									
8	Dust And Clean Ceilings, Ceiling Corners And Ceiling Tiles									
9	Thoroughly Clean Grout And Tiles									
10	Clean Refrigerator Coils To Remove Dust, Unplug First									
11	Run Cleaning & Sanitizing Chemicals Through Coffee Machine									
12	Disinfect And Clean All The Walls From Top To Bottom									
13	Check For Out Of Date Food In Cabinets/Cupboards									
14	Clean Skirting Boards/Baseboards And Corners									
15	Clean Under Refrigerator									
16	Wash And Clean Doors, Door Frames And Glass									
17	Sort Through Leftover Items In The Fridge/Refrigerators									
18	Wash And Clean Windows (Inside And Outside)									
19	Replace Pest Traps									

ESSENTIAL CLEANING NOTES

....

....

....

....

....

....

....

....

ESSENTIAL OFFICE CLEANING *Checklist*

Location/Building	Department	Office Number	Week Number

Start Date & Time	Finnish Date & Time	Name	Signature

	Daily/Weekly Office Cleaning Tasks	M	T	W	T	F	S	S	Cleaned By	Date/Time
1	Clean And Sanitize All The Desks And Tables									
2	Clean And Sanitize All The Counter Tops And Surface Areas									
3	Disinfect All Point-Of-Sale Terminals And Touch Screens									
4	Disinfect Touch Points, Light Switches And Other Switches									
5	Clean And Sanitize All Keyboards And Computer Mice									
6	Wipe Down The Walls Wherever There Are Spills And Splashes									
7	Clean And Disinfect All Doors, Door Handles And Doorknobs									
8	Re-Stock Protective Clothing, Face Masks/Shields, Gloves									
9	Clean And Sanitize All The Chairs, Seats And Benches									
10	Clean All The Mirrors, Glass Cabinets/Displays									
11	Replace And Change Burned Out Light Bulbs/Broken Lights									
12	Sweep The Floors To Ensure They're Free From Debris									
13	Mop Tiled And Laminate Floors With Disinfectant Cleaner									
14	Vacuum And Hoover The Carpets, Mats And Rugs									
15	Place Wet Floor Signs If Floors Are Wet After Mopping									
16	Wash & Clean Dirty Cups, Drinking Bottles And Glasses									
17	Clean & Re-Stock Paper Dispensers & Paper Towel Rolls									
18	Wipe Down Equipment & Sanitize Tea And Coffee Makers									
19	Refill Soap Dispensers, Sanitizers And Hand Gels									
20	Clean And Dust Furniture And Office Equipment									
21	Take Out The Rubbish/Trash, Remove Waste And Recycling									
22	Clean & Disinfectant Bins/Waste Disposal Area & Trash Cans									
23	Clean And Wipe Down Windowsills									
24	Vacuum Furnishings, Cushions, Chairs, Sofas And Couches									
25	Spray Air Freshener									
26	Clean And Disinfect Any Cabinets, Shelves And Units									
27	Clean Surfaces And Desk/Work Dividers									
28	Clean And Disinfect Telephones And Headsets									
29	Polish Any Wooden Furniture And Hardwood Surfaces									

	Monthly Office Cleaning Tasks	M	T	W	T	F	S	S	Cleaned By	Date/Time
1	Clean Skirting Boards/Baseboards And Corners									
2	Clean And Disinfect All The Walls From Top To Bottom									
3	Clean Blinds (Take Down And Wash If Possible)									
4	Wash And Clean Windows (Inside And Outside)									
5	Clean And Disinfect Shared Surfaces									
6	Steam Clean Carpets And Rugs									
7	Dust And Clean Ceilings, Ceiling Corners And Ceiling Tiles									
8	Check For Broken Chairs And Tables									
9	Dust And Wash Radiator Covers									
10	Clean And Disinfect Ceiling Wall Vents									
11	Clean And Vacuum Central Heating Units									
12	Wash And Clean Light Covers									
13	Clean Drapes And Curtains (Take Down And Wash if Possible)									
14	Check Cleaning Supplies And Re-Stock As Necessary									
15	Check Ceiling Fans, Fire Sprinklers And Smoke Alarms									
16	Check Hardware, Door Stops And Lock Mechanisms									
17	Fire Exit Lights And Emergency Lights Checked & Functioning									
18	Organize And De-Clutter Office Drawers									
19	Organize And De-Clutter Storeroom									
	Daily/Weekly Toilets/Restroom Cleaning Tasks	M	T	W	T	F	S	S	Cleaned By	Date/Time
1	Clean And Disinfect All Doors, Door Handles And Doorknobs									
2	Disinfect Touch Points, Light Switches And Other Switches									
3	Toilet Roll Holders Cleaned And Disinfected And Re-Stocked									
4	Wipe Down The Walls Wherever There Are Spills And Splashes									
5	Electric Hand Dryers Cleaned, Disinfected & Operating Correctly									
6	Sweep The Floors To Ensure They're Free From Debris									
7	Mop Tiled And Laminate Floors With Disinfectant Cleaner									
8	Paper Dispensers & Paper Towel Rolls Cleaned & Re-Stocked									
9	Take Out The Rubbish/Trash, Remove Waste And Recycling									
10	Clean & Disinfectant Bins/Waste Disposal Area & Trash Cans									
11	Feminine Hygiene Bins/Containers Cleaned And Disinfected									
12	Toilets Cleaned & Disinfected, Outside, Inside And Handles									
13	Urinals & Urinal Screens Cleaned, Disinfected & Blocks Replaced									
14	Wall Mirrors Cleaned With Glass Cleaner									
15	Clean And Re-Stock Paper Dispensers & Paper Towel Rolls									
16	Refill Soap Dispensers, Sanitizers And Hand Gels									
17	Sinks, Taps, Fixtures, Surface Areas Cleaned And Disinfected									

	Daily/Weekly Toilets/Restroom Cleaning Tasks Con	M	T	W	T	F	S	S	Cleaned By	Date/Time
18	Windowsills Clean And Wiped Down									
19	Check Plumbing And Schedule Work If Required									
20	Air Fresheners Checked And Replaced									
21	Fire Exit Lights And Emergency Lights Checked & Functioning									
22	Place Wet Floor Signs If Floors Are Wet After Mopping									
23	Cabinets Cleaned And Disinfected									
	Monthly Toilets/Restroom Cleaning Tasks	M	T	W	T	F	S	S	Cleaned By	Date/Time
1	Toilet/Restroom Service Storeroom/Cupboard Clean And Tidy									
2	Walls Free Of Graffiti, Stickers, Gum And Residue									
3	Wash And Clean Windows (Inside And Outside)									
4	Check Hardware, Door Stops And Lock Mechanisms									
5	All Fittings Securely Fixed (Schedule Maintenance If Not)									
6	Dust And Clean Ceilings, Ceiling Corners And Ceiling Tiles									
7	Clean Skirting Boards/Baseboards And Corners									
8	Thoroughly Clean Grout And Tiles									
9	Ceiling Wall Vents Cleaned And Disinfected									
10	Clean And Vacuum Central Heating Units									
11	Wash And Clean Light Covers									
12	Wash All Toilet And Restroom Mats									
	Daily/Weekly Kitchen Cleaning Tasks	M	T	W	T	F	S	S	Cleaned By	Date/Time
1	Wash And Sanitize All Counter Tops And Prep Area Surfaces									
2	Empty Dishwasher, Run The Dishwasher/Dish Drainer									
3	Disinfect Touch Points, Light Switches And Other Switches									
4	Take Out The Rubbish/Trash, Remove Waste And Recycling									
5	Clean & Disinfectant Bins/Waste Disposal Area & Trash Cans									
6	Wipe Down The Walls Wherever There Are Spills And Splashes									
7	Sweep The Floors To Ensure They're Free From Debris									
8	Mop Tiled And Laminate Floors With Disinfectant Cleaner									
9	Wet Floor Signs In Place If Floors Are Wet After Mopping									
10	Thoroughly Clean And Disinfect The Sinks And Taps									
11	Clean Exterior Of Appliances, Check For Spilled Food									
12	Replace Empty Paper Towel Rolls And Cloth Roller Towels									
13	Refill Soap Dispensers And Hand Sanitizers/Hand Gels									
14	Wipe Down Equipment, Tea And Coffee Makers, Toasters Etc									
15	Fire Exit Lights And Emergency Lights Checked & Functioning									
16	Pour Drain Cleaner Down Floor And Sink Drains									
17	Clean Inside Microwave, Check For Spilled Food									

	Daily/Weekly Kitchen Cleaning Tasks Continued	M	T	W	T	F	S	S	CLEANED BY	DATE/TIME
18	Replace Wash Rags, Cloths And Tea Towels With Clean Ones									
19	Wash Rags, Cloths, Tea Towels And Towels In Washing Machine									
20	Replace And Change Burned Out Light Bulbs/Broken Lights									
21	Clean Inside Of Dishwasher									
22	Sanitise Sponges Or Replace Damaged Sponges With New									
23	Dishes, Pots, Pans, And Utensils To Be Stored Away Properly									
24	Clean Out Refrigerator And Wipe Down Shelves And Drawers									
	Monthly Kitchen Cleaning Tasks	M	T	W	T	F	S	S	Cleaned By	Date/Time
1	Wash And Clean Air Vents									
2	Sort Through And Organize Cooking Utensils, Pans And Pots									
3	Wash And Clean Air Vents									
4	Check Plates, Cups And Glasses And Bin Anything Chipped									
5	Clean And Vacuum Central Heating Units									
6	Wash And Clean Light Covers									
7	Clean And De-Lime Dishwasher									
8	Dust And Clean Ceilings, Ceiling Corners And Ceiling Tiles									
9	Thoroughly Clean Grout And Tiles									
10	Clean Refrigerator Coils To Remove Dust, Unplug First									
11	Run Cleaning & Sanitizing Chemicals Through Coffee Machine									
12	Disinfect And Clean All The Walls From Top To Bottom									
13	Check For Out Of Date Food In Cabinets/Cupboards									
14	Clean Skirting Boards/Baseboards And Corners									
15	Clean Under Refrigerator									
16	Wash And Clean Doors, Door Frames And Glass									
17	Sort Through Leftover Items In The Fridge/Refrigerators									
18	Wash And Clean Windows (Inside And Outside)									
19	Replace Pest Traps									

ESSENTIAL CLEANING NOTES

....

....

....

....

....

....

....

....

ESSENTIAL OFFICE CLEANING *Checklist*

Location/Building	Department	Office Number	Week Number

Start Date & Time	Finnish Date & Time	Name	Signature

	Daily/Weekly Office Cleaning Tasks	M	T	W	T	F	S	S	Cleaned By	Date/Time
1	Clean And Sanitize All The Desks And Tables									
2	Clean And Sanitize All The Counter Tops And Surface Areas									
3	Disinfect All Point-Of-Sale Terminals And Touch Screens									
4	Disinfect Touch Points, Light Switches And Other Switches									
5	Clean And Sanitize All Keyboards And Computer Mice									
6	Wipe Down The Walls Wherever There Are Spills And Splashes									
7	Clean And Disinfect All Doors, Door Handles And Doorknobs									
8	Re-Stock Protective Clothing, Face Masks/Shields, Gloves									
9	Clean And Sanitize All The Chairs, Seats And Benches									
10	Clean All The Mirrors, Glass Cabinets/Displays									
11	Replace And Change Burned Out Light Bulbs/Broken Lights									
12	Sweep The Floors To Ensure They're Free From Debris									
13	Mop Tiled And Laminate Floors With Disinfectant Cleaner									
14	Vacuum And Hoover The Carpets, Mats And Rugs									
15	Place Wet Floor Signs If Floors Are Wet After Mopping									
16	Wash & Clean Dirty Cups, Drinking Bottles And Glasses									
17	Clean & Re-Stock Paper Dispensers & Paper Towel Rolls									
18	Wipe Down Equipment & Sanitize Tea And Coffee Makers									
19	Refill Soap Dispensers, Sanitizers And Hand Gels									
20	Clean And Dust Furniture And Office Equipment									
21	Take Out The Rubbish/Trash, Remove Waste And Recycling									
22	Clean & Disinfectant Bins/Waste Disposal Area & Trash Cans									
23	Clean And Wipe Down Windowsills									
24	Vacuum Furnishings, Cushions, Chairs, Sofas And Couches									
25	Spray Air Freshener									
26	Clean And Disinfect Any Cabinets, Shelves And Units									
27	Clean Surfaces And Desk/Work Dividers									
28	Clean And Disinfect Telephones And Headsets									
29	Polish Any Wooden Furniture And Hardwood Surfaces									

	Monthly Office Cleaning Tasks	M	T	W	T	F	S	S	Cleaned By	Date/Time
1	Clean Skirting Boards/Baseboards And Corners									
2	Clean And Disinfect All The Walls From Top To Bottom									
3	Clean Blinds (Take Down And Wash If Possible)									
4	Wash And Clean Windows (Inside And Outside)									
5	Clean And Disinfect Shared Surfaces									
6	Steam Clean Carpets And Rugs									
7	Dust And Clean Ceilings, Ceiling Corners And Ceiling Tiles									
8	Check For Broken Chairs And Tables									
9	Dust And Wash Radiator Covers									
10	Clean And Disinfect Ceiling Wall Vents									
11	Clean And Vacuum Central Heating Units									
12	Wash And Clean Light Covers									
13	Clean Drapes And Curtains (Take Down And Wash if Possible)									
14	Check Cleaning Supplies And Re-Stock As Necessary									
15	Check Ceiling Fans, Fire Sprinklers And Smoke Alarms									
16	Check Hardware, Door Stops And Lock Mechanisms									
17	Fire Exit Lights And Emergency Lights Checked & Functioning									
18	Organize And De-Clutter Office Drawers									
19	Organize And De-Clutter Storeroom									
	Daily/Weekly Toilets/Restroom Cleaning Tasks	M	T	W	T	F	S	S	Cleaned By	Date/Time
1	Clean And Disinfect All Doors, Door Handles And Doorknobs									
2	Disinfect Touch Points, Light Switches And Other Switches									
3	Toilet Roll Holders Cleaned And Disinfected And Re-Stocked									
4	Wipe Down The Walls Wherever There Are Spills And Splashes									
5	Electric Hand Dryers Cleaned, Disinfected & Operating Correctly									
6	Sweep The Floors To Ensure They're Free From Debris									
7	Mop Tiled And Laminate Floors With Disinfectant Cleaner									
8	Paper Dispensers & Paper Towel Rolls Cleaned & Re-Stocked									
9	Take Out The Rubbish/Trash, Remove Waste And Recycling									
10	Clean & Disinfectant Bins/Waste Disposal Area & Trash Cans									
11	Feminine Hygiene Bins/Containers Cleaned And Disinfected									
12	Toilets Cleaned & Disinfected, Outside, Inside And Handles									
13	Urinals & Urinal Screens Cleaned, Disinfected & Blocks Replaced									
14	Wall Mirrors Cleaned With Glass Cleaner									
15	Clean And Re-Stock Paper Dispensers & Paper Towel Rolls									
16	Refill Soap Dispensers, Sanitizers And Hand Gels									
17	Sinks, Taps, Fixtures, Surface Areas Cleaned And Disinfected									

	Daily/Weekly Toilets/Restroom Cleaning Tasks Con	M	T	W	T	F	S	S	Cleaned By	Date/Time
18	Windowsills Clean And Wiped Down									
19	Check Plumbing And Schedule Work If Required									
20	Air Fresheners Checked And Replaced									
21	Fire Exit Lights And Emergency Lights Checked & Functioning									
22	Place Wet Floor Signs If Floors Are Wet After Mopping									
23	Cabinets Cleaned And Disinfected									
	Monthly Toilets/Restroom Cleaning Tasks	M	T	W	T	F	S	S	Cleaned By	Date/Time
1	Toilet/Restroom Service Storeroom/Cupboard Clean And Tidy									
2	Walls Free Of Graffiti, Stickers, Gum And Residue									
3	Wash And Clean Windows (Inside And Outside)									
4	Check Hardware, Door Stops And Lock Mechanisms									
5	All Fittings Securely Fixed (Schedule Maintenance If Not)									
6	Dust And Clean Ceilings, Ceiling Corners And Ceiling Tiles									
7	Clean Skirting Boards/Baseboards And Corners									
8	Thoroughly Clean Grout And Tiles									
9	Ceiling Wall Vents Cleaned And Disinfected									
10	Clean And Vacuum Central Heating Units									
11	Wash And Clean Light Covers									
12	Wash All Toilet And Restroom Mats									
	Daily/Weekly Kitchen Cleaning Tasks	M	T	W	T	F	S	S	Cleaned By	Date/Time
1	Wash And Sanitize All Counter Tops And Prep Area Surfaces									
2	Empty Dishwasher, Run The Dishwasher/Dish Drainer									
3	Disinfect Touch Points, Light Switches And Other Switches									
4	Take Out The Rubbish/Trash, Remove Waste And Recycling									
5	Clean & Disinfectant Bins/Waste Disposal Area & Trash Cans									
6	Wipe Down The Walls Wherever There Are Spills And Splashes									
7	Sweep The Floors To Ensure They're Free From Debris									
8	Mop Tiled And Laminate Floors With Disinfectant Cleaner									
9	Wet Floor Signs In Place If Floors Are Wet After Mopping									
10	Thoroughly Clean And Disinfect The Sinks And Taps									
11	Clean Exterior Of Appliances, Check For Spilled Food									
12	Replace Empty Paper Towel Rolls And Cloth Roller Towels									
13	Refill Soap Dispensers And Hand Sanitizers/Hand Gels									
14	Wipe Down Equipment, Tea And Coffee Makers, Toasters Etc									
15	Fire Exit Lights And Emergency Lights Checked & Functioning									
16	Pour Drain Cleaner Down Floor And Sink Drains									
17	Clean Inside Microwave, Check For Spilled Food									

	Daily/Weekly Kitchen Cleaning Tasks Continued	M	T	W	T	F	S	S	CLEANED BY	DATE/TIME
18	Replace Wash Rags, Cloths And Tea Towels With Clean Ones									
19	Wash Rags, Cloths, Tea Towels And Towels In Washing Machine									
20	Replace And Change Burned Out Light Bulbs/Broken Lights									
21	Clean Inside Of Dishwasher									
22	Sanitise Sponges Or Replace Damaged Sponges With New									
23	Dishes, Pots, Pans, And Utensils To Be Stored Away Properly									
24	Clean Out Refrigerator And Wipe Down Shelves And Drawers									
	Monthly Kitchen Cleaning Tasks	M	T	W	T	F	S	S	Cleaned By	Date/Time
1	Wash And Clean Air Vents									
2	Sort Through And Organize Cooking Utensils, Pans And Pots									
3	Wash And Clean Air Vents									
4	Check Plates, Cups And Glasses And Bin Anything Chipped									
5	Clean And Vacuum Central Heating Units									
6	Wash And Clean Light Covers									
7	Clean And De-Lime Dishwasher									
8	Dust And Clean Ceilings, Ceiling Corners And Ceiling Tiles									
9	Thoroughly Clean Grout And Tiles									
10	Clean Refrigerator Coils To Remove Dust, Unplug First									
11	Run Cleaning & Sanitizing Chemicals Through Coffee Machine									
12	Disinfect And Clean All The Walls From Top To Bottom									
13	Check For Out Of Date Food In Cabinets/Cupboards									
14	Clean Skirting Boards/Baseboards And Corners									
15	Clean Under Refrigerator									
16	Wash And Clean Doors, Door Frames And Glass									
17	Sort Through Leftover Items In The Fridge/Refrigerators									
18	Wash And Clean Windows (Inside And Outside)									
19	Replace Pest Traps									

ESSENTIAL CLEANING NOTES

ESSENTIAL OFFICE CLEANING *Checklist*

Location/Building	Department	Office Number	Week Number

Start Date & Time	Finnish Date & Time	Name	Signature

	Daily/Weekly Office Cleaning Tasks	M	T	W	T	F	S	S	Cleaned By	Date/Time
1	Clean And Sanitize All The Desks And Tables									
2	Clean And Sanitize All The Counter Tops And Surface Areas									
3	Disinfect All Point-Of-Sale Terminals And Touch Screens									
4	Disinfect Touch Points, Light Switches And Other Switches									
5	Clean And Sanitize All Keyboards And Computer Mice									
6	Wipe Down The Walls Wherever There Are Spills And Splashes									
7	Clean And Disinfect All Doors, Door Handles And Doorknobs									
8	Re-Stock Protective Clothing, Face Masks/Shields, Gloves									
9	Clean And Sanitize All The Chairs, Seats And Benches									
10	Clean All The Mirrors, Glass Cabinets/Displays									
11	Replace And Change Burned Out Light Bulbs/Broken Lights									
12	Sweep The Floors To Ensure They're Free From Debris									
13	Mop Tiled And Laminate Floors With Disinfectant Cleaner									
14	Vacuum And Hoover The Carpets, Mats And Rugs									
15	Place Wet Floor Signs If Floors Are Wet After Mopping									
16	Wash & Clean Dirty Cups, Drinking Bottles And Glasses									
17	Clean & Re-Stock Paper Dispensers & Paper Towel Rolls									
18	Wipe Down Equipment & Sanitize Tea And Coffee Makers									
19	Refill Soap Dispensers, Sanitizers And Hand Gels									
20	Clean And Dust Furniture And Office Equipment									
21	Take Out The Rubbish/Trash, Remove Waste And Recycling									
22	Clean & Disinfectant Bins/Waste Disposal Area & Trash Cans									
23	Clean And Wipe Down Windowsills									
24	Vacuum Furnishings, Cushions, Chairs, Sofas And Couches									
25	Spray Air Freshener									
26	Clean And Disinfect Any Cabinets, Shelves And Units									
27	Clean Surfaces And Desk/Work Dividers									
28	Clean And Disinfect Telephones And Headsets									
29	Polish Any Wooden Furniture And Hardwood Surfaces									

	Monthly Office Cleaning Tasks	M	T	W	T	F	S	S	Cleaned By	Date/Time
1	Clean Skirting Boards/Baseboards And Corners									
2	Clean And Disinfect All The Walls From Top To Bottom									
3	Clean Blinds (Take Down And Wash If Possible)									
4	Wash And Clean Windows (Inside And Outside)									
5	Clean And Disinfect Shared Surfaces									
6	Steam Clean Carpets And Rugs									
7	Dust And Clean Ceilings, Ceiling Corners And Ceiling Tiles									
8	Check For Broken Chairs And Tables									
9	Dust And Wash Radiator Covers									
10	Clean And Disinfect Ceiling Wall Vents									
11	Clean And Vacuum Central Heating Units									
12	Wash And Clean Light Covers									
13	Clean Drapes And Curtains (Take Down And Wash if Possible)									
14	Check Cleaning Supplies And Re-Stock As Necessary									
15	Check Ceiling Fans, Fire Sprinklers And Smoke Alarms									
16	Check Hardware, Door Stops And Lock Mechanisms									
17	Fire Exit Lights And Emergency Lights Checked & Functioning									
18	Organize And De-Clutter Office Drawers									
19	Organize And De-Clutter Storeroom									
	Daily/Weekly Toilets/Restroom Cleaning Tasks	M	T	W	T	F	S	S	Cleaned By	Date/Time
1	Clean And Disinfect All Doors, Door Handles And Doorknobs									
2	Disinfect Touch Points, Light Switches And Other Switches									
3	Toilet Roll Holders Cleaned And Disinfected And Re-Stocked									
4	Wipe Down The Walls Wherever There Are Spills And Splashes									
5	Electric Hand Dryers Cleaned, Disinfected & Operating Correctly									
6	Sweep The Floors To Ensure They're Free From Debris									
7	Mop Tiled And Laminate Floors With Disinfectant Cleaner									
8	Paper Dispensers & Paper Towel Rolls Cleaned & Re-Stocked									
9	Take Out The Rubbish/Trash, Remove Waste And Recycling									
10	Clean & Disinfectant Bins/Waste Disposal Area & Trash Cans									
11	Feminine Hygiene Bins/Containers Cleaned And Disinfected									
12	Toilets Cleaned & Disinfected, Outside, Inside And Handles									
13	Urinals & Urinal Screens Cleaned, Disinfected & Blocks Replaced									
14	Wall Mirrors Cleaned With Glass Cleaner									
15	Clean And Re-Stock Paper Dispensers & Paper Towel Rolls									
16	Refill Soap Dispensers, Sanitizers And Hand Gels									
17	Sinks, Taps, Fixtures, Surface Areas Cleaned And Disinfected									

	Daily/Weekly Toilets/Restroom Cleaning Tasks Con	M	T	W	T	F	S	S	Cleaned By	Date/Time
18	Windowsills Clean And Wiped Down									
19	Check Plumbing And Schedule Work If Required									
20	Air Fresheners Checked And Replaced									
21	Fire Exit Lights And Emergency Lights Checked & Functioning									
22	Place Wet Floor Signs If Floors Are Wet After Mopping									
23	Cabinets Cleaned And Disinfected									
	Monthly Toilets/Restroom Cleaning Tasks	M	T	W	T	F	S	S	Cleaned By	Date/Time
1	Toilet/Restroom Service Storeroom/Cupboard Clean And Tidy									
2	Walls Free Of Graffiti, Stickers, Gum And Residue									
3	Wash And Clean Windows (Inside And Outside)									
4	Check Hardware, Door Stops And Lock Mechanisms									
5	All Fittings Securely Fixed (Schedule Maintenance If Not)									
6	Dust And Clean Ceilings, Ceiling Corners And Ceiling Tiles									
7	Clean Skirting Boards/Baseboards And Corners									
8	Thoroughly Clean Grout And Tiles									
9	Ceiling Wall Vents Cleaned And Disinfected									
10	Clean And Vacuum Central Heating Units									
11	Wash And Clean Light Covers									
12	Wash All Toilet And Restroom Mats									
	Daily/Weekly Kitchen Cleaning Tasks	M	T	W	T	F	S	S	Cleaned By	Date/Time
1	Wash And Sanitize All Counter Tops And Prep Area Surfaces									
2	Empty Dishwasher, Run The Dishwasher/Dish Drainer									
3	Disinfect Touch Points, Light Switches And Other Switches									
4	Take Out The Rubbish/Trash, Remove Waste And Recycling									
5	Clean & Disinfectant Bins/Waste Disposal Area & Trash Cans									
6	Wipe Down The Walls Wherever There Are Spills And Splashes									
7	Sweep The Floors To Ensure They're Free From Debris									
8	Mop Tiled And Laminate Floors With Disinfectant Cleaner									
9	Wet Floor Signs In Place If Floors Are Wet After Mopping									
10	Thoroughly Clean And Disinfect The Sinks And Taps									
11	Clean Exterior Of Appliances, Check For Spilled Food									
12	Replace Empty Paper Towel Rolls And Cloth Roller Towels									
13	Refill Soap Dispensers And Hand Sanitizers/Hand Gels									
14	Wipe Down Equipment, Tea And Coffee Makers, Toasters Etc									
15	Fire Exit Lights And Emergency Lights Checked & Functioning									
16	Pour Drain Cleaner Down Floor And Sink Drains									
17	Clean Inside Microwave, Check For Spilled Food									

	Daily/Weekly Kitchen Cleaning Tasks Continued	M	T	W	T	F	S	S	CLEANED BY	DATE/TIME
18	Replace Wash Rags, Cloths And Tea Towels With Clean Ones									
19	Wash Rags, Cloths, Tea Towels And Towels In Washing Machine									
20	Replace And Change Burned Out Light Bulbs/Broken Lights									
21	Clean Inside Of Dishwasher									
22	Sanitise Sponges Or Replace Damaged Sponges With New									
23	Dishes, Pots, Pans, And Utensils To Be Stored Away Properly									
24	Clean Out Refrigerator And Wipe Down Shelves And Drawers									
	Monthly Kitchen Cleaning Tasks	M	T	W	T	F	S	S	Cleaned By	Date/Time
1	Wash And Clean Air Vents									
2	Sort Through And Organize Cooking Utensils, Pans And Pots									
3	Wash And Clean Air Vents									
4	Check Plates, Cups And Glasses And Bin Anything Chipped									
5	Clean And Vacuum Central Heating Units									
6	Wash And Clean Light Covers									
7	Clean And De-Lime Dishwasher									
8	Dust And Clean Ceilings, Ceiling Corners And Ceiling Tiles									
9	Thoroughly Clean Grout And Tiles									
10	Clean Refrigerator Coils To Remove Dust, Unplug First									
11	Run Cleaning & Sanitizing Chemicals Through Coffee Machine									
12	Disinfect And Clean All The Walls From Top To Bottom									
13	Check For Out Of Date Food In Cabinets/Cupboards									
14	Clean Skirting Boards/Baseboards And Corners									
15	Clean Under Refrigerator									
16	Wash And Clean Doors, Door Frames And Glass									
17	Sort Through Leftover Items In The Fridge/Refrigerators									
18	Wash And Clean Windows (Inside And Outside)									
19	Replace Pest Traps									

ESSENTIAL CLEANING NOTES

....

....

....

....

....

....

....

....

....

ESSENTIAL OFFICE CLEANING *Checklist*

Location/Building	Department	Office Number	Week Number

Start Date & Time	Finnish Date & Time	Name	Signature

	Daily/Weekly Office Cleaning Tasks	M	T	W	T	F	S	S	Cleaned By	Date/Time
1	Clean And Sanitize All The Desks And Tables									
2	Clean And Sanitize All The Counter Tops And Surface Areas									
3	Disinfect All Point-Of-Sale Terminals And Touch Screens									
4	Disinfect Touch Points, Light Switches And Other Switches									
5	Clean And Sanitize All Keyboards And Computer Mice									
6	Wipe Down The Walls Wherever There Are Spills And Splashes									
7	Clean And Disinfect All Doors, Door Handles And Doorknobs									
8	Re-Stock Protective Clothing, Face Masks/Shields, Gloves									
9	Clean And Sanitize All The Chairs, Seats And Benches									
10	Clean All The Mirrors, Glass Cabinets/Displays									
11	Replace And Change Burned Out Light Bulbs/Broken Lights									
12	Sweep The Floors To Ensure They're Free From Debris									
13	Mop Tiled And Laminate Floors With Disinfectant Cleaner									
14	Vacuum And Hoover The Carpets, Mats And Rugs									
15	Place Wet Floor Signs If Floors Are Wet After Mopping									
16	Wash & Clean Dirty Cups, Drinking Bottles And Glasses									
17	Clean & Re-Stock Paper Dispensers & Paper Towel Rolls									
18	Wipe Down Equipment & Sanitize Tea And Coffee Makers									
19	Refill Soap Dispensers, Sanitizers And Hand Gels									
20	Clean And Dust Furniture And Office Equipment									
21	Take Out The Rubbish/Trash, Remove Waste And Recycling									
22	Clean & Disinfectant Bins/Waste Disposal Area & Trash Cans									
23	Clean And Wipe Down Windowsills									
24	Vacuum Furnishings, Cushions, Chairs, Sofas And Couches									
25	Spray Air Freshener									
26	Clean And Disinfect Any Cabinets, Shelves And Units									
27	Clean Surfaces And Desk/Work Dividers									
28	Clean And Disinfect Telephones And Headsets									
29	Polish Any Wooden Furniture And Hardwood Surfaces									

	Monthly Office Cleaning Tasks	M	T	W	T	F	S	S	Cleaned By	Date/Time
1	Clean Skirting Boards/Baseboards And Corners									
2	Clean And Disinfect All The Walls From Top To Bottom									
3	Clean Blinds (Take Down And Wash If Possible)									
4	Wash And Clean Windows (Inside And Outside)									
5	Clean And Disinfect Shared Surfaces									
6	Steam Clean Carpets And Rugs									
7	Dust And Clean Ceilings, Ceiling Corners And Ceiling Tiles									
8	Check For Broken Chairs And Tables									
9	Dust And Wash Radiator Covers									
10	Clean And Disinfect Ceiling Wall Vents									
11	Clean And Vacuum Central Heating Units									
12	Wash And Clean Light Covers									
13	Clean Drapes And Curtains (Take Down And Wash if Possible)									
14	Check Cleaning Supplies And Re-Stock As Necessary									
15	Check Ceiling Fans, Fire Sprinklers And Smoke Alarms									
16	Check Hardware, Door Stops And Lock Mechanisms									
17	Fire Exit Lights And Emergency Lights Checked & Functioning									
18	Organize And De-Clutter Office Drawers									
19	Organize And De-Clutter Storeroom									
	Daily/Weekly Toilets/Restroom Cleaning Tasks	M	T	W	T	F	S	S	Cleaned By	Date/Time
1	Clean And Disinfect All Doors, Door Handles And Doorknobs									
2	Disinfect Touch Points, Light Switches And Other Switches									
3	Toilet Roll Holders Cleaned And Disinfected And Re-Stocked									
4	Wipe Down The Walls Wherever There Are Spills And Splashes									
5	Electric Hand Dryers Cleaned, Disinfected & Operating Correctly									
6	Sweep The Floors To Ensure They're Free From Debris									
7	Mop Tiled And Laminate Floors With Disinfectant Cleaner									
8	Paper Dispensers & Paper Towel Rolls Cleaned & Re-Stocked									
9	Take Out The Rubbish/Trash, Remove Waste And Recycling									
10	Clean & Disinfectant Bins/Waste Disposal Area & Trash Cans									
11	Feminine Hygiene Bins/Containers Cleaned And Disinfected									
12	Toilets Cleaned & Disinfected, Outside, Inside And Handles									
13	Urinals & Urinal Screens Cleaned, Disinfected & Blocks Replaced									
14	Wall Mirrors Cleaned With Glass Cleaner									
15	Clean And Re-Stock Paper Dispensers & Paper Towel Rolls									
16	Refill Soap Dispensers, Sanitizers And Hand Gels									
17	Sinks, Taps, Fixtures, Surface Areas Cleaned And Disinfected									

	Daily/Weekly Toilets/Restroom Cleaning Tasks Con	M	T	W	T	F	S	S	Cleaned By	Date/Time
18	Windowsills Clean And Wiped Down									
19	Check Plumbing And Schedule Work If Required									
20	Air Fresheners Checked And Replaced									
21	Fire Exit Lights And Emergency Lights Checked & Functioning									
22	Place Wet Floor Signs If Floors Are Wet After Mopping									
23	Cabinets Cleaned And Disinfected									
	Monthly Toilets/Restroom Cleaning Tasks	M	T	W	T	F	S	S	Cleaned By	Date/Time
1	Toilet/Restroom Service Storeroom/Cupboard Clean And Tidy									
2	Walls Free Of Graffiti, Stickers, Gum And Residue									
3	Wash And Clean Windows (Inside And Outside)									
4	Check Hardware, Door Stops And Lock Mechanisms									
5	All Fittings Securely Fixed (Schedule Maintenance If Not)									
6	Dust And Clean Ceilings, Ceiling Corners And Ceiling Tiles									
7	Clean Skirting Boards/Baseboards And Corners									
8	Thoroughly Clean Grout And Tiles									
9	Ceiling Wall Vents Cleaned And Disinfected									
10	Clean And Vacuum Central Heating Units									
11	Wash And Clean Light Covers									
12	Wash All Toilet And Restroom Mats									
	Daily/Weekly Kitchen Cleaning Tasks	M	T	W	T	F	S	S	Cleaned By	Date/Time
1	Wash And Sanitize All Counter Tops And Prep Area Surfaces									
2	Empty Dishwasher, Run The Dishwasher/Dish Drainer									
3	Disinfect Touch Points, Light Switches And Other Switches									
4	Take Out The Rubbish/Trash, Remove Waste And Recycling									
5	Clean & Disinfectant Bins/Waste Disposal Area & Trash Cans									
6	Wipe Down The Walls Wherever There Are Spills And Splashes									
7	Sweep The Floors To Ensure They're Free From Debris									
8	Mop Tiled And Laminate Floors With Disinfectant Cleaner									
9	Wet Floor Signs In Place If Floors Are Wet After Mopping									
10	Thoroughly Clean And Disinfect The Sinks And Taps									
11	Clean Exterior Of Appliances, Check For Spilled Food									
12	Replace Empty Paper Towel Rolls And Cloth Roller Towels									
13	Refill Soap Dispensers And Hand Sanitizers/Hand Gels									
14	Wipe Down Equipment, Tea And Coffee Makers, Toasters Etc									
15	Fire Exit Lights And Emergency Lights Checked & Functioning									
16	Pour Drain Cleaner Down Floor And Sink Drains									
17	Clean Inside Microwave, Check For Spilled Food									

	Daily/Weekly Kitchen Cleaning Tasks Continued	M	T	W	T	F	S	S	CLEANED BY	DATE/TIME
18	Replace Wash Rags, Cloths And Tea Towels With Clean Ones									
19	Wash Rags, Cloths, Tea Towels And Towels In Washing Machine									
20	Replace And Change Burned Out Light Bulbs/Broken Lights									
21	Clean Inside Of Dishwasher									
22	Sanitise Sponges Or Replace Damaged Sponges With New									
23	Dishes, Pots, Pans, And Utensils To Be Stored Away Properly									
24	Clean Out Refrigerator And Wipe Down Shelves And Drawers									
	Monthly Kitchen Cleaning Tasks	M	T	W	T	F	S	S	Cleaned By	Date/Time
1	Wash And Clean Air Vents									
2	Sort Through And Organize Cooking Utensils, Pans And Pots									
3	Wash And Clean Air Vents									
4	Check Plates, Cups And Glasses And Bin Anything Chipped									
5	Clean And Vacuum Central Heating Units									
6	Wash And Clean Light Covers									
7	Clean And De-Lime Dishwasher									
8	Dust And Clean Ceilings, Ceiling Corners And Ceiling Tiles									
9	Thoroughly Clean Grout And Tiles									
10	Clean Refrigerator Coils To Remove Dust, Unplug First									
11	Run Cleaning & Sanitizing Chemicals Through Coffee Machine									
12	Disinfect And Clean All The Walls From Top To Bottom									
13	Check For Out Of Date Food In Cabinets/Cupboards									
14	Clean Skirting Boards/Baseboards And Corners									
15	Clean Under Refrigerator									
16	Wash And Clean Doors, Door Frames And Glass									
17	Sort Through Leftover Items In The Fridge/Refrigerators									
18	Wash And Clean Windows (Inside And Outside)									
19	Replace Pest Traps									

ESSENTIAL CLEANING NOTES

....

....

....

....

....

....

....

....

ESSENTIAL OFFICE CLEANING *Checklist*

Location/Building	Department	Office Number	Week Number

Start Date & Time	Finnish Date & Time	Name	Signature

	Daily/Weekly Office Cleaning Tasks	M	T	W	T	F	S	S	Cleaned By	Date/Time
1	Clean And Sanitize All The Desks And Tables									
2	Clean And Sanitize All The Counter Tops And Surface Areas									
3	Disinfect All Point-Of-Sale Terminals And Touch Screens									
4	Disinfect Touch Points, Light Switches And Other Switches									
5	Clean And Sanitize All Keyboards And Computer Mice									
6	Wipe Down The Walls Wherever There Are Spills And Splashes									
7	Clean And Disinfect All Doors, Door Handles And Doorknobs									
8	Re-Stock Protective Clothing, Face Masks/Shields, Gloves									
9	Clean And Sanitize All The Chairs, Seats And Benches									
10	Clean All The Mirrors, Glass Cabinets/Displays									
11	Replace And Change Burned Out Light Bulbs/Broken Lights									
12	Sweep The Floors To Ensure They're Free From Debris									
13	Mop Tiled And Laminate Floors With Disinfectant Cleaner									
14	Vacuum And Hoover The Carpets, Mats And Rugs									
15	Place Wet Floor Signs If Floors Are Wet After Mopping									
16	Wash & Clean Dirty Cups, Drinking Bottles And Glasses									
17	Clean & Re-Stock Paper Dispensers & Paper Towel Rolls									
18	Wipe Down Equipment & Sanitize Tea And Coffee Makers									
19	Refill Soap Dispensers, Sanitizers And Hand Gels									
20	Clean And Dust Furniture And Office Equipment									
21	Take Out The Rubbish/Trash, Remove Waste And Recycling									
22	Clean & Disinfectant Bins/Waste Disposal Area & Trash Cans									
23	Clean And Wipe Down Windowsills									
24	Vacuum Furnishings, Cushions, Chairs, Sofas And Couches									
25	Spray Air Freshener									
26	Clean And Disinfect Any Cabinets, Shelves And Units									
27	Clean Surfaces And Desk/Work Dividers									
28	Clean And Disinfect Telephones And Headsets									
29	Polish Any Wooden Furniture And Hardwood Surfaces									

	Monthly Office Cleaning Tasks	M	T	W	T	F	S	S	Cleaned By	Date/Time
1	Clean Skirting Boards/Baseboards And Corners									
2	Clean And Disinfect All The Walls From Top To Bottom									
3	Clean Blinds (Take Down And Wash If Possible)									
4	Wash And Clean Windows (Inside And Outside)									
5	Clean And Disinfect Shared Surfaces									
6	Steam Clean Carpets And Rugs									
7	Dust And Clean Ceilings, Ceiling Corners And Ceiling Tiles									
8	Check For Broken Chairs And Tables									
9	Dust And Wash Radiator Covers									
10	Clean And Disinfect Ceiling Wall Vents									
11	Clean And Vacuum Central Heating Units									
12	Wash And Clean Light Covers									
13	Clean Drapes And Curtains (Take Down And Wash if Possible)									
14	Check Cleaning Supplies And Re-Stock As Necessary									
15	Check Ceiling Fans, Fire Sprinklers And Smoke Alarms									
16	Check Hardware, Door Stops And Lock Mechanisms									
17	Fire Exit Lights And Emergency Lights Checked & Functioning									
18	Organize And De-Clutter Office Drawers									
19	Organize And De-Clutter Storeroom									
	Daily/Weekly Toilets/Restroom Cleaning Tasks	M	T	W	T	F	S	S	Cleaned By	Date/Time
1	Clean And Disinfect All Doors, Door Handles And Doorknobs									
2	Disinfect Touch Points, Light Switches And Other Switches									
3	Toilet Roll Holders Cleaned And Disinfected And Re-Stocked									
4	Wipe Down The Walls Wherever There Are Spills And Splashes									
5	Electric Hand Dryers Cleaned, Disinfected & Operating Correctly									
6	Sweep The Floors To Ensure They're Free From Debris									
7	Mop Tiled And Laminate Floors With Disinfectant Cleaner									
8	Paper Dispensers & Paper Towel Rolls Cleaned & Re-Stocked									
9	Take Out The Rubbish/Trash, Remove Waste And Recycling									
10	Clean & Disinfectant Bins/Waste Disposal Area & Trash Cans									
11	Feminine Hygiene Bins/Containers Cleaned And Disinfected									
12	Toilets Cleaned & Disinfected, Outside, Inside And Handles									
13	Urinals & Urinal Screens Cleaned, Disinfected & Blocks Replaced									
14	Wall Mirrors Cleaned With Glass Cleaner									
15	Clean And Re-Stock Paper Dispensers & Paper Towel Rolls									
16	Refill Soap Dispensers, Sanitizers And Hand Gels									
17	Sinks, Taps, Fixtures, Surface Areas Cleaned And Disinfected									

	Daily/Weekly Toilets/Restroom Cleaning Tasks Con	M	T	W	T	F	S	S	Cleaned By	Date/Time
18	Windowsills Clean And Wiped Down									
19	Check Plumbing And Schedule Work If Required									
20	Air Fresheners Checked And Replaced									
21	Fire Exit Lights And Emergency Lights Checked & Functioning									
22	Place Wet Floor Signs If Floors Are Wet After Mopping									
23	Cabinets Cleaned And Disinfected									
	Monthly Toilets/Restroom Cleaning Tasks	M	T	W	T	F	S	S	Cleaned By	Date/Time
1	Toilet/Restroom Service Storeroom/Cupboard Clean And Tidy									
2	Walls Free Of Graffiti, Stickers, Gum And Residue									
3	Wash And Clean Windows (Inside And Outside)									
4	Check Hardware, Door Stops And Lock Mechanisms									
5	All Fittings Securely Fixed (Schedule Maintenance If Not)									
6	Dust And Clean Ceilings, Ceiling Corners And Ceiling Tiles									
7	Clean Skirting Boards/Baseboards And Corners									
8	Thoroughly Clean Grout And Tiles									
9	Ceiling Wall Vents Cleaned And Disinfected									
10	Clean And Vacuum Central Heating Units									
11	Wash And Clean Light Covers									
12	Wash All Toilet And Restroom Mats									
	Daily/Weekly Kitchen Cleaning Tasks	M	T	W	T	F	S	S	Cleaned By	Date/Time
1	Wash And Sanitize All Counter Tops And Prep Area Surfaces									
2	Empty Dishwasher, Run The Dishwasher/Dish Drainer									
3	Disinfect Touch Points, Light Switches And Other Switches									
4	Take Out The Rubbish/Trash, Remove Waste And Recycling									
5	Clean & Disinfectant Bins/Waste Disposal Area & Trash Cans									
6	Wipe Down The Walls Wherever There Are Spills And Splashes									
7	Sweep The Floors To Ensure They're Free From Debris									
8	Mop Tiled And Laminate Floors With Disinfectant Cleaner									
9	Wet Floor Signs In Place If Floors Are Wet After Mopping									
10	Thoroughly Clean And Disinfect The Sinks And Taps									
11	Clean Exterior Of Appliances, Check For Spilled Food									
12	Replace Empty Paper Towel Rolls And Cloth Roller Towels									
13	Refill Soap Dispensers And Hand Sanitizers/Hand Gels									
14	Wipe Down Equipment, Tea And Coffee Makers, Toasters Etc									
15	Fire Exit Lights And Emergency Lights Checked & Functioning									
16	Pour Drain Cleaner Down Floor And Sink Drains									
17	Clean Inside Microwave, Check For Spilled Food									

	Daily/Weekly Kitchen Cleaning Tasks Continued	M	T	W	T	F	S	S	CLEANED BY	DATE/TIME
18	Replace Wash Rags, Cloths And Tea Towels With Clean Ones									
19	Wash Rags, Cloths, Tea Towels And Towels In Washing Machine									
20	Replace And Change Burned Out Light Bulbs/Broken Lights									
21	Clean Inside Of Dishwasher									
22	Sanitise Sponges Or Replace Damaged Sponges With New									
23	Dishes, Pots, Pans, And Utensils To Be Stored Away Properly									
24	Clean Out Refrigerator And Wipe Down Shelves And Drawers									
	Monthly Kitchen Cleaning Tasks	M	T	W	T	F	S	S	Cleaned By	Date/Time
1	Wash And Clean Air Vents									
2	Sort Through And Organize Cooking Utensils, Pans And Pots									
3	Wash And Clean Air Vents									
4	Check Plates, Cups And Glasses And Bin Anything Chipped									
5	Clean And Vacuum Central Heating Units									
6	Wash And Clean Light Covers									
7	Clean And De-Lime Dishwasher									
8	Dust And Clean Ceilings, Ceiling Corners And Ceiling Tiles									
9	Thoroughly Clean Grout And Tiles									
10	Clean Refrigerator Coils To Remove Dust, Unplug First									
11	Run Cleaning & Sanitizing Chemicals Through Coffee Machine									
12	Disinfect And Clean All The Walls From Top To Bottom									
13	Check For Out Of Date Food In Cabinets/Cupboards									
14	Clean Skirting Boards/Baseboards And Corners									
15	Clean Under Refrigerator									
16	Wash And Clean Doors, Door Frames And Glass									
17	Sort Through Leftover Items In The Fridge/Refrigerators									
18	Wash And Clean Windows (Inside And Outside)									
19	Replace Pest Traps									

ESSENTIAL CLEANING NOTES

....

....

....

....

....

....

....

ESSENTIAL OFFICE CLEANING *Checklist*

Location/Building	Department	Office Number	Week Number

Start Date & Time	Finnish Date & Time	Name	Signature

	Daily/Weekly Office Cleaning Tasks	M	T	W	T	F	S	S	Cleaned By	Date/Time
1	Clean And Sanitize All The Desks And Tables									
2	Clean And Sanitize All The Counter Tops And Surface Areas									
3	Disinfect All Point-Of-Sale Terminals And Touch Screens									
4	Disinfect Touch Points, Light Switches And Other Switches									
5	Clean And Sanitize All Keyboards And Computer Mice									
6	Wipe Down The Walls Wherever There Are Spills And Splashes									
7	Clean And Disinfect All Doors, Door Handles And Doorknobs									
8	Re-Stock Protective Clothing, Face Masks/Shields, Gloves									
9	Clean And Sanitize All The Chairs, Seats And Benches									
10	Clean All The Mirrors, Glass Cabinets/Displays									
11	Replace And Change Burned Out Light Bulbs/Broken Lights									
12	Sweep The Floors To Ensure They're Free From Debris									
13	Mop Tiled And Laminate Floors With Disinfectant Cleaner									
14	Vacuum And Hoover The Carpets, Mats And Rugs									
15	Place Wet Floor Signs If Floors Are Wet After Mopping									
16	Wash & Clean Dirty Cups, Drinking Bottles And Glasses									
17	Clean & Re-Stock Paper Dispensers & Paper Towel Rolls									
18	Wipe Down Equipment & Sanitize Tea And Coffee Makers									
19	Refill Soap Dispensers, Sanitizers And Hand Gels									
20	Clean And Dust Furniture And Office Equipment									
21	Take Out The Rubbish/Trash, Remove Waste And Recycling									
22	Clean & Disinfectant Bins/Waste Disposal Area & Trash Cans									
23	Clean And Wipe Down Windowsills									
24	Vacuum Furnishings, Cushions, Chairs, Sofas And Couches									
25	Spray Air Freshener									
26	Clean And Disinfect Any Cabinets, Shelves And Units									
27	Clean Surfaces And Desk/Work Dividers									
28	Clean And Disinfect Telephones And Headsets									
29	Polish Any Wooden Furniture And Hardwood Surfaces									

	Monthly Office Cleaning Tasks	M	T	W	T	F	S	S	Cleaned By	Date/Time
1	Clean Skirting Boards/Baseboards And Corners									
2	Clean And Disinfect All The Walls From Top To Bottom									
3	Clean Blinds (Take Down And Wash If Possible)									
4	Wash And Clean Windows (Inside And Outside)									
5	Clean And Disinfect Shared Surfaces									
6	Steam Clean Carpets And Rugs									
7	Dust And Clean Ceilings, Ceiling Corners And Ceiling Tiles									
8	Check For Broken Chairs And Tables									
9	Dust And Wash Radiator Covers									
10	Clean And Disinfect Ceiling Wall Vents									
11	Clean And Vacuum Central Heating Units									
12	Wash And Clean Light Covers									
13	Clean Drapes And Curtains (Take Down And Wash if Possible)									
14	Check Cleaning Supplies And Re-Stock As Necessary									
15	Check Ceiling Fans, Fire Sprinklers And Smoke Alarms									
16	Check Hardware, Door Stops And Lock Mechanisms									
17	Fire Exit Lights And Emergency Lights Checked & Functioning									
18	Organize And De-Clutter Office Drawers									
19	Organize And De-Clutter Storeroom									
	Daily/Weekly Toilets/Restroom Cleaning Tasks	M	T	W	T	F	S	S	Cleaned By	Date/Time
1	Clean And Disinfect All Doors, Door Handles And Doorknobs									
2	Disinfect Touch Points, Light Switches And Other Switches									
3	Toilet Roll Holders Cleaned And Disinfected And Re-Stocked									
4	Wipe Down The Walls Wherever There Are Spills And Splashes									
5	Electric Hand Dryers Cleaned, Disinfected & Operating Correctly									
6	Sweep The Floors To Ensure They're Free From Debris									
7	Mop Tiled And Laminate Floors With Disinfectant Cleaner									
8	Paper Dispensers & Paper Towel Rolls Cleaned & Re-Stocked									
9	Take Out The Rubbish/Trash, Remove Waste And Recycling									
10	Clean & Disinfectant Bins/Waste Disposal Area & Trash Cans									
11	Feminine Hygiene Bins/Containers Cleaned And Disinfected									
12	Toilets Cleaned & Disinfected, Outside, Inside And Handles									
13	Urinals & Urinal Screens Cleaned, Disinfected & Blocks Replaced									
14	Wall Mirrors Cleaned With Glass Cleaner									
15	Clean And Re-Stock Paper Dispensers & Paper Towel Rolls									
16	Refill Soap Dispensers, Sanitizers And Hand Gels									
17	Sinks, Taps, Fixtures, Surface Areas Cleaned And Disinfected									

	Daily/Weekly Toilets/Restroom Cleaning Tasks Con	M	T	W	T	F	S	S	Cleaned By	Date/Time
18	Windowsills Clean And Wiped Down									
19	Check Plumbing And Schedule Work If Required									
20	Air Fresheners Checked And Replaced									
21	Fire Exit Lights And Emergency Lights Checked & Functioning									
22	Place Wet Floor Signs If Floors Are Wet After Mopping									
23	Cabinets Cleaned And Disinfected									
	Monthly Toilets/Restroom Cleaning Tasks	M	T	W	T	F	S	S	Cleaned By	Date/Time
1	Toilet/Restroom Service Storeroom/Cupboard Clean And Tidy									
2	Walls Free Of Graffiti, Stickers, Gum And Residue									
3	Wash And Clean Windows (Inside And Outside)									
4	Check Hardware, Door Stops And Lock Mechanisms									
5	All Fittings Securely Fixed (Schedule Maintenance If Not)									
6	Dust And Clean Ceilings, Ceiling Corners And Ceiling Tiles									
7	Clean Skirting Boards/Baseboards And Corners									
8	Thoroughly Clean Grout And Tiles									
9	Ceiling Wall Vents Cleaned And Disinfected									
10	Clean And Vacuum Central Heating Units									
11	Wash And Clean Light Covers									
12	Wash All Toilet And Restroom Mats									
	Daily/Weekly Kitchen Cleaning Tasks	M	T	W	T	F	S	S	Cleaned By	Date/Time
1	Wash And Sanitize All Counter Tops And Prep Area Surfaces									
2	Empty Dishwasher, Run The Dishwasher/Dish Drainer									
3	Disinfect Touch Points, Light Switches And Other Switches									
4	Take Out The Rubbish/Trash, Remove Waste And Recycling									
5	Clean & Disinfectant Bins/Waste Disposal Area & Trash Cans									
6	Wipe Down The Walls Wherever There Are Spills And Splashes									
7	Sweep The Floors To Ensure They're Free From Debris									
8	Mop Tiled And Laminate Floors With Disinfectant Cleaner									
9	Wet Floor Signs In Place If Floors Are Wet After Mopping									
10	Thoroughly Clean And Disinfect The Sinks And Taps									
11	Clean Exterior Of Appliances, Check For Spilled Food									
12	Replace Empty Paper Towel Rolls And Cloth Roller Towels									
13	Refill Soap Dispensers And Hand Sanitizers/Hand Gels									
14	Wipe Down Equipment, Tea And Coffee Makers, Toasters Etc									
15	Fire Exit Lights And Emergency Lights Checked & Functioning									
16	Pour Drain Cleaner Down Floor And Sink Drains									
17	Clean Inside Microwave, Check For Spilled Food									

	Daily/Weekly Kitchen Cleaning Tasks Continued	M	T	W	T	F	S	S	CLEANED BY	DATE/TIME
18	Replace Wash Rags, Cloths And Tea Towels With Clean Ones									
19	Wash Rags, Cloths, Tea Towels And Towels In Washing Machine									
20	Replace And Change Burned Out Light Bulbs/Broken Lights									
21	Clean Inside Of Dishwasher									
22	Sanitise Sponges Or Replace Damaged Sponges With New									
23	Dishes, Pots, Pans, And Utensils To Be Stored Away Properly									
24	Clean Out Refrigerator And Wipe Down Shelves And Drawers									
	Monthly Kitchen Cleaning Tasks	M	T	W	T	F	S	S	Cleaned By	Date/Time
1	Wash And Clean Air Vents									
2	Sort Through And Organize Cooking Utensils, Pans And Pots									
3	Wash And Clean Air Vents									
4	Check Plates, Cups And Glasses And Bin Anything Chipped									
5	Clean And Vacuum Central Heating Units									
6	Wash And Clean Light Covers									
7	Clean And De-Lime Dishwasher									
8	Dust And Clean Ceilings, Ceiling Corners And Ceiling Tiles									
9	Thoroughly Clean Grout And Tiles									
10	Clean Refrigerator Coils To Remove Dust, Unplug First									
11	Run Cleaning & Sanitizing Chemicals Through Coffee Machine									
12	Disinfect And Clean All The Walls From Top To Bottom									
13	Check For Out Of Date Food In Cabinets/Cupboards									
14	Clean Skirting Boards/Baseboards And Corners									
15	Clean Under Refrigerator									
16	Wash And Clean Doors, Door Frames And Glass									
17	Sort Through Leftover Items In The Fridge/Refrigerators									
18	Wash And Clean Windows (Inside And Outside)									
19	Replace Pest Traps									

ESSENTIAL CLEANING NOTES

....

....

....

....

....

....

....

ESSENTIAL OFFICE CLEANING *Checklist*

Location/Building	Department	Office Number	Week Number

Start Date & Time	Finnish Date & Time	Name	Signature

	Daily/Weekly Office Cleaning Tasks	M	T	W	T	F	S	S	Cleaned By	Date/Time
1	Clean And Sanitize All The Desks And Tables									
2	Clean And Sanitize All The Counter Tops And Surface Areas									
3	Disinfect All Point-Of-Sale Terminals And Touch Screens									
4	Disinfect Touch Points, Light Switches And Other Switches									
5	Clean And Sanitize All Keyboards And Computer Mice									
6	Wipe Down The Walls Wherever There Are Spills And Splashes									
7	Clean And Disinfect All Doors, Door Handles And Doorknobs									
8	Re-Stock Protective Clothing, Face Masks/Shields, Gloves									
9	Clean And Sanitize All The Chairs, Seats And Benches									
10	Clean All The Mirrors, Glass Cabinets/Displays									
11	Replace And Change Burned Out Light Bulbs/Broken Lights									
12	Sweep The Floors To Ensure They're Free From Debris									
13	Mop Tiled And Laminate Floors With Disinfectant Cleaner									
14	Vacuum And Hoover The Carpets, Mats And Rugs									
15	Place Wet Floor Signs If Floors Are Wet After Mopping									
16	Wash & Clean Dirty Cups, Drinking Bottles And Glasses									
17	Clean & Re-Stock Paper Dispensers & Paper Towel Rolls									
18	Wipe Down Equipment & Sanitize Tea And Coffee Makers									
19	Refill Soap Dispensers, Sanitizers And Hand Gels									
20	Clean And Dust Furniture And Office Equipment									
21	Take Out The Rubbish/Trash, Remove Waste And Recycling									
22	Clean & Disinfectant Bins/Waste Disposal Area & Trash Cans									
23	Clean And Wipe Down Windowsills									
24	Vacuum Furnishings, Cushions, Chairs, Sofas And Couches									
25	Spray Air Freshener									
26	Clean And Disinfect Any Cabinets, Shelves And Units									
27	Clean Surfaces And Desk/Work Dividers									
28	Clean And Disinfect Telephones And Headsets									
29	Polish Any Wooden Furniture And Hardwood Surfaces									

	Monthly Office Cleaning Tasks	M	T	W	T	F	S	S	Cleaned By	Date/Time
1	Clean Skirting Boards/Baseboards And Corners									
2	Clean And Disinfect All The Walls From Top To Bottom									
3	Clean Blinds (Take Down And Wash If Possible)									
4	Wash And Clean Windows (Inside And Outside)									
5	Clean And Disinfect Shared Surfaces									
6	Steam Clean Carpets And Rugs									
7	Dust And Clean Ceilings, Ceiling Corners And Ceiling Tiles									
8	Check For Broken Chairs And Tables									
9	Dust And Wash Radiator Covers									
10	Clean And Disinfect Ceiling Wall Vents									
11	Clean And Vacuum Central Heating Units									
12	Wash And Clean Light Covers									
13	Clean Drapes And Curtains (Take Down And Wash if Possible)									
14	Check Cleaning Supplies And Re-Stock As Necessary									
15	Check Ceiling Fans, Fire Sprinklers And Smoke Alarms									
16	Check Hardware, Door Stops And Lock Mechanisms									
17	Fire Exit Lights And Emergency Lights Checked & Functioning									
18	Organize And De-Clutter Office Drawers									
19	Organize And De-Clutter Storeroom									

	Daily/Weekly Toilets/Restroom Cleaning Tasks	M	T	W	T	F	S	S	Cleaned By	Date/Time
1	Clean And Disinfect All Doors, Door Handles And Doorknobs									
2	Disinfect Touch Points, Light Switches And Other Switches									
3	Toilet Roll Holders Cleaned And Disinfected And Re-Stocked									
4	Wipe Down The Walls Wherever There Are Spills And Splashes									
5	Electric Hand Dryers Cleaned, Disinfected & Operating Correctly									
6	Sweep The Floors To Ensure They're Free From Debris									
7	Mop Tiled And Laminate Floors With Disinfectant Cleaner									
8	Paper Dispensers & Paper Towel Rolls Cleaned & Re-Stocked									
9	Take Out The Rubbish/Trash, Remove Waste And Recycling									
10	Clean & Disinfectant Bins/Waste Disposal Area & Trash Cans									
11	Feminine Hygiene Bins/Containers Cleaned And Disinfected									
12	Toilets Cleaned & Disinfected, Outside, Inside And Handles									
13	Urinals & Urinal Screens Cleaned, Disinfected & Blocks Replaced									
14	Wall Mirrors Cleaned With Glass Cleaner									
15	Clean And Re-Stock Paper Dispensers & Paper Towel Rolls									
16	Refill Soap Dispensers, Sanitizers And Hand Gels									
17	Sinks, Taps, Fixtures, Surface Areas Cleaned And Disinfected									

	Daily/Weekly Toilets/Restroom Cleaning Tasks Con	M	T	W	T	F	S	S	Cleaned By	Date/Time
18	Windowsills Clean And Wiped Down									
19	Check Plumbing And Schedule Work If Required									
20	Air Fresheners Checked And Replaced									
21	Fire Exit Lights And Emergency Lights Checked & Functioning									
22	Place Wet Floor Signs If Floors Are Wet After Mopping									
23	Cabinets Cleaned And Disinfected									
	Monthly Toilets/Restroom Cleaning Tasks	M	T	W	T	F	S	S	Cleaned By	Date/Time
1	Toilet/Restroom Service Storeroom/Cupboard Clean And Tidy									
2	Walls Free Of Graffiti, Stickers, Gum And Residue									
3	Wash And Clean Windows (Inside And Outside)									
4	Check Hardware, Door Stops And Lock Mechanisms									
5	All Fittings Securely Fixed (Schedule Maintenance If Not)									
6	Dust And Clean Ceilings, Ceiling Corners And Ceiling Tiles									
7	Clean Skirting Boards/Baseboards And Corners									
8	Thoroughly Clean Grout And Tiles									
9	Ceiling Wall Vents Cleaned And Disinfected									
10	Clean And Vacuum Central Heating Units									
11	Wash And Clean Light Covers									
12	Wash All Toilet And Restroom Mats									
	Daily/Weekly Kitchen Cleaning Tasks	M	T	W	T	F	S	S	Cleaned By	Date/Time
1	Wash And Sanitize All Counter Tops And Prep Area Surfaces									
2	Empty Dishwasher, Run The Dishwasher/Dish Drainer									
3	Disinfect Touch Points, Light Switches And Other Switches									
4	Take Out The Rubbish/Trash, Remove Waste And Recycling									
5	Clean & Disinfectant Bins/Waste Disposal Area & Trash Cans									
6	Wipe Down The Walls Wherever There Are Spills And Splashes									
7	Sweep The Floors To Ensure They're Free From Debris									
8	Mop Tiled And Laminate Floors With Disinfectant Cleaner									
9	Wet Floor Signs In Place If Floors Are Wet After Mopping									
10	Thoroughly Clean And Disinfect The Sinks And Taps									
11	Clean Exterior Of Appliances, Check For Spilled Food									
12	Replace Empty Paper Towel Rolls And Cloth Roller Towels									
13	Refill Soap Dispensers And Hand Sanitizers/Hand Gels									
14	Wipe Down Equipment, Tea And Coffee Makers, Toasters Etc									
15	Fire Exit Lights And Emergency Lights Checked & Functioning									
16	Pour Drain Cleaner Down Floor And Sink Drains									
17	Clean Inside Microwave, Check For Spilled Food									

	Daily/Weekly Kitchen Cleaning Tasks Continued	M	T	W	T	F	S	S	CLEANED BY	DATE/TIME
18	Replace Wash Rags, Cloths And Tea Towels With Clean Ones									
19	Wash Rags, Cloths, Tea Towels And Towels In Washing Machine									
20	Replace And Change Burned Out Light Bulbs/Broken Lights									
21	Clean Inside Of Dishwasher									
22	Sanitise Sponges Or Replace Damaged Sponges With New									
23	Dishes, Pots, Pans, And Utensils To Be Stored Away Properly									
24	Clean Out Refrigerator And Wipe Down Shelves And Drawers									
	Monthly Kitchen Cleaning Tasks	M	T	W	T	F	S	S	Cleaned By	Date/Time
1	Wash And Clean Air Vents									
2	Sort Through And Organize Cooking Utensils, Pans And Pots									
3	Wash And Clean Air Vents									
4	Check Plates, Cups And Glasses And Bin Anything Chipped									
5	Clean And Vacuum Central Heating Units									
6	Wash And Clean Light Covers									
7	Clean And De-Lime Dishwasher									
8	Dust And Clean Ceilings, Ceiling Corners And Ceiling Tiles									
9	Thoroughly Clean Grout And Tiles									
10	Clean Refrigerator Coils To Remove Dust, Unplug First									
11	Run Cleaning & Sanitizing Chemicals Through Coffee Machine									
12	Disinfect And Clean All The Walls From Top To Bottom									
13	Check For Out Of Date Food In Cabinets/Cupboards									
14	Clean Skirting Boards/Baseboards And Corners									
15	Clean Under Refrigerator									
16	Wash And Clean Doors, Door Frames And Glass									
17	Sort Through Leftover Items In The Fridge/Refrigerators									
18	Wash And Clean Windows (Inside And Outside)									
19	Replace Pest Traps									

ESSENTIAL CLEANING NOTES

....

....

....

....

....

....

....

ESSENTIAL OFFICE CLEANING *Checklist*

Location/Building	Department	Office Number	Week Number

Start Date & Time	Finnish Date & Time	Name	Signature

	Daily/Weekly Office Cleaning Tasks	M	T	W	T	F	S	S	Cleaned By	Date/Time
1	Clean And Sanitize All The Desks And Tables									
2	Clean And Sanitize All The Counter Tops And Surface Areas									
3	Disinfect All Point-Of-Sale Terminals And Touch Screens									
4	Disinfect Touch Points, Light Switches And Other Switches									
5	Clean And Sanitize All Keyboards And Computer Mice									
6	Wipe Down The Walls Wherever There Are Spills And Splashes									
7	Clean And Disinfect All Doors, Door Handles And Doorknobs									
8	Re-Stock Protective Clothing, Face Masks/Shields, Gloves									
9	Clean And Sanitize All The Chairs, Seats And Benches									
10	Clean All The Mirrors, Glass Cabinets/Displays									
11	Replace And Change Burned Out Light Bulbs/Broken Lights									
12	Sweep The Floors To Ensure They're Free From Debris									
13	Mop Tiled And Laminate Floors With Disinfectant Cleaner									
14	Vacuum And Hoover The Carpets, Mats And Rugs									
15	Place Wet Floor Signs If Floors Are Wet After Mopping									
16	Wash & Clean Dirty Cups, Drinking Bottles And Glasses									
17	Clean & Re-Stock Paper Dispensers & Paper Towel Rolls									
18	Wipe Down Equipment & Sanitize Tea And Coffee Makers									
19	Refill Soap Dispensers, Sanitizers And Hand Gels									
20	Clean And Dust Furniture And Office Equipment									
21	Take Out The Rubbish/Trash, Remove Waste And Recycling									
22	Clean & Disinfectant Bins/Waste Disposal Area & Trash Cans									
23	Clean And Wipe Down Windowsills									
24	Vacuum Furnishings, Cushions, Chairs, Sofas And Couches									
25	Spray Air Freshener									
26	Clean And Disinfect Any Cabinets, Shelves And Units									
27	Clean Surfaces And Desk/Work Dividers									
28	Clean And Disinfect Telephones And Headsets									
29	Polish Any Wooden Furniture And Hardwood Surfaces									

	Monthly Office Cleaning Tasks	M	T	W	T	F	S	S	Cleaned By	Date/Time
1	Clean Skirting Boards/Baseboards And Corners									
2	Clean And Disinfect All The Walls From Top To Bottom									
3	Clean Blinds (Take Down And Wash If Possible)									
4	Wash And Clean Windows (Inside And Outside)									
5	Clean And Disinfect Shared Surfaces									
6	Steam Clean Carpets And Rugs									
7	Dust And Clean Ceilings, Ceiling Corners And Ceiling Tiles									
8	Check For Broken Chairs And Tables									
9	Dust And Wash Radiator Covers									
10	Clean And Disinfect Ceiling Wall Vents									
11	Clean And Vacuum Central Heating Units									
12	Wash And Clean Light Covers									
13	Clean Drapes And Curtains (Take Down And Wash if Possible)									
14	Check Cleaning Supplies And Re-Stock As Necessary									
15	Check Ceiling Fans, Fire Sprinklers And Smoke Alarms									
16	Check Hardware, Door Stops And Lock Mechanisms									
17	Fire Exit Lights And Emergency Lights Checked & Functioning									
18	Organize And De-Clutter Office Drawers									
19	Organize And De-Clutter Storeroom									

	Daily/Weekly Toilets/Restroom Cleaning Tasks	M	T	W	T	F	S	S	Cleaned By	Date/Time
1	Clean And Disinfect All Doors, Door Handles And Doorknobs									
2	Disinfect Touch Points, Light Switches And Other Switches									
3	Toilet Roll Holders Cleaned And Disinfected And Re-Stocked									
4	Wipe Down The Walls Wherever There Are Spills And Splashes									
5	Electric Hand Dryers Cleaned, Disinfected & Operating Correctly									
6	Sweep The Floors To Ensure They're Free From Debris									
7	Mop Tiled And Laminate Floors With Disinfectant Cleaner									
8	Paper Dispensers & Paper Towel Rolls Cleaned & Re-Stocked									
9	Take Out The Rubbish/Trash, Remove Waste And Recycling									
10	Clean & Disinfectant Bins/Waste Disposal Area & Trash Cans									
11	Feminine Hygiene Bins/Containers Cleaned And Disinfected									
12	Toilets Cleaned & Disinfected, Outside, Inside And Handles									
13	Urinals & Urinal Screens Cleaned, Disinfected & Blocks Replaced									
14	Wall Mirrors Cleaned With Glass Cleaner									
15	Clean And Re-Stock Paper Dispensers & Paper Towel Rolls									
16	Refill Soap Dispensers, Sanitizers And Hand Gels									
17	Sinks, Taps, Fixtures, Surface Areas Cleaned And Disinfected									

	Daily/Weekly Toilets/Restroom Cleaning Tasks Con	M	T	W	T	F	S	S	Cleaned By	Date/Time
18	Windowsills Clean And Wiped Down									
19	Check Plumbing And Schedule Work If Required									
20	Air Fresheners Checked And Replaced									
21	Fire Exit Lights And Emergency Lights Checked & Functioning									
22	Place Wet Floor Signs If Floors Are Wet After Mopping									
23	Cabinets Cleaned And Disinfected									
	Monthly Toilets/Restroom Cleaning Tasks	M	T	W	T	F	S	S	Cleaned By	Date/Time
1	Toilet/Restroom Service Storeroom/Cupboard Clean And Tidy									
2	Walls Free Of Graffiti, Stickers, Gum And Residue									
3	Wash And Clean Windows (Inside And Outside)									
4	Check Hardware, Door Stops And Lock Mechanisms									
5	All Fittings Securely Fixed (Schedule Maintenance If Not)									
6	Dust And Clean Ceilings, Ceiling Corners And Ceiling Tiles									
7	Clean Skirting Boards/Baseboards And Corners									
8	Thoroughly Clean Grout And Tiles									
9	Ceiling Wall Vents Cleaned And Disinfected									
10	Clean And Vacuum Central Heating Units									
11	Wash And Clean Light Covers									
12	Wash All Toilet And Restroom Mats									
	Daily/Weekly Kitchen Cleaning Tasks	M	T	W	T	F	S	S	Cleaned By	Date/Time
1	Wash And Sanitize All Counter Tops And Prep Area Surfaces									
2	Empty Dishwasher, Run The Dishwasher/Dish Drainer									
3	Disinfect Touch Points, Light Switches And Other Switches									
4	Take Out The Rubbish/Trash, Remove Waste And Recycling									
5	Clean & Disinfectant Bins/Waste Disposal Area & Trash Cans									
6	Wipe Down The Walls Wherever There Are Spills And Splashes									
7	Sweep The Floors To Ensure They're Free From Debris									
8	Mop Tiled And Laminate Floors With Disinfectant Cleaner									
9	Wet Floor Signs In Place If Floors Are Wet After Mopping									
10	Thoroughly Clean And Disinfect The Sinks And Taps									
11	Clean Exterior Of Appliances, Check For Spilled Food									
12	Replace Empty Paper Towel Rolls And Cloth Roller Towels									
13	Refill Soap Dispensers And Hand Sanitizers/Hand Gels									
14	Wipe Down Equipment, Tea And Coffee Makers, Toasters Etc									
15	Fire Exit Lights And Emergency Lights Checked & Functioning									
16	Pour Drain Cleaner Down Floor And Sink Drains									
17	Clean Inside Microwave, Check For Spilled Food									

	Daily/Weekly Kitchen Cleaning Tasks Continued	M	T	W	T	F	S	S	CLEANED BY	DATE/TIME
18	Replace Wash Rags, Cloths And Tea Towels With Clean Ones									
19	Wash Rags, Cloths, Tea Towels And Towels In Washing Machine									
20	Replace And Change Burned Out Light Bulbs/Broken Lights									
21	Clean Inside Of Dishwasher									
22	Sanitise Sponges Or Replace Damaged Sponges With New									
23	Dishes, Pots, Pans, And Utensils To Be Stored Away Properly									
24	Clean Out Refrigerator And Wipe Down Shelves And Drawers									
	Monthly Kitchen Cleaning Tasks	M	T	W	T	F	S	S	Cleaned By	Date/Time
1	Wash And Clean Air Vents									
2	Sort Through And Organize Cooking Utensils, Pans And Pots									
3	Wash And Clean Air Vents									
4	Check Plates, Cups And Glasses And Bin Anything Chipped									
5	Clean And Vacuum Central Heating Units									
6	Wash And Clean Light Covers									
7	Clean And De-Lime Dishwasher									
8	Dust And Clean Ceilings, Ceiling Corners And Ceiling Tiles									
9	Thoroughly Clean Grout And Tiles									
10	Clean Refrigerator Coils To Remove Dust, Unplug First									
11	Run Cleaning & Sanitizing Chemicals Through Coffee Machine									
12	Disinfect And Clean All The Walls From Top To Bottom									
13	Check For Out Of Date Food In Cabinets/Cupboards									
14	Clean Skirting Boards/Baseboards And Corners									
15	Clean Under Refrigerator									
16	Wash And Clean Doors, Door Frames And Glass									
17	Sort Through Leftover Items In The Fridge/Refrigerators									
18	Wash And Clean Windows (Inside And Outside)									
19	Replace Pest Traps									

ESSENTIAL CLEANING NOTES

....

....

....

....

....

....

....

....

....

....

ESSENTIAL OFFICE CLEANING *Checklist*

Location/Building	Department	Office Number	Week Number

Start Date & Time	Finnish Date & Time	Name	Signature

	Daily/Weekly Office Cleaning Tasks	M	T	W	T	F	S	S	Cleaned By	Date/Time
1	Clean And Sanitize All The Desks And Tables									
2	Clean And Sanitize All The Counter Tops And Surface Areas									
3	Disinfect All Point-Of-Sale Terminals And Touch Screens									
4	Disinfect Touch Points, Light Switches And Other Switches									
5	Clean And Sanitize All Keyboards And Computer Mice									
6	Wipe Down The Walls Wherever There Are Spills And Splashes									
7	Clean And Disinfect All Doors, Door Handles And Doorknobs									
8	Re-Stock Protective Clothing, Face Masks/Shields, Gloves									
9	Clean And Sanitize All The Chairs, Seats And Benches									
10	Clean All The Mirrors, Glass Cabinets/Displays									
11	Replace And Change Burned Out Light Bulbs/Broken Lights									
12	Sweep The Floors To Ensure They're Free From Debris									
13	Mop Tiled And Laminate Floors With Disinfectant Cleaner									
14	Vacuum And Hoover The Carpets, Mats And Rugs									
15	Place Wet Floor Signs If Floors Are Wet After Mopping									
16	Wash & Clean Dirty Cups, Drinking Bottles And Glasses									
17	Clean & Re-Stock Paper Dispensers & Paper Towel Rolls									
18	Wipe Down Equipment & Sanitize Tea And Coffee Makers									
19	Refill Soap Dispensers, Sanitizers And Hand Gels									
20	Clean And Dust Furniture And Office Equipment									
21	Take Out The Rubbish/Trash, Remove Waste And Recycling									
22	Clean & Disinfectant Bins/Waste Disposal Area & Trash Cans									
23	Clean And Wipe Down Windowsills									
24	Vacuum Furnishings, Cushions, Chairs, Sofas And Couches									
25	Spray Air Freshener									
26	Clean And Disinfect Any Cabinets, Shelves And Units									
27	Clean Surfaces And Desk/Work Dividers									
28	Clean And Disinfect Telephones And Headsets									
29	Polish Any Wooden Furniture And Hardwood Surfaces									

	Monthly Office Cleaning Tasks	M	T	W	T	F	S	S	Cleaned By	Date/Time
1	Clean Skirting Boards/Baseboards And Corners									
2	Clean And Disinfect All The Walls From Top To Bottom									
3	Clean Blinds (Take Down And Wash If Possible)									
4	Wash And Clean Windows (Inside And Outside)									
5	Clean And Disinfect Shared Surfaces									
6	Steam Clean Carpets And Rugs									
7	Dust And Clean Ceilings, Ceiling Corners And Ceiling Tiles									
8	Check For Broken Chairs And Tables									
9	Dust And Wash Radiator Covers									
10	Clean And Disinfect Ceiling Wall Vents									
11	Clean And Vacuum Central Heating Units									
12	Wash And Clean Light Covers									
13	Clean Drapes And Curtains (Take Down And Wash if Possible)									
14	Check Cleaning Supplies And Re-Stock As Necessary									
15	Check Ceiling Fans, Fire Sprinklers And Smoke Alarms									
16	Check Hardware, Door Stops And Lock Mechanisms									
17	Fire Exit Lights And Emergency Lights Checked & Functioning									
18	Organize And De-Clutter Office Drawers									
19	Organize And De-Clutter Storeroom									

	Daily/Weekly Toilets/Restroom Cleaning Tasks	M	T	W	T	F	S	S	Cleaned By	Date/Time
1	Clean And Disinfect All Doors, Door Handles And Doorknobs									
2	Disinfect Touch Points, Light Switches And Other Switches									
3	Toilet Roll Holders Cleaned And Disinfected And Re-Stocked									
4	Wipe Down The Walls Wherever There Are Spills And Splashes									
5	Electric Hand Dryers Cleaned, Disinfected & Operating Correctly									
6	Sweep The Floors To Ensure They're Free From Debris									
7	Mop Tiled And Laminate Floors With Disinfectant Cleaner									
8	Paper Dispensers & Paper Towel Rolls Cleaned & Re-Stocked									
9	Take Out The Rubbish/Trash, Remove Waste And Recycling									
10	Clean & Disinfectant Bins/Waste Disposal Area & Trash Cans									
11	Feminine Hygiene Bins/Containers Cleaned And Disinfected									
12	Toilets Cleaned & Disinfected, Outside, Inside And Handles									
13	Urinals & Urinal Screens Cleaned, Disinfected & Blocks Replaced									
14	Wall Mirrors Cleaned With Glass Cleaner									
15	Clean And Re-Stock Paper Dispensers & Paper Towel Rolls									
16	Refill Soap Dispensers, Sanitizers And Hand Gels									
17	Sinks, Taps, Fixtures, Surface Areas Cleaned And Disinfected									

	Daily/Weekly Toilets/Restroom Cleaning Tasks Con	M	T	W	T	F	S	S	Cleaned By	Date/Time
18	Windowsills Clean And Wiped Down									
19	Check Plumbing And Schedule Work If Required									
20	Air Fresheners Checked And Replaced									
21	Fire Exit Lights And Emergency Lights Checked & Functioning									
22	Place Wet Floor Signs If Floors Are Wet After Mopping									
23	Cabinets Cleaned And Disinfected									
	Monthly Toilets/Restroom Cleaning Tasks	M	T	W	T	F	S	S	Cleaned By	Date/Time
1	Toilet/Restroom Service Storeroom/Cupboard Clean And Tidy									
2	Walls Free Of Graffiti, Stickers, Gum And Residue									
3	Wash And Clean Windows (Inside And Outside)									
4	Check Hardware, Door Stops And Lock Mechanisms									
5	All Fittings Securely Fixed (Schedule Maintenance If Not)									
6	Dust And Clean Ceilings, Ceiling Corners And Ceiling Tiles									
7	Clean Skirting Boards/Baseboards And Corners									
8	Thoroughly Clean Grout And Tiles									
9	Ceiling Wall Vents Cleaned And Disinfected									
10	Clean And Vacuum Central Heating Units									
11	Wash And Clean Light Covers									
12	Wash All Toilet And Restroom Mats									
	Daily/Weekly Kitchen Cleaning Tasks	M	T	W	T	F	S	S	Cleaned By	Date/Time
1	Wash And Sanitize All Counter Tops And Prep Area Surfaces									
2	Empty Dishwasher, Run The Dishwasher/Dish Drainer									
3	Disinfect Touch Points, Light Switches And Other Switches									
4	Take Out The Rubbish/Trash, Remove Waste And Recycling									
5	Clean & Disinfectant Bins/Waste Disposal Area & Trash Cans									
6	Wipe Down The Walls Wherever There Are Spills And Splashes									
7	Sweep The Floors To Ensure They're Free From Debris									
8	Mop Tiled And Laminate Floors With Disinfectant Cleaner									
9	Wet Floor Signs In Place If Floors Are Wet After Mopping									
10	Thoroughly Clean And Disinfect The Sinks And Taps									
11	Clean Exterior Of Appliances, Check For Spilled Food									
12	Replace Empty Paper Towel Rolls And Cloth Roller Towels									
13	Refill Soap Dispensers And Hand Sanitizers/Hand Gels									
14	Wipe Down Equipment, Tea And Coffee Makers, Toasters Etc									
15	Fire Exit Lights And Emergency Lights Checked & Functioning									
16	Pour Drain Cleaner Down Floor And Sink Drains									
17	Clean Inside Microwave, Check For Spilled Food									

	Daily/Weekly Kitchen Cleaning Tasks Continued	M	T	W	T	F	S	S	CLEANED BY	DATE/TIME
18	Replace Wash Rags, Cloths And Tea Towels With Clean Ones									
19	Wash Rags, Cloths, Tea Towels And Towels In Washing Machine									
20	Replace And Change Burned Out Light Bulbs/Broken Lights									
21	Clean Inside Of Dishwasher									
22	Sanitise Sponges Or Replace Damaged Sponges With New									
23	Dishes, Pots, Pans, And Utensils To Be Stored Away Properly									
24	Clean Out Refrigerator And Wipe Down Shelves And Drawers									
	Monthly Kitchen Cleaning Tasks	M	T	W	T	F	S	S	Cleaned By	Date/Time
1	Wash And Clean Air Vents									
2	Sort Through And Organize Cooking Utensils, Pans And Pots									
3	Wash And Clean Air Vents									
4	Check Plates, Cups And Glasses And Bin Anything Chipped									
5	Clean And Vacuum Central Heating Units									
6	Wash And Clean Light Covers									
7	Clean And De-Lime Dishwasher									
8	Dust And Clean Ceilings, Ceiling Corners And Ceiling Tiles									
9	Thoroughly Clean Grout And Tiles									
10	Clean Refrigerator Coils To Remove Dust, Unplug First									
11	Run Cleaning & Sanitizing Chemicals Through Coffee Machine									
12	Disinfect And Clean All The Walls From Top To Bottom									
13	Check For Out Of Date Food In Cabinets/Cupboards									
14	Clean Skirting Boards/Baseboards And Corners									
15	Clean Under Refrigerator									
16	Wash And Clean Doors, Door Frames And Glass									
17	Sort Through Leftover Items In The Fridge/Refrigerators									
18	Wash And Clean Windows (Inside And Outside)									
19	Replace Pest Traps									

ESSENTIAL CLEANING NOTES

....

....

....

....

....

....

....

....

ESSENTIAL OFFICE CLEANING *Checklist*

Location/Building	Department	Office Number	Week Number

Start Date & Time	Finnish Date & Time	Name	Signature

	Daily/Weekly Office Cleaning Tasks	M	T	W	T	F	S	S	Cleaned By	Date/Time
1	Clean And Sanitize All The Desks And Tables									
2	Clean And Sanitize All The Counter Tops And Surface Areas									
3	Disinfect All Point-Of-Sale Terminals And Touch Screens									
4	Disinfect Touch Points, Light Switches And Other Switches									
5	Clean And Sanitize All Keyboards And Computer Mice									
6	Wipe Down The Walls Wherever There Are Spills And Splashes									
7	Clean And Disinfect All Doors, Door Handles And Doorknobs									
8	Re-Stock Protective Clothing, Face Masks/Shields, Gloves									
9	Clean And Sanitize All The Chairs, Seats And Benches									
10	Clean All The Mirrors, Glass Cabinets/Displays									
11	Replace And Change Burned Out Light Bulbs/Broken Lights									
12	Sweep The Floors To Ensure They're Free From Debris									
13	Mop Tiled And Laminate Floors With Disinfectant Cleaner									
14	Vacuum And Hoover The Carpets, Mats And Rugs									
15	Place Wet Floor Signs If Floors Are Wet After Mopping									
16	Wash & Clean Dirty Cups, Drinking Bottles And Glasses									
17	Clean & Re-Stock Paper Dispensers & Paper Towel Rolls									
18	Wipe Down Equipment & Sanitize Tea And Coffee Makers									
19	Refill Soap Dispensers, Sanitizers And Hand Gels									
20	Clean And Dust Furniture And Office Equipment									
21	Take Out The Rubbish/Trash, Remove Waste And Recycling									
22	Clean & Disinfectant Bins/Waste Disposal Area & Trash Cans									
23	Clean And Wipe Down Windowsills									
24	Vacuum Furnishings, Cushions, Chairs, Sofas And Couches									
25	Spray Air Freshener									
26	Clean And Disinfect Any Cabinets, Shelves And Units									
27	Clean Surfaces And Desk/Work Dividers									
28	Clean And Disinfect Telephones And Headsets									
29	Polish Any Wooden Furniture And Hardwood Surfaces									

	Monthly Office Cleaning Tasks	M	T	W	T	F	S	S	Cleaned By	Date/Time
1	Clean Skirting Boards/Baseboards And Corners									
2	Clean And Disinfect All The Walls From Top To Bottom									
3	Clean Blinds (Take Down And Wash If Possible)									
4	Wash And Clean Windows (Inside And Outside)									
5	Clean And Disinfect Shared Surfaces									
6	Steam Clean Carpets And Rugs									
7	Dust And Clean Ceilings, Ceiling Corners And Ceiling Tiles									
8	Check For Broken Chairs And Tables									
9	Dust And Wash Radiator Covers									
10	Clean And Disinfect Ceiling Wall Vents									
11	Clean And Vacuum Central Heating Units									
12	Wash And Clean Light Covers									
13	Clean Drapes And Curtains (Take Down And Wash if Possible)									
14	Check Cleaning Supplies And Re-Stock As Necessary									
15	Check Ceiling Fans, Fire Sprinklers And Smoke Alarms									
16	Check Hardware, Door Stops And Lock Mechanisms									
17	Fire Exit Lights And Emergency Lights Checked & Functioning									
18	Organize And De-Clutter Office Drawers									
19	Organize And De-Clutter Storeroom									

	Daily/Weekly Toilets/Restroom Cleaning Tasks	M	T	W	T	F	S	S	Cleaned By	Date/Time
1	Clean And Disinfect All Doors, Door Handles And Doorknobs									
2	Disinfect Touch Points, Light Switches And Other Switches									
3	Toilet Roll Holders Cleaned And Disinfected And Re-Stocked									
4	Wipe Down The Walls Wherever There Are Spills And Splashes									
5	Electric Hand Dryers Cleaned, Disinfected & Operating Correctly									
6	Sweep The Floors To Ensure They're Free From Debris									
7	Mop Tiled And Laminate Floors With Disinfectant Cleaner									
8	Paper Dispensers & Paper Towel Rolls Cleaned & Re-Stocked									
9	Take Out The Rubbish/Trash, Remove Waste And Recycling									
10	Clean & Disinfectant Bins/Waste Disposal Area & Trash Cans									
11	Feminine Hygiene Bins/Containers Cleaned And Disinfected									
12	Toilets Cleaned & Disinfected, Outside, Inside And Handles									
13	Urinals & Urinal Screens Cleaned, Disinfected & Blocks Replaced									
14	Wall Mirrors Cleaned With Glass Cleaner									
15	Clean And Re-Stock Paper Dispensers & Paper Towel Rolls									
16	Refill Soap Dispensers, Sanitizers And Hand Gels									
17	Sinks, Taps, Fixtures, Surface Areas Cleaned And Disinfected									

	Daily/Weekly Toilets/Restroom Cleaning Tasks Con	M	T	W	T	F	S	S	Cleaned By	Date/Time
18	Windowsills Clean And Wiped Down									
19	Check Plumbing And Schedule Work If Required									
20	Air Fresheners Checked And Replaced									
21	Fire Exit Lights And Emergency Lights Checked & Functioning									
22	Place Wet Floor Signs If Floors Are Wet After Mopping									
23	Cabinets Cleaned And Disinfected									
	Monthly Toilets/Restroom Cleaning Tasks	M	T	W	T	F	S	S	Cleaned By	Date/Time
1	Toilet/Restroom Service Storeroom/Cupboard Clean And Tidy									
2	Walls Free Of Graffiti, Stickers, Gum And Residue									
3	Wash And Clean Windows (Inside And Outside)									
4	Check Hardware, Door Stops And Lock Mechanisms									
5	All Fittings Securely Fixed (Schedule Maintenance If Not)									
6	Dust And Clean Ceilings, Ceiling Corners And Ceiling Tiles									
7	Clean Skirting Boards/Baseboards And Corners									
8	Thoroughly Clean Grout And Tiles									
9	Ceiling Wall Vents Cleaned And Disinfected									
10	Clean And Vacuum Central Heating Units									
11	Wash And Clean Light Covers									
12	Wash All Toilet And Restroom Mats									
	Daily/Weekly Kitchen Cleaning Tasks	M	T	W	T	F	S	S	Cleaned By	Date/Time
1	Wash And Sanitize All Counter Tops And Prep Area Surfaces									
2	Empty Dishwasher, Run The Dishwasher/Dish Drainer									
3	Disinfect Touch Points, Light Switches And Other Switches									
4	Take Out The Rubbish/Trash, Remove Waste And Recycling									
5	Clean & Disinfectant Bins/Waste Disposal Area & Trash Cans									
6	Wipe Down The Walls Wherever There Are Spills And Splashes									
7	Sweep The Floors To Ensure They're Free From Debris									
8	Mop Tiled And Laminate Floors With Disinfectant Cleaner									
9	Wet Floor Signs In Place If Floors Are Wet After Mopping									
10	Thoroughly Clean And Disinfect The Sinks And Taps									
11	Clean Exterior Of Appliances, Check For Spilled Food									
12	Replace Empty Paper Towel Rolls And Cloth Roller Towels									
13	Refill Soap Dispensers And Hand Sanitizers/Hand Gels									
14	Wipe Down Equipment, Tea And Coffee Makers, Toasters Etc									
15	Fire Exit Lights And Emergency Lights Checked & Functioning									
16	Pour Drain Cleaner Down Floor And Sink Drains									
17	Clean Inside Microwave, Check For Spilled Food									

	Daily/Weekly Kitchen Cleaning Tasks Continued	M	T	W	T	F	S	S	CLEANED BY	DATE/TIME
18	Replace Wash Rags, Cloths And Tea Towels With Clean Ones									
19	Wash Rags, Cloths, Tea Towels And Towels In Washing Machine									
20	Replace And Change Burned Out Light Bulbs/Broken Lights									
21	Clean Inside Of Dishwasher									
22	Sanitise Sponges Or Replace Damaged Sponges With New									
23	Dishes, Pots, Pans, And Utensils To Be Stored Away Properly									
24	Clean Out Refrigerator And Wipe Down Shelves And Drawers									
	Monthly Kitchen Cleaning Tasks	M	T	W	T	F	S	S	Cleaned By	Date/Time
1	Wash And Clean Air Vents									
2	Sort Through And Organize Cooking Utensils, Pans And Pots									
3	Wash And Clean Air Vents									
4	Check Plates, Cups And Glasses And Bin Anything Chipped									
5	Clean And Vacuum Central Heating Units									
6	Wash And Clean Light Covers									
7	Clean And De-Lime Dishwasher									
8	Dust And Clean Ceilings, Ceiling Corners And Ceiling Tiles									
9	Thoroughly Clean Grout And Tiles									
10	Clean Refrigerator Coils To Remove Dust, Unplug First									
11	Run Cleaning & Sanitizing Chemicals Through Coffee Machine									
12	Disinfect And Clean All The Walls From Top To Bottom									
13	Check For Out Of Date Food In Cabinets/Cupboards									
14	Clean Skirting Boards/Baseboards And Corners									
15	Clean Under Refrigerator									
16	Wash And Clean Doors, Door Frames And Glass									
17	Sort Through Leftover Items In The Fridge/Refrigerators									
18	Wash And Clean Windows (Inside And Outside)									
19	Replace Pest Traps									

ESSENTIAL CLEANING NOTES

....

....

....

....

....

....

....

....

....

ESSENTIAL OFFICE CLEANING *Checklist*

Location/Building	Department	Office Number	Week Number

Start Date & Time	Finnish Date & Time	Name	Signature

	Daily/Weekly Office Cleaning Tasks	M	T	W	T	F	S	S	Cleaned By	Date/Time
1	Clean And Sanitize All The Desks And Tables									
2	Clean And Sanitize All The Counter Tops And Surface Areas									
3	Disinfect All Point-Of-Sale Terminals And Touch Screens									
4	Disinfect Touch Points, Light Switches And Other Switches									
5	Clean And Sanitize All Keyboards And Computer Mice									
6	Wipe Down The Walls Wherever There Are Spills And Splashes									
7	Clean And Disinfect All Doors, Door Handles And Doorknobs									
8	Re-Stock Protective Clothing, Face Masks/Shields, Gloves									
9	Clean And Sanitize All The Chairs, Seats And Benches									
10	Clean All The Mirrors, Glass Cabinets/Displays									
11	Replace And Change Burned Out Light Bulbs/Broken Lights									
12	Sweep The Floors To Ensure They're Free From Debris									
13	Mop Tiled And Laminate Floors With Disinfectant Cleaner									
14	Vacuum And Hoover The Carpets, Mats And Rugs									
15	Place Wet Floor Signs If Floors Are Wet After Mopping									
16	Wash & Clean Dirty Cups, Drinking Bottles And Glasses									
17	Clean & Re-Stock Paper Dispensers & Paper Towel Rolls									
18	Wipe Down Equipment & Sanitize Tea And Coffee Makers									
19	Refill Soap Dispensers, Sanitizers And Hand Gels									
20	Clean And Dust Furniture And Office Equipment									
21	Take Out The Rubbish/Trash, Remove Waste And Recycling									
22	Clean & Disinfectant Bins/Waste Disposal Area & Trash Cans									
23	Clean And Wipe Down Windowsills									
24	Vacuum Furnishings, Cushions, Chairs, Sofas And Couches									
25	Spray Air Freshener									
26	Clean And Disinfect Any Cabinets, Shelves And Units									
27	Clean Surfaces And Desk/Work Dividers									
28	Clean And Disinfect Telephones And Headsets									
29	Polish Any Wooden Furniture And Hardwood Surfaces									

	Monthly Office Cleaning Tasks	M	T	W	T	F	S	S	Cleaned By	Date/Time
1	Clean Skirting Boards/Baseboards And Corners									
2	Clean And Disinfect All The Walls From Top To Bottom									
3	Clean Blinds (Take Down And Wash If Possible)									
4	Wash And Clean Windows (Inside And Outside)									
5	Clean And Disinfect Shared Surfaces									
6	Steam Clean Carpets And Rugs									
7	Dust And Clean Ceilings, Ceiling Corners And Ceiling Tiles									
8	Check For Broken Chairs And Tables									
9	Dust And Wash Radiator Covers									
10	Clean And Disinfect Ceiling Wall Vents									
11	Clean And Vacuum Central Heating Units									
12	Wash And Clean Light Covers									
13	Clean Drapes And Curtains (Take Down And Wash if Possible)									
14	Check Cleaning Supplies And Re-Stock As Necessary									
15	Check Ceiling Fans, Fire Sprinklers And Smoke Alarms									
16	Check Hardware, Door Stops And Lock Mechanisms									
17	Fire Exit Lights And Emergency Lights Checked & Functioning									
18	Organize And De-Clutter Office Drawers									
19	Organize And De-Clutter Storeroom									

	Daily/Weekly Toilets/Restroom Cleaning Tasks	M	T	W	T	F	S	S	Cleaned By	Date/Time
1	Clean And Disinfect All Doors, Door Handles And Doorknobs									
2	Disinfect Touch Points, Light Switches And Other Switches									
3	Toilet Roll Holders Cleaned And Disinfected And Re-Stocked									
4	Wipe Down The Walls Wherever There Are Spills And Splashes									
5	Electric Hand Dryers Cleaned, Disinfected & Operating Correctly									
6	Sweep The Floors To Ensure They're Free From Debris									
7	Mop Tiled And Laminate Floors With Disinfectant Cleaner									
8	Paper Dispensers & Paper Towel Rolls Cleaned & Re-Stocked									
9	Take Out The Rubbish/Trash, Remove Waste And Recycling									
10	Clean & Disinfectant Bins/Waste Disposal Area & Trash Cans									
11	Feminine Hygiene Bins/Containers Cleaned And Disinfected									
12	Toilets Cleaned & Disinfected, Outside, Inside And Handles									
13	Urinals & Urinal Screens Cleaned, Disinfected & Blocks Replaced									
14	Wall Mirrors Cleaned With Glass Cleaner									
15	Clean And Re-Stock Paper Dispensers & Paper Towel Rolls									
16	Refill Soap Dispensers, Sanitizers And Hand Gels									
17	Sinks, Taps, Fixtures, Surface Areas Cleaned And Disinfected									

	Daily/Weekly Toilets/Restroom Cleaning Tasks Con	M	T	W	T	F	S	S	Cleaned By	Date/Time
18	Windowsills Clean And Wiped Down									
19	Check Plumbing And Schedule Work If Required									
20	Air Fresheners Checked And Replaced									
21	Fire Exit Lights And Emergency Lights Checked & Functioning									
22	Place Wet Floor Signs If Floors Are Wet After Mopping									
23	Cabinets Cleaned And Disinfected									
	Monthly Toilets/Restroom Cleaning Tasks	M	T	W	T	F	S	S	Cleaned By	Date/Time
1	Toilet/Restroom Service Storeroom/Cupboard Clean And Tidy									
2	Walls Free Of Graffiti, Stickers, Gum And Residue									
3	Wash And Clean Windows (Inside And Outside)									
4	Check Hardware, Door Stops And Lock Mechanisms									
5	All Fittings Securely Fixed (Schedule Maintenance If Not)									
6	Dust And Clean Ceilings, Ceiling Corners And Ceiling Tiles									
7	Clean Skirting Boards/Baseboards And Corners									
8	Thoroughly Clean Grout And Tiles									
9	Ceiling Wall Vents Cleaned And Disinfected									
10	Clean And Vacuum Central Heating Units									
11	Wash And Clean Light Covers									
12	Wash All Toilet And Restroom Mats									
	Daily/Weekly Kitchen Cleaning Tasks	M	T	W	T	F	S	S	Cleaned By	Date/Time
1	Wash And Sanitize All Counter Tops And Prep Area Surfaces									
2	Empty Dishwasher, Run The Dishwasher/Dish Drainer									
3	Disinfect Touch Points, Light Switches And Other Switches									
4	Take Out The Rubbish/Trash, Remove Waste And Recycling									
5	Clean & Disinfectant Bins/Waste Disposal Area & Trash Cans									
6	Wipe Down The Walls Wherever There Are Spills And Splashes									
7	Sweep The Floors To Ensure They're Free From Debris									
8	Mop Tiled And Laminate Floors With Disinfectant Cleaner									
9	Wet Floor Signs In Place If Floors Are Wet After Mopping									
10	Thoroughly Clean And Disinfect The Sinks And Taps									
11	Clean Exterior Of Appliances, Check For Spilled Food									
12	Replace Empty Paper Towel Rolls And Cloth Roller Towels									
13	Refill Soap Dispensers And Hand Sanitizers/Hand Gels									
14	Wipe Down Equipment, Tea And Coffee Makers, Toasters Etc									
15	Fire Exit Lights And Emergency Lights Checked & Functioning									
16	Pour Drain Cleaner Down Floor And Sink Drains									
17	Clean Inside Microwave, Check For Spilled Food									

	Daily/Weekly Kitchen Cleaning Tasks Continued	M	T	W	T	F	S	S	CLEANED BY	DATE/TIME
18	Replace Wash Rags, Cloths And Tea Towels With Clean Ones									
19	Wash Rags, Cloths, Tea Towels And Towels In Washing Machine									
20	Replace And Change Burned Out Light Bulbs/Broken Lights									
21	Clean Inside Of Dishwasher									
22	Sanitise Sponges Or Replace Damaged Sponges With New									
23	Dishes, Pots, Pans, And Utensils To Be Stored Away Properly									
24	Clean Out Refrigerator And Wipe Down Shelves And Drawers									
	Monthly Kitchen Cleaning Tasks	M	T	W	T	F	S	S	Cleaned By	Date/Time
1	Wash And Clean Air Vents									
2	Sort Through And Organize Cooking Utensils, Pans And Pots									
3	Wash And Clean Air Vents									
4	Check Plates, Cups And Glasses And Bin Anything Chipped									
5	Clean And Vacuum Central Heating Units									
6	Wash And Clean Light Covers									
7	Clean And De-Lime Dishwasher									
8	Dust And Clean Ceilings, Ceiling Corners And Ceiling Tiles									
9	Thoroughly Clean Grout And Tiles									
10	Clean Refrigerator Coils To Remove Dust, Unplug First									
11	Run Cleaning & Sanitizing Chemicals Through Coffee Machine									
12	Disinfect And Clean All The Walls From Top To Bottom									
13	Check For Out Of Date Food In Cabinets/Cupboards									
14	Clean Skirting Boards/Baseboards And Corners									
15	Clean Under Refrigerator									
16	Wash And Clean Doors, Door Frames And Glass									
17	Sort Through Leftover Items In The Fridge/Refrigerators									
18	Wash And Clean Windows (Inside And Outside)									
19	Replace Pest Traps									

ESSENTIAL CLEANING NOTES

....
....
....
....
....
....
....
....

ESSENTIAL OFFICE CLEANING *Checklist*

Location/Building	Department	Office Number	Week Number

Start Date & Time	Finnish Date & Time	Name	Signature

	Daily/Weekly Office Cleaning Tasks	M	T	W	T	F	S	S	Cleaned By	Date/Time
1	Clean And Sanitize All The Desks And Tables									
2	Clean And Sanitize All The Counter Tops And Surface Areas									
3	Disinfect All Point-Of-Sale Terminals And Touch Screens									
4	Disinfect Touch Points, Light Switches And Other Switches									
5	Clean And Sanitize All Keyboards And Computer Mice									
6	Wipe Down The Walls Wherever There Are Spills And Splashes									
7	Clean And Disinfect All Doors, Door Handles And Doorknobs									
8	Re-Stock Protective Clothing, Face Masks/Shields, Gloves									
9	Clean And Sanitize All The Chairs, Seats And Benches									
10	Clean All The Mirrors, Glass Cabinets/Displays									
11	Replace And Change Burned Out Light Bulbs/Broken Lights									
12	Sweep The Floors To Ensure They're Free From Debris									
13	Mop Tiled And Laminate Floors With Disinfectant Cleaner									
14	Vacuum And Hoover The Carpets, Mats And Rugs									
15	Place Wet Floor Signs If Floors Are Wet After Mopping									
16	Wash & Clean Dirty Cups, Drinking Bottles And Glasses									
17	Clean & Re-Stock Paper Dispensers & Paper Towel Rolls									
18	Wipe Down Equipment & Sanitize Tea And Coffee Makers									
19	Refill Soap Dispensers, Sanitizers And Hand Gels									
20	Clean And Dust Furniture And Office Equipment									
21	Take Out The Rubbish/Trash, Remove Waste And Recycling									
22	Clean & Disinfectant Bins/Waste Disposal Area & Trash Cans									
23	Clean And Wipe Down Windowsills									
24	Vacuum Furnishings, Cushions, Chairs, Sofas And Couches									
25	Spray Air Freshener									
26	Clean And Disinfect Any Cabinets, Shelves And Units									
27	Clean Surfaces And Desk/Work Dividers									
28	Clean And Disinfect Telephones And Headsets									
29	Polish Any Wooden Furniture And Hardwood Surfaces									

	Monthly Office Cleaning Tasks	M	T	W	T	F	S	S	Cleaned By	Date/Time
1	Clean Skirting Boards/Baseboards And Corners									
2	Clean And Disinfect All The Walls From Top To Bottom									
3	Clean Blinds (Take Down And Wash If Possible)									
4	Wash And Clean Windows (Inside And Outside)									
5	Clean And Disinfect Shared Surfaces									
6	Steam Clean Carpets And Rugs									
7	Dust And Clean Ceilings, Ceiling Corners And Ceiling Tiles									
8	Check For Broken Chairs And Tables									
9	Dust And Wash Radiator Covers									
10	Clean And Disinfect Ceiling Wall Vents									
11	Clean And Vacuum Central Heating Units									
12	Wash And Clean Light Covers									
13	Clean Drapes And Curtains (Take Down And Wash if Possible)									
14	Check Cleaning Supplies And Re-Stock As Necessary									
15	Check Ceiling Fans, Fire Sprinklers And Smoke Alarms									
16	Check Hardware, Door Stops And Lock Mechanisms									
17	Fire Exit Lights And Emergency Lights Checked & Functioning									
18	Organize And De-Clutter Office Drawers									
19	Organize And De-Clutter Storeroom									
	Daily/Weekly Toilets/Restroom Cleaning Tasks	M	T	W	T	F	S	S	Cleaned By	Date/Time
1	Clean And Disinfect All Doors, Door Handles And Doorknobs									
2	Disinfect Touch Points, Light Switches And Other Switches									
3	Toilet Roll Holders Cleaned And Disinfected And Re-Stocked									
4	Wipe Down The Walls Wherever There Are Spills And Splashes									
5	Electric Hand Dryers Cleaned, Disinfected & Operating Correctly									
6	Sweep The Floors To Ensure They're Free From Debris									
7	Mop Tiled And Laminate Floors With Disinfectant Cleaner									
8	Paper Dispensers & Paper Towel Rolls Cleaned & Re-Stocked									
9	Take Out The Rubbish/Trash, Remove Waste And Recycling									
10	Clean & Disinfectant Bins/Waste Disposal Area & Trash Cans									
11	Feminine Hygiene Bins/Containers Cleaned And Disinfected									
12	Toilets Cleaned & Disinfected, Outside, Inside And Handles									
13	Urinals & Urinal Screens Cleaned, Disinfected & Blocks Replaced									
14	Wall Mirrors Cleaned With Glass Cleaner									
15	Clean And Re-Stock Paper Dispensers & Paper Towel Rolls									
16	Refill Soap Dispensers, Sanitizers And Hand Gels									
17	Sinks, Taps, Fixtures, Surface Areas Cleaned And Disinfected									

	Daily/Weekly Toilets/Restroom Cleaning Tasks Con	M	T	W	T	F	S	S	Cleaned By	Date/Time
18	Windowsills Clean And Wiped Down									
19	Check Plumbing And Schedule Work If Required									
20	Air Fresheners Checked And Replaced									
21	Fire Exit Lights And Emergency Lights Checked & Functioning									
22	Place Wet Floor Signs If Floors Are Wet After Mopping									
23	Cabinets Cleaned And Disinfected									
	Monthly Toilets/Restroom Cleaning Tasks	M	T	W	T	F	S	S	Cleaned By	Date/Time
1	Toilet/Restroom Service Storeroom/Cupboard Clean And Tidy									
2	Walls Free Of Graffiti, Stickers, Gum And Residue									
3	Wash And Clean Windows (Inside And Outside)									
4	Check Hardware, Door Stops And Lock Mechanisms									
5	All Fittings Securely Fixed (Schedule Maintenance If Not)									
6	Dust And Clean Ceilings, Ceiling Corners And Ceiling Tiles									
7	Clean Skirting Boards/Baseboards And Corners									
8	Thoroughly Clean Grout And Tiles									
9	Ceiling Wall Vents Cleaned And Disinfected									
10	Clean And Vacuum Central Heating Units									
11	Wash And Clean Light Covers									
12	Wash All Toilet And Restroom Mats									
	Daily/Weekly Kitchen Cleaning Tasks	M	T	W	T	F	S	S	Cleaned By	Date/Time
1	Wash And Sanitize All Counter Tops And Prep Area Surfaces									
2	Empty Dishwasher, Run The Dishwasher/Dish Drainer									
3	Disinfect Touch Points, Light Switches And Other Switches									
4	Take Out The Rubbish/Trash, Remove Waste And Recycling									
5	Clean & Disinfectant Bins/Waste Disposal Area & Trash Cans									
6	Wipe Down The Walls Wherever There Are Spills And Splashes									
7	Sweep The Floors To Ensure They're Free From Debris									
8	Mop Tiled And Laminate Floors With Disinfectant Cleaner									
9	Wet Floor Signs In Place If Floors Are Wet After Mopping									
10	Thoroughly Clean And Disinfect The Sinks And Taps									
11	Clean Exterior Of Appliances, Check For Spilled Food									
12	Replace Empty Paper Towel Rolls And Cloth Roller Towels									
13	Refill Soap Dispensers And Hand Sanitizers/Hand Gels									
14	Wipe Down Equipment, Tea And Coffee Makers, Toasters Etc									
15	Fire Exit Lights And Emergency Lights Checked & Functioning									
16	Pour Drain Cleaner Down Floor And Sink Drains									
17	Clean Inside Microwave, Check For Spilled Food									

	Daily/Weekly Kitchen Cleaning Tasks Continued	M	T	W	T	F	S	S	CLEANED BY	DATE/TIME
18	Replace Wash Rags, Cloths And Tea Towels With Clean Ones									
19	Wash Rags, Cloths, Tea Towels And Towels In Washing Machine									
20	Replace And Change Burned Out Light Bulbs/Broken Lights									
21	Clean Inside Of Dishwasher									
22	Sanitise Sponges Or Replace Damaged Sponges With New									
23	Dishes, Pots, Pans, And Utensils To Be Stored Away Properly									
24	Clean Out Refrigerator And Wipe Down Shelves And Drawers									
	Monthly Kitchen Cleaning Tasks	M	T	W	T	F	S	S	Cleaned By	Date/Time
1	Wash And Clean Air Vents									
2	Sort Through And Organize Cooking Utensils, Pans And Pots									
3	Wash And Clean Air Vents									
4	Check Plates, Cups And Glasses And Bin Anything Chipped									
5	Clean And Vacuum Central Heating Units									
6	Wash And Clean Light Covers									
7	Clean And De-Lime Dishwasher									
8	Dust And Clean Ceilings, Ceiling Corners And Ceiling Tiles									
9	Thoroughly Clean Grout And Tiles									
10	Clean Refrigerator Coils To Remove Dust, Unplug First									
11	Run Cleaning & Sanitizing Chemicals Through Coffee Machine									
12	Disinfect And Clean All The Walls From Top To Bottom									
13	Check For Out Of Date Food In Cabinets/Cupboards									
14	Clean Skirting Boards/Baseboards And Corners									
15	Clean Under Refrigerator									
16	Wash And Clean Doors, Door Frames And Glass									
17	Sort Through Leftover Items In The Fridge/Refrigerators									
18	Wash And Clean Windows (Inside And Outside)									
19	Replace Pest Traps									

ESSENTIAL CLEANING NOTES

....

....

....

....

....

....

....

ESSENTIAL OFFICE CLEANING *Checklist*

Location/Building	Department	Office Number	Week Number

Start Date & Time	Finnish Date & Time	Name	Signature

	Daily/Weekly Office Cleaning Tasks	M	T	W	T	F	S	S	Cleaned By	Date/Time
1	Clean And Sanitize All The Desks And Tables									
2	Clean And Sanitize All The Counter Tops And Surface Areas									
3	Disinfect All Point-Of-Sale Terminals And Touch Screens									
4	Disinfect Touch Points, Light Switches And Other Switches									
5	Clean And Sanitize All Keyboards And Computer Mice									
6	Wipe Down The Walls Wherever There Are Spills And Splashes									
7	Clean And Disinfect All Doors, Door Handles And Doorknobs									
8	Re-Stock Protective Clothing, Face Masks/Shields, Gloves									
9	Clean And Sanitize All The Chairs, Seats And Benches									
10	Clean All The Mirrors, Glass Cabinets/Displays									
11	Replace And Change Burned Out Light Bulbs/Broken Lights									
12	Sweep The Floors To Ensure They're Free From Debris									
13	Mop Tiled And Laminate Floors With Disinfectant Cleaner									
14	Vacuum And Hoover The Carpets, Mats And Rugs									
15	Place Wet Floor Signs If Floors Are Wet After Mopping									
16	Wash & Clean Dirty Cups, Drinking Bottles And Glasses									
17	Clean & Re-Stock Paper Dispensers & Paper Towel Rolls									
18	Wipe Down Equipment & Sanitize Tea And Coffee Makers									
19	Refill Soap Dispensers, Sanitizers And Hand Gels									
20	Clean And Dust Furniture And Office Equipment									
21	Take Out The Rubbish/Trash, Remove Waste And Recycling									
22	Clean & Disinfectant Bins/Waste Disposal Area & Trash Cans									
23	Clean And Wipe Down Windowsills									
24	Vacuum Furnishings, Cushions, Chairs, Sofas And Couches									
25	Spray Air Freshener									
26	Clean And Disinfect Any Cabinets, Shelves And Units									
27	Clean Surfaces And Desk/Work Dividers									
28	Clean And Disinfect Telephones And Headsets									
29	Polish Any Wooden Furniture And Hardwood Surfaces									

	Monthly Office Cleaning Tasks	M	T	W	T	F	S	S	Cleaned By	Date/Time
1	Clean Skirting Boards/Baseboards And Corners									
2	Clean And Disinfect All The Walls From Top To Bottom									
3	Clean Blinds (Take Down And Wash If Possible)									
4	Wash And Clean Windows (Inside And Outside)									
5	Clean And Disinfect Shared Surfaces									
6	Steam Clean Carpets And Rugs									
7	Dust And Clean Ceilings, Ceiling Corners And Ceiling Tiles									
8	Check For Broken Chairs And Tables									
9	Dust And Wash Radiator Covers									
10	Clean And Disinfect Ceiling Wall Vents									
11	Clean And Vacuum Central Heating Units									
12	Wash And Clean Light Covers									
13	Clean Drapes And Curtains (Take Down And Wash if Possible)									
14	Check Cleaning Supplies And Re-Stock As Necessary									
15	Check Ceiling Fans, Fire Sprinklers And Smoke Alarms									
16	Check Hardware, Door Stops And Lock Mechanisms									
17	Fire Exit Lights And Emergency Lights Checked & Functioning									
18	Organize And De-Clutter Office Drawers									
19	Organize And De-Clutter Storeroom									
	Daily/Weekly Toilets/Restroom Cleaning Tasks	M	T	W	T	F	S	S	Cleaned By	Date/Time
1	Clean And Disinfect All Doors, Door Handles And Doorknobs									
2	Disinfect Touch Points, Light Switches And Other Switches									
3	Toilet Roll Holders Cleaned And Disinfected And Re-Stocked									
4	Wipe Down The Walls Wherever There Are Spills And Splashes									
5	Electric Hand Dryers Cleaned, Disinfected & Operating Correctly									
6	Sweep The Floors To Ensure They're Free From Debris									
7	Mop Tiled And Laminate Floors With Disinfectant Cleaner									
8	Paper Dispensers & Paper Towel Rolls Cleaned & Re-Stocked									
9	Take Out The Rubbish/Trash, Remove Waste And Recycling									
10	Clean & Disinfectant Bins/Waste Disposal Area & Trash Cans									
11	Feminine Hygiene Bins/Containers Cleaned And Disinfected									
12	Toilets Cleaned & Disinfected, Outside, Inside And Handles									
13	Urinals & Urinal Screens Cleaned, Disinfected & Blocks Replaced									
14	Wall Mirrors Cleaned With Glass Cleaner									
15	Clean And Re-Stock Paper Dispensers & Paper Towel Rolls									
16	Refill Soap Dispensers, Sanitizers And Hand Gels									
17	Sinks, Taps, Fixtures, Surface Areas Cleaned And Disinfected									

	Daily/Weekly Toilets/Restroom Cleaning Tasks Con	M	T	W	T	F	S	S	Cleaned By	Date/Time
18	Windowsills Clean And Wiped Down									
19	Check Plumbing And Schedule Work If Required									
20	Air Fresheners Checked And Replaced									
21	Fire Exit Lights And Emergency Lights Checked & Functioning									
22	Place Wet Floor Signs If Floors Are Wet After Mopping									
23	Cabinets Cleaned And Disinfected									
	Monthly Toilets/Restroom Cleaning Tasks	M	T	W	T	F	S	S	Cleaned By	Date/Time
1	Toilet/Restroom Service Storeroom/Cupboard Clean And Tidy									
2	Walls Free Of Graffiti, Stickers, Gum And Residue									
3	Wash And Clean Windows (Inside And Outside)									
4	Check Hardware, Door Stops And Lock Mechanisms									
5	All Fittings Securely Fixed (Schedule Maintenance If Not)									
6	Dust And Clean Ceilings, Ceiling Corners And Ceiling Tiles									
7	Clean Skirting Boards/Baseboards And Corners									
8	Thoroughly Clean Grout And Tiles									
9	Ceiling Wall Vents Cleaned And Disinfected									
10	Clean And Vacuum Central Heating Units									
11	Wash And Clean Light Covers									
12	Wash All Toilet And Restroom Mats									
	Daily/Weekly Kitchen Cleaning Tasks	M	T	W	T	F	S	S	Cleaned By	Date/Time
1	Wash And Sanitize All Counter Tops And Prep Area Surfaces									
2	Empty Dishwasher, Run The Dishwasher/Dish Drainer									
3	Disinfect Touch Points, Light Switches And Other Switches									
4	Take Out The Rubbish/Trash, Remove Waste And Recycling									
5	Clean & Disinfectant Bins/Waste Disposal Area & Trash Cans									
6	Wipe Down The Walls Wherever There Are Spills And Splashes									
7	Sweep The Floors To Ensure They're Free From Debris									
8	Mop Tiled And Laminate Floors With Disinfectant Cleaner									
9	Wet Floor Signs In Place If Floors Are Wet After Mopping									
10	Thoroughly Clean And Disinfect The Sinks And Taps									
11	Clean Exterior Of Appliances, Check For Spilled Food									
12	Replace Empty Paper Towel Rolls And Cloth Roller Towels									
13	Refill Soap Dispensers And Hand Sanitizers/Hand Gels									
14	Wipe Down Equipment, Tea And Coffee Makers, Toasters Etc									
15	Fire Exit Lights And Emergency Lights Checked & Functioning									
16	Pour Drain Cleaner Down Floor And Sink Drains									
17	Clean Inside Microwave, Check For Spilled Food									

	Daily/Weekly Kitchen Cleaning Tasks Continued	M	T	W	T	F	S	S	CLEANED BY	DATE/TIME
18	Replace Wash Rags, Cloths And Tea Towels With Clean Ones									
19	Wash Rags, Cloths, Tea Towels And Towels In Washing Machine									
20	Replace And Change Burned Out Light Bulbs/Broken Lights									
21	Clean Inside Of Dishwasher									
22	Sanitise Sponges Or Replace Damaged Sponges With New									
23	Dishes, Pots, Pans, And Utensils To Be Stored Away Properly									
24	Clean Out Refrigerator And Wipe Down Shelves And Drawers									
	Monthly Kitchen Cleaning Tasks	M	T	W	T	F	S	S	Cleaned By	Date/Time
1	Wash And Clean Air Vents									
2	Sort Through And Organize Cooking Utensils, Pans And Pots									
3	Wash And Clean Air Vents									
4	Check Plates, Cups And Glasses And Bin Anything Chipped									
5	Clean And Vacuum Central Heating Units									
6	Wash And Clean Light Covers									
7	Clean And De-Lime Dishwasher									
8	Dust And Clean Ceilings, Ceiling Corners And Ceiling Tiles									
9	Thoroughly Clean Grout And Tiles									
10	Clean Refrigerator Coils To Remove Dust, Unplug First									
11	Run Cleaning & Sanitizing Chemicals Through Coffee Machine									
12	Disinfect And Clean All The Walls From Top To Bottom									
13	Check For Out Of Date Food In Cabinets/Cupboards									
14	Clean Skirting Boards/Baseboards And Corners									
15	Clean Under Refrigerator									
16	Wash And Clean Doors, Door Frames And Glass									
17	Sort Through Leftover Items In The Fridge/Refrigerators									
18	Wash And Clean Windows (Inside And Outside)									
19	Replace Pest Traps									

ESSENTIAL CLEANING NOTES

....
....
....
....
....
....
....
....
....

ESSENTIAL OFFICE CLEANING *Checklist*

Location/Building	Department	Office Number	Week Number

Start Date & Time	Finnish Date & Time	Name	Signature

	Daily/Weekly Office Cleaning Tasks	M	T	W	T	F	S	S	Cleaned By	Date/Time
1	Clean And Sanitize All The Desks And Tables									
2	Clean And Sanitize All The Counter Tops And Surface Areas									
3	Disinfect All Point-Of-Sale Terminals And Touch Screens									
4	Disinfect Touch Points, Light Switches And Other Switches									
5	Clean And Sanitize All Keyboards And Computer Mice									
6	Wipe Down The Walls Wherever There Are Spills And Splashes									
7	Clean And Disinfect All Doors, Door Handles And Doorknobs									
8	Re-Stock Protective Clothing, Face Masks/Shields, Gloves									
9	Clean And Sanitize All The Chairs, Seats And Benches									
10	Clean All The Mirrors, Glass Cabinets/Displays									
11	Replace And Change Burned Out Light Bulbs/Broken Lights									
12	Sweep The Floors To Ensure They're Free From Debris									
13	Mop Tiled And Laminate Floors With Disinfectant Cleaner									
14	Vacuum And Hoover The Carpets, Mats And Rugs									
15	Place Wet Floor Signs If Floors Are Wet After Mopping									
16	Wash & Clean Dirty Cups, Drinking Bottles And Glasses									
17	Clean & Re-Stock Paper Dispensers & Paper Towel Rolls									
18	Wipe Down Equipment & Sanitize Tea And Coffee Makers									
19	Refill Soap Dispensers, Sanitizers And Hand Gels									
20	Clean And Dust Furniture And Office Equipment									
21	Take Out The Rubbish/Trash, Remove Waste And Recycling									
22	Clean & Disinfectant Bins/Waste Disposal Area & Trash Cans									
23	Clean And Wipe Down Windowsills									
24	Vacuum Furnishings, Cushions, Chairs, Sofas And Couches									
25	Spray Air Freshener									
26	Clean And Disinfect Any Cabinets, Shelves And Units									
27	Clean Surfaces And Desk/Work Dividers									
28	Clean And Disinfect Telephones And Headsets									
29	Polish Any Wooden Furniture And Hardwood Surfaces									

	Monthly Office Cleaning Tasks	M	T	W	T	F	S	S	Cleaned By	Date/Time
1	Clean Skirting Boards/Baseboards And Corners									
2	Clean And Disinfect All The Walls From Top To Bottom									
3	Clean Blinds (Take Down And Wash If Possible)									
4	Wash And Clean Windows (Inside And Outside)									
5	Clean And Disinfect Shared Surfaces									
6	Steam Clean Carpets And Rugs									
7	Dust And Clean Ceilings, Ceiling Corners And Ceiling Tiles									
8	Check For Broken Chairs And Tables									
9	Dust And Wash Radiator Covers									
10	Clean And Disinfect Ceiling Wall Vents									
11	Clean And Vacuum Central Heating Units									
12	Wash And Clean Light Covers									
13	Clean Drapes And Curtains (Take Down And Wash if Possible)									
14	Check Cleaning Supplies And Re-Stock As Necessary									
15	Check Ceiling Fans, Fire Sprinklers And Smoke Alarms									
16	Check Hardware, Door Stops And Lock Mechanisms									
17	Fire Exit Lights And Emergency Lights Checked & Functioning									
18	Organize And De-Clutter Office Drawers									
19	Organize And De-Clutter Storeroom									
	Daily/Weekly Toilets/Restroom Cleaning Tasks	M	T	W	T	F	S	S	Cleaned By	Date/Time
1	Clean And Disinfect All Doors, Door Handles And Doorknobs									
2	Disinfect Touch Points, Light Switches And Other Switches									
3	Toilet Roll Holders Cleaned And Disinfected And Re-Stocked									
4	Wipe Down The Walls Wherever There Are Spills And Splashes									
5	Electric Hand Dryers Cleaned, Disinfected & Operating Correctly									
6	Sweep The Floors To Ensure They're Free From Debris									
7	Mop Tiled And Laminate Floors With Disinfectant Cleaner									
8	Paper Dispensers & Paper Towel Rolls Cleaned & Re-Stocked									
9	Take Out The Rubbish/Trash, Remove Waste And Recycling									
10	Clean & Disinfectant Bins/Waste Disposal Area & Trash Cans									
11	Feminine Hygiene Bins/Containers Cleaned And Disinfected									
12	Toilets Cleaned & Disinfected, Outside, Inside And Handles									
13	Urinals & Urinal Screens Cleaned, Disinfected & Blocks Replaced									
14	Wall Mirrors Cleaned With Glass Cleaner									
15	Clean And Re-Stock Paper Dispensers & Paper Towel Rolls									
16	Refill Soap Dispensers, Sanitizers And Hand Gels									
17	Sinks, Taps, Fixtures, Surface Areas Cleaned And Disinfected									

	Daily/Weekly Toilets/Restroom Cleaning Tasks Con	M	T	W	T	F	S	S	Cleaned By	Date/Time
18	Windowsills Clean And Wiped Down									
19	Check Plumbing And Schedule Work If Required									
20	Air Fresheners Checked And Replaced									
21	Fire Exit Lights And Emergency Lights Checked & Functioning									
22	Place Wet Floor Signs If Floors Are Wet After Mopping									
23	Cabinets Cleaned And Disinfected									
	Monthly Toilets/Restroom Cleaning Tasks	M	T	W	T	F	S	S	Cleaned By	Date/Time
1	Toilet/Restroom Service Storeroom/Cupboard Clean And Tidy									
2	Walls Free Of Graffiti, Stickers, Gum And Residue									
3	Wash And Clean Windows (Inside And Outside)									
4	Check Hardware, Door Stops And Lock Mechanisms									
5	All Fittings Securely Fixed (Schedule Maintenance If Not)									
6	Dust And Clean Ceilings, Ceiling Corners And Ceiling Tiles									
7	Clean Skirting Boards/Baseboards And Corners									
8	Thoroughly Clean Grout And Tiles									
9	Ceiling Wall Vents Cleaned And Disinfected									
10	Clean And Vacuum Central Heating Units									
11	Wash And Clean Light Covers									
12	Wash All Toilet And Restroom Mats									
	Daily/Weekly Kitchen Cleaning Tasks	M	T	W	T	F	S	S	Cleaned By	Date/Time
1	Wash And Sanitize All Counter Tops And Prep Area Surfaces									
2	Empty Dishwasher, Run The Dishwasher/Dish Drainer									
3	Disinfect Touch Points, Light Switches And Other Switches									
4	Take Out The Rubbish/Trash, Remove Waste And Recycling									
5	Clean & Disinfectant Bins/Waste Disposal Area & Trash Cans									
6	Wipe Down The Walls Wherever There Are Spills And Splashes									
7	Sweep The Floors To Ensure They're Free From Debris									
8	Mop Tiled And Laminate Floors With Disinfectant Cleaner									
9	Wet Floor Signs In Place If Floors Are Wet After Mopping									
10	Thoroughly Clean And Disinfect The Sinks And Taps									
11	Clean Exterior Of Appliances, Check For Spilled Food									
12	Replace Empty Paper Towel Rolls And Cloth Roller Towels									
13	Refill Soap Dispensers And Hand Sanitizers/Hand Gels									
14	Wipe Down Equipment, Tea And Coffee Makers, Toasters Etc									
15	Fire Exit Lights And Emergency Lights Checked & Functioning									
16	Pour Drain Cleaner Down Floor And Sink Drains									
17	Clean Inside Microwave, Check For Spilled Food									

	Daily/Weekly Kitchen Cleaning Tasks Continued	M	T	W	T	F	S	S	CLEANED BY	DATE/TIME
18	Replace Wash Rags, Cloths And Tea Towels With Clean Ones									
19	Wash Rags, Cloths, Tea Towels And Towels In Washing Machine									
20	Replace And Change Burned Out Light Bulbs/Broken Lights									
21	Clean Inside Of Dishwasher									
22	Sanitise Sponges Or Replace Damaged Sponges With New									
23	Dishes, Pots, Pans, And Utensils To Be Stored Away Properly									
24	Clean Out Refrigerator And Wipe Down Shelves And Drawers									
	Monthly Kitchen Cleaning Tasks	M	T	W	T	F	S	S	Cleaned By	Date/Time
1	Wash And Clean Air Vents									
2	Sort Through And Organize Cooking Utensils, Pans And Pots									
3	Wash And Clean Air Vents									
4	Check Plates, Cups And Glasses And Bin Anything Chipped									
5	Clean And Vacuum Central Heating Units									
6	Wash And Clean Light Covers									
7	Clean And De-Lime Dishwasher									
8	Dust And Clean Ceilings, Ceiling Corners And Ceiling Tiles									
9	Thoroughly Clean Grout And Tiles									
10	Clean Refrigerator Coils To Remove Dust, Unplug First									
11	Run Cleaning & Sanitizing Chemicals Through Coffee Machine									
12	Disinfect And Clean All The Walls From Top To Bottom									
13	Check For Out Of Date Food In Cabinets/Cupboards									
14	Clean Skirting Boards/Baseboards And Corners									
15	Clean Under Refrigerator									
16	Wash And Clean Doors, Door Frames And Glass									
17	Sort Through Leftover Items In The Fridge/Refrigerators									
18	Wash And Clean Windows (Inside And Outside)									
19	Replace Pest Traps									

ESSENTIAL CLEANING NOTES

....

....

....

....

....

....

....

ESSENTIAL OFFICE CLEANING *Checklist*

Location/Building	Department	Office Number	Week Number

Start Date & Time	Finnish Date & Time	Name	Signature

	Daily/Weekly Office Cleaning Tasks	M	T	W	T	F	S	S	Cleaned By	Date/Time
1	Clean And Sanitize All The Desks And Tables									
2	Clean And Sanitize All The Counter Tops And Surface Areas									
3	Disinfect All Point-Of-Sale Terminals And Touch Screens									
4	Disinfect Touch Points, Light Switches And Other Switches									
5	Clean And Sanitize All Keyboards And Computer Mice									
6	Wipe Down The Walls Wherever There Are Spills And Splashes									
7	Clean And Disinfect All Doors, Door Handles And Doorknobs									
8	Re-Stock Protective Clothing, Face Masks/Shields, Gloves									
9	Clean And Sanitize All The Chairs, Seats And Benches									
10	Clean All The Mirrors, Glass Cabinets/Displays									
11	Replace And Change Burned Out Light Bulbs/Broken Lights									
12	Sweep The Floors To Ensure They're Free From Debris									
13	Mop Tiled And Laminate Floors With Disinfectant Cleaner									
14	Vacuum And Hoover The Carpets, Mats And Rugs									
15	Place Wet Floor Signs If Floors Are Wet After Mopping									
16	Wash & Clean Dirty Cups, Drinking Bottles And Glasses									
17	Clean & Re-Stock Paper Dispensers & Paper Towel Rolls									
18	Wipe Down Equipment & Sanitize Tea And Coffee Makers									
19	Refill Soap Dispensers, Sanitizers And Hand Gels									
20	Clean And Dust Furniture And Office Equipment									
21	Take Out The Rubbish/Trash, Remove Waste And Recycling									
22	Clean & Disinfectant Bins/Waste Disposal Area & Trash Cans									
23	Clean And Wipe Down Windowsills									
24	Vacuum Furnishings, Cushions, Chairs, Sofas And Couches									
25	Spray Air Freshener									
26	Clean And Disinfect Any Cabinets, Shelves And Units									
27	Clean Surfaces And Desk/Work Dividers									
28	Clean And Disinfect Telephones And Headsets									
29	Polish Any Wooden Furniture And Hardwood Surfaces									

	Monthly Office Cleaning Tasks	M	T	W	T	F	S	S	Cleaned By	Date/Time
1	Clean Skirting Boards/Baseboards And Corners									
2	Clean And Disinfect All The Walls From Top To Bottom									
3	Clean Blinds (Take Down And Wash If Possible)									
4	Wash And Clean Windows (Inside And Outside)									
5	Clean And Disinfect Shared Surfaces									
6	Steam Clean Carpets And Rugs									
7	Dust And Clean Ceilings, Ceiling Corners And Ceiling Tiles									
8	Check For Broken Chairs And Tables									
9	Dust And Wash Radiator Covers									
10	Clean And Disinfect Ceiling Wall Vents									
11	Clean And Vacuum Central Heating Units									
12	Wash And Clean Light Covers									
13	Clean Drapes And Curtains (Take Down And Wash if Possible)									
14	Check Cleaning Supplies And Re-Stock As Necessary									
15	Check Ceiling Fans, Fire Sprinklers And Smoke Alarms									
16	Check Hardware, Door Stops And Lock Mechanisms									
17	Fire Exit Lights And Emergency Lights Checked & Functioning									
18	Organize And De-Clutter Office Drawers									
19	Organize And De-Clutter Storeroom									
	Daily/Weekly Toilets/Restroom Cleaning Tasks	M	T	W	T	F	S	S	Cleaned By	Date/Time
1	Clean And Disinfect All Doors, Door Handles And Doorknobs									
2	Disinfect Touch Points, Light Switches And Other Switches									
3	Toilet Roll Holders Cleaned And Disinfected And Re-Stocked									
4	Wipe Down The Walls Wherever There Are Spills And Splashes									
5	Electric Hand Dryers Cleaned, Disinfected & Operating Correctly									
6	Sweep The Floors To Ensure They're Free From Debris									
7	Mop Tiled And Laminate Floors With Disinfectant Cleaner									
8	Paper Dispensers & Paper Towel Rolls Cleaned & Re-Stocked									
9	Take Out The Rubbish/Trash, Remove Waste And Recycling									
10	Clean & Disinfectant Bins/Waste Disposal Area & Trash Cans									
11	Feminine Hygiene Bins/Containers Cleaned And Disinfected									
12	Toilets Cleaned & Disinfected, Outside, Inside And Handles									
13	Urinals & Urinal Screens Cleaned, Disinfected & Blocks Replaced									
14	Wall Mirrors Cleaned With Glass Cleaner									
15	Clean And Re-Stock Paper Dispensers & Paper Towel Rolls									
16	Refill Soap Dispensers, Sanitizers And Hand Gels									
17	Sinks, Taps, Fixtures, Surface Areas Cleaned And Disinfected									

	Daily/Weekly Toilets/Restroom Cleaning Tasks Con	M	T	W	T	F	S	S	Cleaned By	Date/Time
18	Windowsills Clean And Wiped Down									
19	Check Plumbing And Schedule Work If Required									
20	Air Fresheners Checked And Replaced									
21	Fire Exit Lights And Emergency Lights Checked & Functioning									
22	Place Wet Floor Signs If Floors Are Wet After Mopping									
23	Cabinets Cleaned And Disinfected									
	Monthly Toilets/Restroom Cleaning Tasks	M	T	W	T	F	S	S	Cleaned By	Date/Time
1	Toilet/Restroom Service Storeroom/Cupboard Clean And Tidy									
2	Walls Free Of Graffiti, Stickers, Gum And Residue									
3	Wash And Clean Windows (Inside And Outside)									
4	Check Hardware, Door Stops And Lock Mechanisms									
5	All Fittings Securely Fixed (Schedule Maintenance If Not)									
6	Dust And Clean Ceilings, Ceiling Corners And Ceiling Tiles									
7	Clean Skirting Boards/Baseboards And Corners									
8	Thoroughly Clean Grout And Tiles									
9	Ceiling Wall Vents Cleaned And Disinfected									
10	Clean And Vacuum Central Heating Units									
11	Wash And Clean Light Covers									
12	Wash All Toilet And Restroom Mats									
	Daily/Weekly Kitchen Cleaning Tasks	M	T	W	T	F	S	S	Cleaned By	Date/Time
1	Wash And Sanitize All Counter Tops And Prep Area Surfaces									
2	Empty Dishwasher, Run The Dishwasher/Dish Drainer									
3	Disinfect Touch Points, Light Switches And Other Switches									
4	Take Out The Rubbish/Trash, Remove Waste And Recycling									
5	Clean & Disinfectant Bins/Waste Disposal Area & Trash Cans									
6	Wipe Down The Walls Wherever There Are Spills And Splashes									
7	Sweep The Floors To Ensure They're Free From Debris									
8	Mop Tiled And Laminate Floors With Disinfectant Cleaner									
9	Wet Floor Signs In Place If Floors Are Wet After Mopping									
10	Thoroughly Clean And Disinfect The Sinks And Taps									
11	Clean Exterior Of Appliances, Check For Spilled Food									
12	Replace Empty Paper Towel Rolls And Cloth Roller Towels									
13	Refill Soap Dispensers And Hand Sanitizers/Hand Gels									
14	Wipe Down Equipment, Tea And Coffee Makers, Toasters Etc									
15	Fire Exit Lights And Emergency Lights Checked & Functioning									
16	Pour Drain Cleaner Down Floor And Sink Drains									
17	Clean Inside Microwave, Check For Spilled Food									

	Daily/Weekly Kitchen Cleaning Tasks Continued	M	T	W	T	F	S	S	CLEANED BY	DATE/TIME
18	Replace Wash Rags, Cloths And Tea Towels With Clean Ones									
19	Wash Rags, Cloths, Tea Towels And Towels In Washing Machine									
20	Replace And Change Burned Out Light Bulbs/Broken Lights									
21	Clean Inside Of Dishwasher									
22	Sanitise Sponges Or Replace Damaged Sponges With New									
23	Dishes, Pots, Pans, And Utensils To Be Stored Away Properly									
24	Clean Out Refrigerator And Wipe Down Shelves And Drawers									
	Monthly Kitchen Cleaning Tasks	M	T	W	T	F	S	S	Cleaned By	Date/Time
1	Wash And Clean Air Vents									
2	Sort Through And Organize Cooking Utensils, Pans And Pots									
3	Wash And Clean Air Vents									
4	Check Plates, Cups And Glasses And Bin Anything Chipped									
5	Clean And Vacuum Central Heating Units									
6	Wash And Clean Light Covers									
7	Clean And De-Lime Dishwasher									
8	Dust And Clean Ceilings, Ceiling Corners And Ceiling Tiles									
9	Thoroughly Clean Grout And Tiles									
10	Clean Refrigerator Coils To Remove Dust, Unplug First									
11	Run Cleaning & Sanitizing Chemicals Through Coffee Machine									
12	Disinfect And Clean All The Walls From Top To Bottom									
13	Check For Out Of Date Food In Cabinets/Cupboards									
14	Clean Skirting Boards/Baseboards And Corners									
15	Clean Under Refrigerator									
16	Wash And Clean Doors, Door Frames And Glass									
17	Sort Through Leftover Items In The Fridge/Refrigerators									
18	Wash And Clean Windows (Inside And Outside)									
19	Replace Pest Traps									

ESSENTIAL CLEANING NOTES

....
....
....
....
....
....
....
....

ESSENTIAL OFFICE CONTACT *Details*

Name:

Company:

Address:

Phone:

Phone:

Email:

Email:

Web:

Name:

Company:

Address:

Phone:

Phone:

Email:

Email:

Web:

Name:

Company:

Address:

Phone:

Phone:

Email:

Email:

Web:

Name:

Company:

Address:

Phone:

Phone:

Email:

Email:

Web:

Name:

Company:

Address:

Phone:

Phone:

Email:

Email:

Web:

Name:

Company:

Address:

Phone:

Phone:

Email:

Email:

Web:

ESSENTIAL OFFICE CONTACT *Details*

Name:

Company:

Address:

Phone:

Phone:

Email:

Email:

Web:

Name:

Company:

Address:

Phone:

Phone:

Email:

Email:

Web:

Name:

Company:

Address:

Phone:

Phone:

Email:

Email:

Web:

Name:

Company:

Address:

Phone:

Phone:

Email:

Email:

Web:

Name:

Company:

Address:

Phone:

Phone:

Email:

Email:

Web:

Name:

Company:

Address:

Phone:

Phone:

Email:

Email:

Web:

ESSENTIAL OFFICE CONTACT *Details*

Name:

Company:

Address:

Phone:

Phone:

Email:

Email:

Web:

Name:

Company:

Address:

Phone:

Phone:

Email:

Email:

Web:

Name:

Company:

Address:

Phone:

Phone:

Email:

Email:

Web:

Name:

Company:

Address:

Phone:

Phone:

Email:

Email:

Web:

Name:

Company:

Address:

Phone:

Phone:

Email:

Email:

Web:

Name:

Company:

Address:

Phone:

Phone:

Email:

Email:

Web:

ESSENTIAL OFFICE CONTACT *Details*

Name: ....
Company: ....
Address: ....
....
....

Phone: ....
Phone: ....
Email: ....
Email: ....
Web: ....

Name: ....
Company: ....
Address: ....
....
....

Phone: ....
Phone: ....
Email: ....
Email: ....
Web: ....

Name: ....
Company: ....
Address: ....
....
....

Phone: ....
Phone: ....
Email: ....
Email: ....
Web: ....

Name: ....
Company: ....
Address: ....
....
....

Phone: ....
Phone: ....
Email: ....
Email: ....
Web: ....

Name: ....
Company: ....
Address: ....
....
....

Phone: ....
Phone: ....
Email: ....
Email: ....
Web: ....

Name: ....
Company: ....
Address: ....
....
....

Phone: ....
Phone: ....
Email: ....
Email: ....
Web: ....

OFFICE TO DO TASKS *Checklist*

Name:............................ Location:................................ Date:........................ Week No:...................

HIGH PRIORITY - To Do List... ☆☆☆	DATE	DONE
1.		○
2.		○
3.		○
4.		○
5.		○
6.		○
7.		○
8.		○
9.		○
10.		○

MEDIUM PRIORITY - To Do List... ☆☆	DATE	DONE
1.		○
2.		○
3.		○
4.		○
5.		○
6.		○
7.		○
8.		○
9.		○
10.		○

LOW PRIORITY - To Do List... ☆	DATE	DONE
1.		○
2.		○
3.		○
4.		○
5.		○
6.		○
7.		○
8.		○
9.		○
10.		○

OFFICE TO DO TASKS *Checklist*

Name: .... Location: .... Date: .... Week No: ....

HIGH PRIORITY - To Do List... ⭐⭐⭐	DATE	DONE
1.	....	◯
2.	....	◯
3.	....	◯
4.	....	◯
5.	....	◯
6.	....	◯
7.	....	◯
8.	....	◯
9.	....	◯
10.	....	◯

MEDIUM PRIORITY - To Do List... ⭐⭐	DATE	DONE
1.	....	◯
2.	....	◯
3.	....	◯
4.	....	◯
5.	....	◯
6.	....	◯
7.	....	◯
8.	....	◯
9.	....	◯
10.	....	◯

LOW PRIORITY - To Do List... ⭐	DATE	DONE
1.	....	◯
2.	....	◯
3.	....	◯
4.	....	◯
5.	....	◯
6.	....	◯
7.	....	◯
8.	....	◯
9.	....	◯
10.	....	◯

OFFICE TO DO TASKS *Checklist*

Name: .... Location: .... Date: .... Week No: ....

HIGH PRIORITY - To Do List... ⭐⭐⭐	DATE	DONE
1.	....	◯
2.	....	◯
3.	....	◯
4.	....	◯
5.	....	◯
6.	....	◯
7.	....	◯
8.	....	◯
9.	....	◯
10.	....	◯

MEDIUM PRIORITY - To Do List... ⭐⭐	DATE	DONE
1.	....	◯
2.	....	◯
3.	....	◯
4.	....	◯
5.	....	◯
6.	....	◯
7.	....	◯
8.	....	◯
9.	....	◯
10.	....	◯

LOW PRIORITY - To Do List... ⭐	DATE	DONE
1.	....	◯
2.	....	◯
3.	....	◯
4.	....	◯
5.	....	◯
6.	....	◯
7.	....	◯
8.	....	◯
9.	....	◯
10.	....	◯

OFFICE TO DO TASKS *Checklist*

Name:.. Location:.................................... Date:.................................... Week No:....................................

HIGH PRIORITY - To Do List... ⭐✓⭐✓⭐✓	DATE	DONE
1.	....	◯
2.	....	◯
3.	....	◯
4.	....	◯
5.	....	◯
6.	....	◯
7.	....	◯
8.	....	◯
9.	....	◯
10.	....	◯

MEDIUM PRIORITY - To Do List... ⭐✓⭐✓	DATE	DONE
1.	....	◯
2.	....	◯
3.	....	◯
4.	....	◯
5.	....	◯
6.	....	◯
7.	....	◯
8.	....	◯
9.	....	◯
10.	....	◯

LOW PRIORITY - To Do List... ⭐✓	DATE	DONE
1.	....	◯
2.	....	◯
3.	....	◯
4.	....	◯
5.	....	◯
6.	....	◯
7.	....	◯
8.	....	◯
9.	....	◯
10.	....	◯

IMPORTANT DATES AND EVENTS *Checklist*

Name: ....   **Date:** ....

Event/Occasion: ....   **Time:** ....

Location: ....   **Phone:** ....

....   **Email:** ....

....   **Web:** ....

Name: ....   **Date:** ....

Event/Occasion: ....   **Time:** ....

Location: ....   **Phone:** ....

....   **Email:** ....

....   **Web:** ....

Name: ....   **Date:** ....

Event/Occasion: ....   **Time:** ....

Location: ....   **Phone:** ....

....   **Email:** ....

....   **Web:** ....

Name: ....   **Date:** ....

Event/Occasion: ....   **Time:** ....

Location: ....   **Phone:** ....

....   **Email:** ....

....   **Web:** ....

Name: ....   **Date:** ....

Event/Occasion: ....   **Time:** ....

Location: ....   **Phone:** ....

....   **Email:** ....

....   **Web:** ....

Name: ....   **Date:** ....

Event/Occasion: ....   **Time:** ....

Location: ....   **Phone:** ....

....   **Email:** ....

....   **Web:** ....

IMPORTANT DATES AND EVENTS *Checklist*

Name:

Event/Occasion:

Location:

Date:

Time:

Phone:

Email:

Web:

Name:

Event/Occasion:

Location:

Date:

Time:

Phone:

Email:

Web:

Name:

Event/Occasion:

Location:

Date:

Time:

Phone:

Email:

Web:

Name:

Event/Occasion:

Location:

Date:

Time:

Phone:

Email:

Web:

Name:

Event/Occasion:

Location:

Date:

Time:

Phone:

Email:

Web:

Name:

Event/Occasion:

Location:

Date:

Time:

Phone:

Email:

Web:

IMPORTANT DATES AND EVENTS *Checklist*

Name: ....   **Date:** ....

Event/Occasion: ....   **Time:** ....

Location: ....   **Phone:** ....

....   **Email:** ....

....   **Web:** ....

Name: ....   **Date:** ....

Event/Occasion: ....   **Time:** ....

Location: ....   **Phone:** ....

....   **Email:** ....

....   **Web:** ....

Name: ....   **Date:** ....

Event/Occasion: ....   **Time:** ....

Location: ....   **Phone:** ....

....   **Email:** ....

....   **Web:** ....

Name: ....   **Date:** ....

Event/Occasion: ....   **Time:** ....

Location: ....   **Phone:** ....

....   **Email:** ....

....   **Web:** ....

Name: ....   **Date:** ....

Event/Occasion: ....   **Time:** ....

Location: ....   **Phone:** ....

....   **Email:** ....

....   **Web:** ....

Name: ....   **Date:** ....

Event/Occasion: ....   **Time:** ....

Location: ....   **Phone:** ....

....   **Email:** ....

....   **Web:** ....

IMPORTANT DATES AND EVENTS *Checklist*

Name:

Event/Occasion:

Location:

Date:

Time:

Phone:

Email:

Web:

Name:

Event/Occasion:

Location:

Date:

Time:

Phone:

Email:

Web:

Name:

Event/Occasion:

Location:

Date:

Time:

Phone:

Email:

Web:

Name:

Event/Occasion:

Location:

Date:

Time:

Phone:

Email:

Web:

Name:

Event/Occasion:

Location:

Date:

Time:

Phone:

Email:

Web:

Name:

Event/Occasion:

Location:

Date:

Time:

Phone:

Email:

Web:

ESSENTIAL CLEANING INVENTORY *Checklist*

Date	Establishment/Location	Counted By

SKU/Product No	Product/Description	Quantity	Price	Reorder Date

ESSENTIAL CLEANING INVENTORY *Checklist*

Date	Establishment/Location	Counted By

SKU/Product No	Product/Description	Quantity	Price	Reorder Date

ESSENTIAL CLEANING INVENTORY *Checklist*

Date	Establishment/Location	Counted By

SKU/Product No	Product/Description	Quantity	Price	Reorder Date

ESSENTIAL CLEANING INVENTORY *Checklist*

Date	Establishment/Location	Counted By

SKU/Product No	Product/Description	Quantity	Price	Reorder Date

ESSENTIAL CLEANING INVENTORY *Checklist*

Date	Establishment/Location	Counted By

SKU/Product No	Product/Description	Quantity	Price	Reorder Date

ESSENTIAL CLEANING INVENTORY *Checklist*

Date	Establishment/Location	Counted By

SKU/Product No	Product/Description	Quantity	Price	Reorder Date

FYLDE
MERCHANDISE

"Thank you for being an exceptional customer."

We hope that your notebook exceeded your expectations.

Creating notebook ideas is what we do.

Notebooks designed with love for you and your business.

If you have any notebook ideas, big or small, we would love to hear from you.

And maybe we can make those ideas come to life!

Additional pages adding?
New features or sections creating?
Other notebook sizes?
Any covers or page design ideas?
Any industries or sectors you require notebooks for?

Please email any notebook suggestions to:

sales@FyldeMerchandise.com

→] LOG BOOKS [←

FOLLOW US ON

www.FyldeMerchandise.com

Made in United States
Orlando, FL
24 April 2022